Work and Mental Illness

The Johns Hopkins Series in Contemporary Medicine and Public Health

also of interest in this series:

Family Management of Schizophrenia: A Study of Clinical, Social, Family, and Economic Benefits, Ian R. H. Falloon and Others

Neuropsychological Rehabilitation after Brain Injury, George P. Prigatano and Others

Work and Mental Illness

Transitions to Employment

Bertram J. Black

Professor Emeritus, Departments of Psychiatry and of Epidemiology and Social Medicine, and

Senior Advisor, Rehabilitation Research and Training Center for Psychiatrically Disabled Individuals

Albert Einstein College of Medicine

The Johns Hopkins University Press
Baltimore and London

To Rose

Printed in the United States of America

The Johns Hopkins University Press
701 West 40th Street
Baltimore, Maryland 21211
The Johns Hopkins Press Ltd., London

∞

The paper used in this publication meets the minimum requirements of American National Standard for Information Sciences—Permanence of Paper for Printed Library Materials, ANSI Z39.48-1984.

LIBRARY OF CONGRESS CATALOGING-IN-PUBLICATION DATA

Black, Bertram J.

Work and mental illness.

(The Johns Hopkins series in contemporary medicine and public health)

Bibliography: p.

Includes index.

1. Vocational rehabilitation. 2. Mentally ill—Employment. 3. Mentally ill—Rehabilitation. I. Title. II. Series. [DNLM: 1. Employment. 2. Mental Disorders—rehabilitation. WM 29.1 B627w]

HD7255.B56 1988 362.2′0425 87-26084

ISBN 0-8018-3565-8 (alk. paper)

Contents

Foreword

The right to employment is as much a symbol of full citizenship in modern society as is the right to vote. Work has been a focus of the struggle for the civil rights of women, ethnic groups, age groups, and groups of people who have suffered discrimination in the workplace because of a history of cancer, or diabetes, or epilepsy. Persons with developmental disabilities and physical disabilities have made notable gains in employment in the past few years by forcing societal recognition of their legitimate rights and needs in the workplace. Opening employment opportunities for the psychiatrically disabled will be no less difficult. It calls for sweeping away entrenched, taken-for-granted discriminatory practices and indifference to the problems. Ignorance, intolerance of difference, and fear all contribute to shunning the psychiatrically disabled. Professor Black reminds us how great is the underlying fear of mental illness in the general population, and how pervasive that fear and stigma is throughout the world. Fortunately, visionaries are among us who see what is right, and possible. Bert Black is one of these. He tells us the story of the development of work opportunities for mentally ill persons, often from a first-person perspective: he implemented those programs. We have much to learn from him, and from this book with its wealth of descriptions of the development of employment programs.

The language of the 1986 Amendments to the Rehabilitation Act of 1973, mandating that supported employment be extended to the chronically mentally ill, dramatically expands opportunities for these persons. Implementing the act, creating work roles for the severely mentally ill person, will call on the most creative and collegial responses from professionals in the areas of work, mental health, and the social services. Collaboration between vocational rehabilitation and mental health agencies will be crucial for the success of the venture. Can these two unlike services be brought together? Vocational rehabilitation has a long history with the testing, training, and placement of the physically disabled. Working effectively with the psychiatrically disabled will demand new concepts of testing, training, and placement: more attention to the work environment, more on-site training and support, and more attention to support in retention in the job. Mental health practitioners will have to think of work as part of the rehabilitation process, not as the end point of rehabilitation. New liaisons with vocational rehabilitation programs and contact persons, new arrangements for following clients on a long-term basis and stepping in when warning signs develop at the job placement—these are some of the new and challenging tasks in store for the mental health specialists.

Professor Black's work is invaluable in providing examples of policies and programs, with note taken of the successes, the partial successes, and pitfalls encountered. One begins to see the degree of interorganizational and interdisciplinary change and cooperation that may come of this new initiative. This book will serve as a reference for a long time to come. Professor Black shows us the state of the art around the world: the United States in welcome detail, but also important but too-little-known countries like the Peoples' Republic of China and European Eastern Bloc countries. These descriptions throw into sharp relief the degree to which social, economic, and political forces, as well as specific beliefs about mental illness, shape programs of work and therapy and care.

The federal initiative to create community support services systems lagged by too many years the beginning of deinstitutionalization which moved large numbers of patients into the community and limited hospitalization for new cases of mental illness. The new federal initiative that opens the possibilities of employment to the psychiatrically disabled is a natural extension of the idea of deinstitutionalization: that the person who lives in the community should have a full sharing of the life of the community. The truth of Professor Black's thesis—that for the psychiatrically disabled, work is in many ways indistinguishable from therapy, and is therapeutic for the psychiatrically disabled—applies to most of us in our everyday lives. There is ample evidence that carefully planned employment for the psychiatrically disabled person can be a successful experience leading to a better life. The challenge to a caring professional, and to a caring society, is to keep the tragedy of unrealized potential stemming from a severe and chronic mental illness from turning into catastrophe.

SEYMOUR R. KAPLAN, M.D., *Professor of Psychiatry and Director of Rehabilitation Research and Training Center for Psychiatrically Disabled Individuals, Albert Einstein College of Medicine*

Preface

Using programs of work as a modality of treatment and rehabilitation of the mentally ill is an idea whose time has come—again! Twenty years ago, when I reviewed what was then a decade of experience with sheltered work for psychiatric patients discharged from hospitals, it seemed as though this would be a rapidly growing field. However, it took a back seat during the 1970s to the burgeoning developments in community psychiatry, day hospitals, and mental health centers, and then to the deinstitutionalization of the large mental hospitals. Now that the locus of service for mental illness rests firmly in the communities, the question of what the former patient can and should do in his or her working years comes again to the forefront.

A number of kinds of work programs have evolved for the disabled, including the mentally ill, in this country and abroad. I have described them and have tried to place them in the context of the welfare, health, and mental-health delivery systems of which they are part, and have described the techniques and methods they use. Since work programs are also part of the economic and business life of their societies, I have also described the issues they raise in that sphere of life as well as the balance required between business and therapy.

Over the years I have worked with and learned from so many leaders in psychiatry, social work, psychology, public health, rehabilitation medicine, rehabilitation counseling, and the other disciplines in mental health that it is impossible to recognize and thank them individually. I can only express my gratitude *en masse*. I am indebted to the van Ameringen Foundation for its grant in support of the fact gathering, field visits, and preparation of manuscript and to the Medical and Health Research Association of New York City for serving as my sponsor. I appreciate the capable assistance of my wife at every stage of this work, and thank the many colleagues here and overseas who supplied information for my use. Any errors of fact are mine alone, as are opinions about programs, and their relation to the politics and economics of their settings.

Work and Mental Illness

1
The Value of Work for the Mentally Ill

As the locus of services to the mentally ill, particularly the chronically mentally ill, has moved from the state hospitals to the community, the question of participation by patients in the labor market has taken on new meaning. There is a dichotomy of opinion by professionals who provide treatment and rehabilitation of this population: on the one hand, there are those who believe that the ultimate goal for all those recovered from or stabilized in psychiatric disorders should be remunerative employment; on the other are those who insist that entry or reentry into the competitive labor market is impossible or at best wishful thinking for the majority of their patients or clients. Before discussing the kinds of work programs which are being developed to meet the needs of the mentally ill, I will consider the arguments as to the value of work or the lack thereof and examine the epidemiological and environmental circumstances that surround them.

The Meaning of Work

Work consumes at least a third of the daily time of a wage earner. Where work life has been interrupted, as is the case for many mental patients, its reestablishment becomes an important step in their cure or rehabilitation. Actually, work of some kind has played a large part in the treatment of the mentally ill for over a century. Before the large state hospitals evolved in the late 1800s, but after Pinel had removed the chains from his lunatics in the closing years of the previous century, the mentally ill were housed in small institutions. Their illness was looked upon as a moral failure, and forms of "moral therapy" were much in vogue. Idleness was considered dissonant with godliness. Prayer, good manners, and occupied hands and minds were prescribed by the institutional directors, more often clergymen than physicians. In 1812 Dr. Benjamin Rush, who directed one such insane asylum, quoted the poet William Cowper in support of work as moral therapy: "Absence of occupation is not rest; / A mind quite vacant is a mind distress'd." Particularly in New England and on the eastern seaboard, the cradle of American institutional care for the insane, the Calvinistic philosophy prevailed on the virtue of work, both physical and mental (see Black 1970). Thomas Eddy, in his report to the governors of the New York Hospital in 1815, said, "Of all the modes by which maniacs may be induced to restrain themselves, regular employment is perhaps the most efficacious; and those kind of employments are to be preferred, both on a moral and physical account, which are accompanied by considerable bodily action, most agreeable to the patient, and most opposite of his disease. In short the patient should be always treated as much like a *rational* being as the state of his mind will possibly allow" (p. 9).

As time went on, the findings of Kraepelin and others brought an increasing shift to a "medical" rather than a "moral" explanation for insanity. Dorothea Dix and her followers exposed the jailing and the mistreatment of the mentally ill, and the efforts of Clifford Beers and the National Committee for Mental Hygiene brought about the establishment of the state mental hospital system. The numbers of patients increased, almost exponentially. The majority of patients were treated with physical restraints, but a goodly number were ambulatory and capable of working. The work provided was tailored to the needs of the hospital—work in the laundry, on the grounds and on the farms, in sewing and upholstery repairs, on the maintenance force, and to a limited extent in the library and offices. Indeed, these large institutions, with patients numbering from 2,000 to 20,000 each, could hardly have functioned without the work done by patients, since staffs were never large enough to run the hospitals without this help. Not surprisingly, however, efficiency was always at a low ebb. In 1962 the Program Area Committee of the American Public Health Association reported on the place of work in mental hospitals:

> For many years in America any patient able to work was expected to do so *in the service of the hospital.* If he was not desocialized to the point where it was considered useless to attempt to make him work or if he was not physically ill, he was expected to perform one of a series of tasks supposed to benefit the hospital. Frequently the work was sheerest drudgery, and often had to be performed under conditions of danger or discomfort, making impossible the obtaining of other workers.
>
> It was often said that these hospitals "could not operate without patient labor." It is unfortunate that in many cases this was a true statement. The

> hospitals reached an unhappy equilibrium where a great deal of inefficient patient labor was necessary to keep the hospital going, since the hospital had neither adequate equipment nor trained staff for getting essential work done. On the one hand these were usually the best preserved of the chronic patients, many of whom could have been rehabilitated or discharged from the hospital. In many cases their usefulness to the hospital, together with the absence of any source of appreciation and satisfaction for them in the community, was a factor in their continued hospitalization. On the other hand their labor with inadequate tools was so inefficient that, even at the cost of their maintenance, it was uneconomic. Revulsion over the abuses of this system has led, in some quarters, to a complete about-face, where it is felt that patients should not be forced to work for their keep and should not even be allowed to do so. The potentially beneficial value of work under proper clinical supervision is easily lost from view in this controversy. (Williams 1962, p. 16)

A few of the medical superintendents described the work of patients as "industrial therapy" and really believed in the concept, but quite a number gave only lip service to the idea and exploited patient labor under this rubric. It was not until ten years later that a federal judge decided the issue in favor of denying work to patients in mental hospitals unless they were paid going wages for their employment (Souder vs. Brennan 1973). In this country the term *industrial therapy* came to be equated with exploitation, as with prison labor. Elsewhere in the world this was not so, and the term *industrial therapy* is still in use (for example, in Great Britain) to mean a mode of treatment using work tasks.

Work has more than one function in the human condition. In his series of essays on community psychiatry, Dr. Sol Ginsburg outlined many of these quite clearly. To quote selectively,

> We live in a work-conscious and work-oriented world . . . One of our highest American values is that of success, especially when achieved through the sweat of one's own efforts . . . Work affords an opportunity for the discharge and binding of a multitude of instinctual tendencies, narcissistic, partial instinctual, object libidinal, and aggressive . . . In addition, work occupies a central position in the formation of the structure of the ego, because it is one of the most important visible manifestations of adulthood; in other words, it is a major vehicle of identification with the role of the adult . . .
>
> There are other aspects of work which show how closely allied work activity is to essential ego functions. Foremost among them is the fact that work is directed toward reality: it aims at changing it. Freud (1953) said, "Laying stress upon the importance of work has a greater effect on binding the individual more closely to reality than any other technique of living . . . In his work he [the individual] is at least securely attached to a part of reality, the human community." (Ginsburg 1963, pp. 162–72)

Ginsburg pointed out, too, that

> a successful occupational choice must lead to work which will provide the wealth of potential ego satisfactions . . . mastery of the assigned task, satisfying job (work) social relations; fulfillment of the adult and appropriate sexual roles, gains in prestige and rewards, and others . . . Work is a basic part of everyone's life. It supplies the means not only to support life, but to afford leisure pursuits which are gratifying and meaningful to the individual. Work is a social activity, and the end products of the worker's efforts have a social value . . . Work is a vital and basic instrument whereby one achieves and maintains one's role and status in the family group; security and pleasure in this role are an indirect but basic part of a man's work "satisfaction" . . . To have work to do is to be needed and to be needed is essential for life. (Ibid., pp. 172 and 182)

Work as an Unhappy Necessity

Notwithstanding the values ascribed to work, questions continually arise as to why we should be so concerned with work in the treatment and rehabilitation of the mentally ill. A goodly number of those who serve the chronically mentally ill keep questioning the ability of their patients ever to be productive in the workplace. A number of those who deal with the severely handicapped seem convinced that the changes in the economics of Western society, at any rate, will so diminish the availability of the kinds of work utilized in sheltered work conditions as to necessitate finding alternatives to work altogether. There are also those who look upon the drive to work as representing the worst features of a "Protestant ethic" and unnecessary in modern society; they view work as a "curse," an unhappy necessity for most people that should be avoided by those, including the severely handicapped, for whom it would be difficult.

The questions regarding the abilities of patients to perform work and the changing economics will be dealt with later. At this point let us consider the ethical issue of work as a necessity. Work as a sacred duty to God is built into the concept of orthodox Christianity. Neff (1968) pointed out that these ideas, although usually ascribed to Protestantism, began as early as the sixth century as doctrine of the Catholic orders. During recent decades we have come to question the idea of working as the will of God. As Neff put it, "We are becoming sensitive to the fact that workers are not born but *made*" (p. 64). Some social scientists have taken the view that in our alienated work world there is no satisfaction in working, that work is a "curse," demoralizing and destructive in its influences on the workers (see Erikson 1950). Ginsburg (1963, p. 183) challenged this: "The notion that work represents a 'curse' for most people is one that I cannot easily accept and which . . . is hardly tenable on either theoretical or practical grounds." Neff (1968, pp. 258–59) said:

> Probably few people still see work as the path to Godliness, for revealed religion is no longer a powerful social force. Work may also be losing some of its intrinsic virtues, with the development of mass production and intrinsic pervasiveness of machinery. We may even be approaching a situation where the clear nexus between work and money may become somewhat diluted, so that our incomes and styles of life may no longer so unequivocally reflect the particular kinds of work we do. It is also quite possible that formal education may have to give more concern to the constructive use of leisure. But none of this implies any immediate risk that work will become a negligible part of human existence.

Written almost twenty years ago, Neff's perspectives are almost predictive, except that a shift toward fundamentalism in religion is reemphasizing the "duty" of the individual to work and be productive.

Productive Participation

Another way of describing work that does not derogate paid employment is the anthropological concept of "productive participation." Chapple (1970, p. 48) wrote: "If rehabilitation is to mean competent performance by the standards of the group, not of the rehabilitators, then work needs to be redefined, from an anthropological point of view, as productive participation to the degree the individual is capable. Such productivity does imply reciprocity, yet in no way does it need to be symbolized by money exchange. For value received, say our legal documents of exchange. Such values are a consequence of all types of productive participation."

Chapple further pointed out that in all cultures, including our own, there are acceptable productive activities not involving payment in monetary wages. He referred to the work of Navajo Indians in tending sheep, tending crops, hauling wood or water, necessary to family and survival. He mentioned the "singer of ballads, the preacher, the healer or even the blacksmith in less affluent societies." He continued:

> If, then, we accept the anthropologist's point that our cultural definition of work is too limited and that a more general term, usable in every cultural group, can be called something like productive participation, all the anomalies of our own society fall in place: children doing the chores (if they still do), the mother managing home and community involvements, the retirees, still dependent on one another, even the criminals in their illegal activities and at the very bottom, the sporadic participation of addicts and

Skid Row outcasts intermittently active in the search for oblivion. (Ibid., p. 50)

It is true that in the field of rehabilitation of the disabled the tasks of homemaking and caring for little children have been looked upon as acceptable alternatives to gainful employment. Volunteer activities, unless the individual is quite elderly or with independent income, are usually considered questionable, or at best transitional to paid employment. Chapple urged reconsideration of the definition of work in the rehabilitation of the disabled. "Unwillingness to broaden the concept of work to include all forms of what we have here called productive participation is to a large extent a consequence of our own culture of rehabilitation. It is a product of our middle class orientations, our habitual roles as professionals and institutional and symbolic frameworks in which we work. All of these need to be looked at with the eye of the anthropologist to make clear how much of what we do has scientific validity and how much is simply the habits and customs of a tribe of rehabilitators" (ibid.). The concept of productive participation might be a more palatable concept than that of work to the mental health professionals dealing with the more chronically mentally ill. In fact, an international conference on rehabilitation of the mentally ill held in Helsinki in 1973 was deliberately given that title for its attractiveness to psychiatrists and others in the mental health disciplines (*Productive Participation* 1973).

The Value of Work in Rehabilitation

With all the discussion as to the changing values of work in our society and other societies, and the doubts of its value by some mental health practitioners, the balance of belief is nevertheless that work has an important place in the rehabilitation of the mentally ill. A survey of community programs for the mentally ill, conducted in 1977/78, for ICD concluded:

> Work is a critical factor in the rehabilitation of mental health patients, ranging from its immediate therapeutic value to ultimate financial independence. For some psychologically disabled clients, work enhances their self-esteem and self-concept to the point of acting as a bulwark against too easily accepting a "patient" role. Other clients find that meaningful vocational activity provides them with an opportunity to deny their illness, since through work they are fulfilling an expected adult role—that of "worker." Therefore, meaningful work must replace the "busy" work that in the past has too often been offered to MH clients. It can provide a core of valuable learning experiences and a measure of status against which the rehabilitant may assess his own values. In fact, the relationship between employment

> and the adjustment of the post-hospitalized patient goes beyond the specific need for earning a living. It bears directly on the ability of an individual to remain in the community, whether or not he is self-supporting, and whether or not he is able to accomplish other social roles. Thus, the capacity to work for even severely emotionally handicapped individuals is often surprising. (Robinault and Weisinger 1978, p. 76)

A report of the Royal College of Psychiatrists of England (1980, p. 12) states:

> The values of paid work in relation to mentally ill people in industrial societies need to be distinguished. The first is as a means of rehabilitation, gradually acquiring or regaining the necessary confidence and skills, the ability to get on with supervisors and workmates, and to work full hours. The second is as an end in itself, evidence of wellness and citizenship. In this sense, a person *is* well if he or she can hold down a paid job. Being in work demonstrates to the individual and to others the fact of monetary and social independence, or membership in a working community, of not having patient status. Satisfactory resettlement into work is therefore the culmination of a substantial part of the process of social adjustment which enables people who have suffered from mental illness to play their full part in the community.

Milton Greenblatt (1983, p. 531) makes the case for the therapeutic value of work:

> Countless patients, acute and chronic, have benefited from work rehabilitation, and to many it has been *the* vital, effective therapy. In fact, for many patients, work rehabilitation has been more powerful medicine than drugs, psychotherapy, social therapy, or any other kind of intervention. It has been the *sine qua non*, without which other therapies would have little or no effectiveness. We point this out because, to some professionals, rehabilitation is adjunctive, accessory, low on the scale of our therapeutic armamentarium. It is sometimes pejoratively belittled as "non-dynamic" intervention. Perhaps it may be granted that the dynamics of personality development on the ego-syntonic side of life are incompletely understood; however, the empirical rationale for use of work rehabilitation stands solidly on its own merits.

An additional viewpoint is that of Anthony and colleagues, who say: "The primary focus of psychiatric rehabilitation is on improving the psychiatrically disabled person's capabilities and competence. Rehabilitation is directed primarily at maximizing health rather than minimizing sickness, i.e., health induction, not simply symptom reduction. . . . Put another way, the emphasis is on coping rather than succumbing, i.e., on the challenge for meaningful adaptation or change rather than on the difficulties and heartbreak of the disability. Or . . . a fundamental message of rehabilitation is the belief in the potential productivity of the most severely disabled client" (Anthony, Cohen, and Cohen 1984, p. 139). Similar views are held by Lamb (1976) and Kunce (1970). It would be nice to say that these are the prevailing opinions today among the mental health professions. However, my experience shows that it is the minority of leading psychiatrists and others among mental health practitioners who hold these views, and an even smaller group who try to put them into practice.

The opinion that most of the seriously mentally ill are incapable of working or gaining much from efforts to put them to work is very prevalent. Combatting this viewpoint has been difficult. The ICD study tried: "Attaining a reasonable level of financial independence may not be a feasible goal for many clients. However, its impact on those who are successful is considerable" (Robinault and Weisinger 1978, p. 76). The British report said also:

> The more disabled the individual, the less likely is full settlement into open employment, and a time will come when little further progress seems to be being made. The preventive value of regular occupation is then often forgotten by staff, who may become disheartened and reflect this attitude to the patient or client. An important part of training should be to help staff to recognize that a central aim of rehabilitation is not only to allow progress up to an optimal level but to maintain performance there by preventing deterioration. Moreover, the preservation of good working habits may prove very useful, because the process of improvement can be very slow and at times imperceptible, but may eventually accelerate again. Experienced staff are well aware that the process of rehabilitation can take several years, but still end in the achievement of normal social performance. (Royal College of Psychiatrists 1980, pp. 12–13)

The emphasis of most day treatment programs has been on group or individual therapy. Many of the programs have included maintenance of medication, providing alternate living arrangements, and socialization. Where work programs have been provided at all in mental health agencies or clinics, they have been of the "work activity" variety, of which more will be said later. Little emphasis has been placed on preparation for open employment. The idea that with adequate rehabilitative efforts saleable productivity is possible for most chronically mentally ill is only slowly permeating mental health practices.

The Extent of the Problem

It is difficult to estimate the numbers of persons with mental illness for whom work as therapy or rehabilitation would be beneficial. Various studies of the extent of mental illness in the population of the United States have put the proportion with diagnosable problems at one out of five. Such a percentage is borne out in the recent reports of a three-community prevalence study (Myers et al. 1984), which extrapolates to a rate of 18.7 percent, or over 29 million people age 18 or older in the United States (standardizing rates to the 1980 U.S. Census on age, sex, and race). The largest number are in the diagnostic categories of substance abuse (alcohol and drugs); however, the classifications of schizophrenia alone account for 1 percent, or 1.5 million people age 18 or over.

Disabling mental illness is not restricted to the schizophrenic/schizophreniform diagnoses. Many patients with affective disorders could benefit from vocational rehabilitation, as could many with serious phobic, cognitive, addictive, and other problems. What is clear is that the apparent volume of need, using any reasonable proportion of the total number of disabled—as, for example, 10 or 20 percent—is overwhelming in relation to the resources available. I estimate that the total number of places now in use in sheltered, transitional, supported work or work activity for those with mental illness in this country to be not more than five thousand. Since the epidemiological findings in the U.S. study are reported to agree with prevalence studies abroad, the availability of work-related services for rehabilitation seems bleak across the world.

Kramer (1980) points to expected increases in mental health problems over the next decades resulting from

- increasing numbers of separations and divorces,
- increases in numbers of one-person households,
- a rise in the number of unmarried couples living together,
- an increasing older population,
- increasing numbers of minority population,
- an increasing population economically below the poverty level,
- increasing numbers of women entering the labor force,
- greater spatial mobility of the population,
- disruptions in employment as the economy changes.

He says: "Although there are many shortcomings and gaps in currently available morbidity and mortality statistics, those that are available are sufficient to illustrate the extraordinary increases that can be expected in the number of persons who will be affected by major problems of disease and disability that are of concern to mental health. This includes persons in every age group, from youngest to the oldest. This worldwide increase in the prevalence of chronic disease may be best characterized as a rising chronic disease pandemic. Prevalence rates of mental disorders, Down's Syndrome, hypertensive disease, cerebrovascular disease, cirrhosis of the liver, diabetes, blindness and other chronic conditions are increasing throughout the world" (pp. 17–18).

In view of the continuing reliance on community treatment and care for the mentally ill, in place of the large institutions of the past, I forecast much greater use of work programs both for therapy and vocational rehabilitation in the years ahead.

The Nature of the Problem

When rehabilitation of the mentally ill was introduced into Altro Work Shops in the early 1950s, the first such program in the United States, the aim was to demonstrate that dischargees from mental hospitals could be productive in a protected work setting and could return eventually to competitive employment. In retrospect it seems that the few people who were able to leave the state institutions in those days were either fairly well functioning or had reached "burned-out" stability after long years of hospital residence. There was little difficulty, therefore, in demonstrating that mental patients could work and that vocational rehabilitation should be extended to this ill and handicapped population (Black 1956; Bellak et al. 1956; Black, Meyer, and Borgatta 1960).

Our experiences, and those abroad (Black 1966), served to convince U.S. federal authorities to include mental illness among the major handicaps eligible for financial support in the federal-state vocational rehabilitation system. Programs for the identification of and service to patients eligible for vocational rehabilitation were set up in and adjacent to many state hospitals. Sheltered workshops were established in a number of state institutions, and state vocational rehabilitation agencies provided counseling services.

By the 1960s the push to discharge patients from the state hospitals, the process that came to be known as "deinstitutionalization," reduced the numbers of patients remaining in the institutions. Moreover, it reduced the number of those patients with higher functional capabilities, for they were no longer available to be referred to the sheltered workshops and the vocational rehabilitation agencies. Even though assessment of the remaining patients in the hospitals found that 20–30 percent of them were capable of living in the community outside the hospital, their greatest need was judged to be housing: work was rarely considered.

Goals of returning to or being prepared for competitive employment became more difficult or unattainable. Disenchantment with vocational rehabilitation set in among the mental health services providers and interest in the mentally ill waned among the practitioners of rehabilitation. The community services that were necessary to serve the larger numbers of mentally ill who were discharged from the hospitals or who, with the aid of medication and therapeutic supports, did not require hospitalization were very slow in coming. Community mental health centers placed vocational rehabilitation services low on the list of those they believed their patients had to have. The more recently developed community support programs have only begun to pay attention to the use of work activity and other vocational rehabilitation approaches. Of this, more later. It is a measure of how low rehabilitation of the mentally ill had fallen that in 1983 the U.S. Department of Education omitted rehabilitation of the mentally ill from its priority list for its National Institute of Handicapped Research. It took strong protests to have it reinstated the following year.

Three concepts are important to keep in mind in discussing the use of work programs in the United States in therapy and rehabilitation of the mentally ill. First of all, mental illness is not a single illness or disability. The range of diagnoses of psychiatric conditions fills a book (*Diagnostic and Statistical Manual of Mental Disorders* [American Psychiatric Association 1980]), and any of these may be present in a person for whom vocational rehabilitation is justified. I am inclined, however, to focus on the more seriously disabling categories, and these, apart from the alcohol- and drug-related illnesses (also covered under the psychiatric rubric), are mainly the schizophrenic and affective (depressive) disorders.

Second, the public health and mental health services are more concerned with the more seriously disabled among the mentally ill, primarily those who before deinstitutionalization would without doubt have sojourned in state hospitals. Thus, the pressure from funding sources has been upon whatever community services have been established to turn their attention from "the walking wounded" to the chronically mentally ill. This has greatly influenced the referrals to vocational rehabilitation resources as well. Third, the concept of chronicity has been changing. In the past it was sufficient to point to number of hospital stays and their duration as the determinant of chronicity. Today, with more mentally ill people out of hospitals than in them, and with increasing attention to services in the community, chronicity is increasingly becoming a medical determination, identified along diagnostic and/or functional parameters.

A decade ago I described the persons who were being referred to vocational rehabilitation as follows:

> Many are mentally or cognitively defective. Few have much schooling or significant, if any, work experience. As is common among schizophrenics, many have serious deficits in social performance and considerable impairment of social and leisure time activities. They need a lot of supervision to insure that they follow such normal routines as getting up in the morning, keeping clean, and eating adequately or even regularly. They are often

frightened, withdrawn, queer, and in semi-professional lingo, fragile . . . These are not great prospects for making the grade in our competitive society; nor do these people have any assets that would induce employers to put up with them. (Black 1977, p. 32)

While in the epidemiological studies of mental illness in the total population the most severe diagnoses occur in less than half of those reported (Myers et al. 1984), the Census of the Camberwell Register (Royal College of Psychiatrists 1980) shows that of those known to the mental health service system nearly 80 percent are suffering from schizophrenia or are manic depressives. The register is a more adequate expression of the population with which we are here concerned.

The Royal College report (1980, pp. 6–7) further describes the problem for these patients:

> Some of the commonest problems in rehabilitation are concerned with lethargy, and unacceptable behaviour, lack of awareness of handicaps and disturbance in social relationships. These may be present in various psychiatric disorders and may lead to problems or conflicts within the family, at work, with neighbours or with the public generally. The commonest syndrome associated with chronic schizophrenia consists of social withdrawal, flatness of affect, slowness, underactivity, poverty of speech, apathy, self-neglect, and difficulty in using non-verbal as well as verbal means of communication. At its most severe, the syndrome includes muteness, incontinence, and an inability to eat, drink or dress, although this degree of severity is rare if medication and the social environment are adequate. At the other end of the scale, minor degrees of the syndrome are quite common and are most evident, not so much in behaviour as in the individual's report of subjective feelings. One of the chief problems in rehabilitation is to reduce the resulting inertia by trying to stimulate the individual to some worthwhile activity and to maintain progress towards a realistic goal.

As I indicated earlier, there are differences of opinion between mental health practitioners and rehabilitation experts with regard to the work ability of the chronically mentally ill, the latter being of the opinion that their potential is much greater than the former assume. Such statements as "Rehabilitation therefore necessitates a long-term commitment to the individual patient" (Royal College of Psychiatrists 1980, p. 7) and "A person with chronic mental illness has a disability that often lasts half a century" (Lamb and Peele 1984, p. 801) are commonly made. Lamb and Peele paraphrase the British psychiatrist J. K. Wing in suggesting what seems an almost "no win" situation:

> For a number of the chronically mentally ill, too many demands—and for some, any demands at all—will reactivate symptoms and perhaps necessitate a hospitalization. Conversely, however, too few demands, and too low

expectations may result in regression. The work of Wing suggests that many patients who have experienced schizophrenia remain vulnerable to two extremes of social stimulation. On the one hand, too much stimulation, experienced by the patient as social intrusiveness, may lead to an acute relapse. On the other hand, too little stimulation will solidify tendencies toward social withdrawal, underactivity, and apathy. Thus the patient has to walk a careful line between two types of danger; we need to recognize both in deciding how much and in what ways to support and protect patients. (P. 798)

Lamb and Peele go on to say: "Nevertheless, normalization of the patient's environment and rehabilitation to the greatest extent possible should be the goal of treatment. Attention to the environment should include consideration of the social milieu, the living situation, and the work situation. As far as possible, the patient's condition should not be allowed to set him or her apart from other citizens in our society" (p. 799). Nevertheless, most therapists are inclined to protect against too much stimulation rather than too little.

The problem was graphically illustrated at a meeting of patients and therapists with friends and relatives of the mentally ill held at Bronx Psychiatric Center (Evans 1984). An anguished mother said: "You want to get them to be busy with some sort of useful work—to make a life. After all, as parents we are not going to be around forever. I have a 34-year-old son who is housebound, hasn't gone out for years—more than half his life. Are there any programs for people who just stay in bed all the time?" A therapist commented: "To say to the person living at home, 'You should go to the program because it's good for you'—they don't understand that. The fear of moving out of the house into society, even in a sheltered program, can be very great." And a patient suggested: "You have to take it slowly. After all, [patients] are having a difficult time without your trying to make them perfect, which they can never be."

The prospective referring mental health hospital or clinic is more likely than not to heed the attitudes of therapist and patient just expressed and consider the patient too fearful and unmotivated. The rehabilitation services are not inclined to try to deal with someone they also consider to be without sufficient motivation. Yet Lamb and Peele (1984) question whether the issue is really motivation: "A closer look reveals that these patients are afraid they will fail if they attempt such activities, and their apprehension is often well founded. To save face, they let others believe (and they themselves believe) that they have decided not to participate rather than admit that they are victims of their low self-esteem and are afraid to try. They would rather appear lazy than fearful and inadequate" (p. 801).

There are those with a somewhat different set of concepts and experiences relating to the seriously and chronic mentally ill: that the length of chronicity is not lifelong nor of fifty years' duration and that the possibilities of return or development to higher levels of functioning in the workaday world are greater than supposed. As I will explain in describing programs, I am inclined to stand with this group. As Kanter (1985, p. 55) put it, "By definition, 'long-term' or 'chronic' suggests an unchanging condition . . . there is still a common belief that the prognosis for such conditions is poor without adequate psychopharmacological and psychosocial treatment . . . changes in life-styles and personal habits are believed to occur only after prolonged periods of continuing psychosocial intervention." He pointed out, however, that "the psychiatric literature contains a small number of studies that examine the long-term course of psychotic disorders apart from any treatment approach . . . Working independently, these researchers all concluded that the course of schizophrenic disorders generally progresses unpredictably to a mild end state of recovery" (p. 56; see Bleuler 1978; Ciompi 1980; Huber et al. 1980). A more recent twenty-year follow-up of back-ward patients discharged from Vermont State Hospital (Harding et al. 1984) presents a much more hopeful picture of the future for schizophrenic patients. As *Science News* described the findings, "One-half to two-thirds of these once chronic schizophrenics showed—or had shown before their deaths—varied degrees of productivity and social involvement. Most displayed slight or no schizophrenic symptoms, had one or more moderately to very close friends, required little or no help meeting basic needs and led relatively full lives. Only 40 percent of the subjects reported full-time employment in the previous year, but this may have been due to their age, which averaged 61 years at follow-up" (*Science News* 1985, p. 340). In referring to the European studies as well, the report concludes, "Together, these findings offer a powerful argument for a shift to a stance of rational optimism from the demoralizing pessimism which pervades case conferences, plenary addresses at national meetings, influential journal articles, and consultations with families of patients" (Harding et al. 1984, p. 30).

In support of optimism has been the contention over many years by rehabilitation professionals that there is very little or no correlation between psychiatric symptoms and ability to work. Bellak (Bellak et al. 1956) pointed this out in the early Altro experience. Turner, in his studies of the relationship between work failure and psychiatric disorder, concluded that "the capacity to perform the work role cannot be wholly or even largely accounted for on the basis of the presence or degree of disorder. Indeed, data are presented suggesting that employment status is a somewhat better predictor of symptom level than is symptom level a predictor of employment status" (1973, Abstract). In the terms in which Ginsburg (1963) and other psychoanalytically oriented psychiatrists would describe it, the capacity to work is one of the last damaged areas of the ego. More recently, examination of a large number of employment settings in which mental patients were placed led Wansbrough and Cooper (1980) to conclude that loss of jobs by employees with mental illness occurred when productivity fell too low, rarely because of any increase in symptomatic behavior. The advice of Altro Work Shops to its psychotic employees many years ago—"If the machine talks to you, just don't talk back"—is adhered to by many workers who remain productive in spite of their symptoms.

In an interesting demonstration in which patients from Creedmoor Psychiatric Center (a state hospital) ran an off-track betting parlor, compared to an identical parlor run by nonpatients, Howard (1975) reported: "None of the criterion values distinguishes between ex-patients and non-patient employees. That is, there is no difference in work performance, absence, tardiness, human relations, objectivity (relationship to supervisor), appearance, personality, or overall employee's rating . . . This study, then, strongly refutes the prevailing negative attitude toward hiring the mentally restored and indicates that such attitudes are founded in bias and lack of knowledge." Howard stated vehemently, "Since mental illness is so closely related to expectancy of failure, low self-esteem, and feelings of lack of competence, the ex-mental patient who, based upon unfounded bias and stigma, is prevented from returning to employment commensurate with his skills, interests, and abilities is in effect being deprived of the opportunity to fully restore his mental health"(p. 482).

In justice to the more conservative viewpoint about the ability of the chronic mental patient to enter competitive employment, it is only fair to point out that Howard's patients had special supports. They were a highly selected group, who, given preparatory training for the job, had continued counseling available to them as well as necessary medications and therapy. A psychiatrist has suggested that "it is important to reverse the trend that requires schizophrenics to adjust to the workplace. As it does with other disabled groups, the workplace must accommodate to the schizophrenic" (Cohen 1984, p. 1042). Cohen used the term *schizophrenia* "as the prime representative of severe mental illness." "Some feasible preliminary solutions are possible," he said, "such as governmental aid to establish not-for-profit businesses operated by patients as work cooperatives, flexible public works job, and tax incentives for companies that are willing to accept schizophrenics who are less productive and can work fewer hours." He concluded: "Significantly, employment has been found to be one of the three principal predictors of outcome in schizophrenia. Perhaps it is time to look to the workplace for some of the keys for understanding and treating schizophrenia" (pp. 1040–42). As I will show in succeeding chapters, all of these solutions and others are being used in many settings in this country and abroad to meet the wide range of needs of the seriously mentally ill.

I cannot leave the discussion of the nature of the problem for those who design and operate programs for the rehabilitation of the mentally ill without noting a trend that is both important and poignant. Increasing numbers of young patients are coming to the attention of the community mental health services. McCreath (1984) relates: "A new image comes to mind for a growing number of mental health practitioners. This image might be of a man in his early twenties who is appropriately dressed and articulate. The man dropped out of college in his first or second year and has a work history that includes numerous jobs, none lasting more than a few months. He has been hospitalized about once a year since age eighteen, is self-medicating, a substance abuser, and fails to keep or cancels out-patient appointments that he agreed to in the hospital" (p. 436).

In a study of 100 consecutive patients admitted to the partial care program of a community mental health center over an eighteen-month period, McCreath (1984) found that 78 fell into this young adult group (18–35 years of age). There were somewhat more males than females (58% to 42%); almost all were single (87%), separated, or divorced (6.5%). Ninety-one percent lived with their parents. Over 90 percent had finished high school; over 36 percent had some college or more. Schizophrenic disorders accounted for over 48 percent, and nearly 36 percent had major affective disorders. It is significant that in a survey of parents who are members of NAMI, the national association for parents and relatives of the mentally ill, 75 percent were found to be parents of young adult mentally ill (Anthony 1983). The majority of these young patients, however, were male (79%), and 67 percent were diagnosed schizophrenic; 91 percent had at least a high school education, and 68 percent had attended college.

There is a great deal of concern with this new group of what are labeled "young chronics," considered to include patients as young as 17 and as old as 35. The general findings are that this is a very difficult population to serve. Their behavior is noncooperative, with violent outbursts, demanding services and attention beyond availability and then refusing to use them even if provided. (For a more complete description, see Pepper, Ryglewicz, and Kirshner 1982; Sheets, Prevost, and Reichman 1982.)

The survey of NAMI (Anthony 1983) showed that 48 percent of these young patients had been placed in sheltered workshops but that only 26 percent of them had been even moderately or more satisfied. Seventy percent of them had received vocational rehabilitation counseling, but only one-fourth of them reported being satisfied with the service. Truly, this is a population for whom work-relatedness is important for the long lives ahead of them, but the field of work rehabilitation services will have to develop programs to catch and hold such patients. McCreath (1984) recommended a series of approaches with which, out of my own experience, I would concur:

- Develop new advocacy and outreach strategies.
- "Provide sheltered workshops for the psychiatrically disabled who although stable, cannot maintain competitive employment."
- Do not expect one program element to engage the patient. Have a range—"stratified programming."
- Expand coverage to provide for earlier identification.
- Provide services for family members.
- Broaden eligibility criteria for the community support programs.
- Be guided by developmental theory.
- Take into account the client's (patient's) struggle to master normal developmental tasks.
- Recognize that assistance will be needed throughout the life cycle.

Disincentives to Work

I have already mentioned two factors that operate as disincentives to the use of work programs in rehabilitation of the mentally ill. One of these develops from the set of characteristics of chronic mental illness just described, which results in a "built-in" lack of motivation on the part of the patient/client. The other is the apparent lack of interest on the part of many mental health practitioners in referring their patients for vocational rehabilitation. This latter is a composite of attitudes: that the patients are too ill and disabled ever to develop the ability to work productively; that the kinds of work activities offered are too demeaning or too far below the patient's past experience or expressed interests (or what the therapist believes should be the patient's interests); that the people with whom the patient will have to associate in the workshop (crippled or mentally retarded or neurologically damaged) will be too distressing; or even that the time spent at work tasks would be better utilized in the patient's interest in clinical therapy.

Added to these is the disincentive presented by the attitude of the general public, and many employees, toward mental illness. While educational efforts and experience in work settings are overcoming negative attitudes in part, most people still equate mental illness with erratic, unexpected, and dangerous behavior. In my experience, a label of schizophrenia or other major psychiatric condition has been tantamount to a barrier to employment; many rehabilitation practitioners have counseled use of the term *nervous breakdown,* which has a much less ominous import. Even sheltered workshops for the disabled, in this country and abroad, have resisted for years including the mentally ill among their clientele. How unnecessary this attitude is was exemplified in the experience of Altro Work Shops thirty years ago, after it added psychiatric patients to the tuberculous and cardiac-disabled patients it was then serving. Two years after its psychiatric program was well under way, some of the physically disabled clients demanded to know when the new clientele would be admitted.

Perhaps the most difficult disincentive to deal with is economic—the loss of benefits if rehabilitation to competitive employment should be successful. Ever since the Great Depression, the United States has been providing income and services to insure a floor under dire economic need and to see that minimal protections are afforded wage earners and their families. By the 1970s, federal laws and regulations included provisions for a minimum wage, recognition of union contracts, workers' compensation, social security pensions (including disability), health coverage (Medicare and Medicaid), and a number of other benefits. The Social Security Amendments of 1972 provided a nationally guaranteed income for the poor aged, the blind, and the disabled. This program, Supplemental Security Income (popularly referred to as SSI), superseded state welfare programs of old-age assistance, aid to the blind, and aid to the permanently and totally disabled. The SSI benefits are available for most of the mentally ill discharged from state mental hospitals and for many of the patients in community mental health service programs. It supplies a basic economic support for more mentally ill persons than does any other "transfer payment" program (as economists refer to them), and it is the very possible loss of these benefits that is threatened by return to the world of work.

As one economist has pointed out (Berkowitz 1981, p. 43), "It is not only transfer payments, but medical payments as well that may be lost with rehabilitation. In addition, a whole host of benefits from direct service programs are available to disabled people who have limited income or assets . . . Thus, a person receiving disability insurance payments may be eligible for Medicare, food stamps, housing subsidies, possibly service-connected Veterans' Administration benefits, and a series of social services. Most might be lost should that person return to work." While some countries, notably in Europe, link sheltered work for the disabled to their social security systems so that health and other benefits are not lost, that is not true in the United States (Black 1977).

In a discerning analysis of SSI in its services for the mentally ill,

Ozawa and Lindsey (1977) asked the question, "Is it a rehabilitative or ameliorative function? That is, is SSI designed to help rehabilitate disabled recipients and return them to the 'mainstream' of society? Or is the government using SSI to solve a major social problem, an inability to provide employment opportunities to marginal persons, by offering income support to those who are diagnosed as physically or mentally 'disabled'? As we shall see, evidence builds to sustain the latter conclusion" (p. 51). For all its value as an income transfer for those unable to supply income through their own efforts, Ozawa and Lindsey "question the long-range effects of SSI on the mentally ill. The perceived answer is danger—a danger that SSI's essentially benign program may provide a permanent dumping ground for the mentally ill, with no prospect for their recovery" (p. 51). I suspect that many involved in therapy, day care, or residential services for the more seriously mentally ill combine their fears for the capabilities of their clients with the fear of loss of income support through SSI and other transfer payments, and make very little effort to refer to rehabilitation programs.

There has been no real research as to the conditions under which psychiatric patients would be willing to risk the loss of insurance and other benefits to undertake rehabilitation to the workaday world. It is true that many counselors report their clients unwilling to take the risk. On the other hand, in programs using manpower training programs to provide transitional work preparation for jobs in the competitive world I have found very few mental patients, most of them with diagnoses of schizophrenia, who have not been willing to try. It may be that the job prospects from such a program held promise of wage payments sufficiently above the minimum wage to balance in favor of the worth of the transfer payment and service benefits. I have heard estimates of the value of SSI or Social Security Disability Insurance and their concomitant benefits as $4.50 to $4.85 per hour, compared to the federal minimum hourly wage of $3.35.

Berkowitz (1981, p. 56) recommends: "Managers of rehabilitation programs may have to face the problem and understand that if disincentives are to be overcome, persons must be rehabilitated to jobs in the competitive labor market that will make them at least as well off psychologically and economically as they were prior to entering the rehabilitation program. For those persons for whom this is not a feasible objective, all of the services might be given to them on some other basis designed to improve their status and well-being, but with full recognition that the goal will not be termination from benefit rolls." The following chapters will describe just such efforts by rehabilitation programs in this country and abroad.

1
The American Scene

2
Sheltered Workshops and Work Activity Centers

The first facilities for the vocational rehabilitation of the mentally ill were the sheltered workshops. Sheltered workshops had their origin in services for the physically handicapped. Nelson (1971) described the use of work in the almshouses and poorhouses of medieval Europe and their later specialization in programs for the blind. Schools for the blind were well organized in the United Kingdom by the early 1800s, and some of them incorporated workshops in their facilities. The idea was carried over into the United States, where shops were set up to manufacture such items as mattresses, cushions, pillows, brushes, and brooms, much as many workshops for the blind still do today. Later in the nineteenth century, religious organizations like the Salvation Army and the Society of Saint Vincent de Paul set up workshops for the salvation of the poor and handicapped. They used the salvaging of discarded goods as the medium of work. Later they were joined by the Volunteers of America (an offshoot of the Salvation Army), the Goodwill Industries, and the Deseret Industries (for the handicapped members of the Church of Jesus Christ of Latter-Day Saints).

The Origins of Sheltered Workshops

It might be said that sheltered work programs, because they dealt with a large cross section of the needy, disadvantaged, and handicapped, perforce served the mentally ill as well. However, this was decreasingly so as the years brought the development of the large state mental institutions. By the third decade of this century the greater likelihood was that the identifiable mentally ill were incarcerated in state hospitals. In the late 1930s and early 1940s "freestanding" sheltered workshops for the handicapped, independent of any special religious organization, were organized to serve all categories of disabled persons, but these, too, provided help for very few, if any, of the mentally ill.

Nelson (1971), for example, described the Sheltered Workshop for the Disabled, Inc., founded in 1942 in Binghamton, New York. This "freestanding" community workshop advertised that it accepted all disabilities, with the purposes of employing "handicapped persons who are not capable of adjusting industrially on a competitive basis" and of evaluating and training "disabled persons to become capable of competitive employment by increasing physical improvement and endurance, developing interest, skills, work habits, and psychological adaptation." The Binghamton workshop is located in the shadow of one of the large mental hospitals of New York State, but took no known mental patients. In fact, by the late 1960s, when I visited to urge the workshop to open its doors to the increasing number of patients being discharged from Binghamton State Hospital, the board of directors of the Sheltered Workshop refused to do so. We must turn to the state institutions themselves for origins of the use of work in the therapy of the mentally ill.

I have already recounted the use of work by patients in the large state institutions. Only a very small number of the thousands incarcerated each year ever left the hospitals. Most of those who became stabilized, though with symptoms such that return to community living was not possible, and many who reached good remission but had no home to return to, were put to work at tasks that benefited the hospital. In fact, a goodly part of the economic support of the physically difficult duties (cleaning, laundry, yard work, and the like) came to be performed by patients.

With the passage of the Borden-LaFollette Act by Congress in 1943, the provisions of the vocational rehabilitation sections of the Social Security Act were expanded to include mental as well as physical disability (Public Law 78-113). This allowed the federal-state vocational rehabilitation system to offer services to the mentally ill. All fifty states, the District of Columbia, and Puerto Rico have state governmental bureaus or divisions, approved by the federal agency (presently the Rehabilitation Services Administration of the U.S. Department of Education). The staffs of these divisions include vocational rehabilitation counselors, professionally trained in vocational counseling, employment guidance, psychology, social work, the social sciences, or education. Increasingly their ranks are being filled by graduates of professional schools of vocational rehabilitation counseling, and in recent years there have been added staff with specialized training in vocational evaluation, work assessment, and the management of work-related facilities, including sheltered workshops.

During the 1940s a few of the state programs offered services to the mentally ill. There is little documentation of these experiences. For the most part they seem to have involved testing and counseling of patients referred from a cooperative state hospital. Two examples illustrate these programs and how the ground was laid for the later development of community rehabilitation services.

The Vocational Rehabilitation Division of the Vermont State Department of Education in 1944 appointed a neuropsychiatric advisory committee. A vocational rehabilitation counselor who was a graduate psychologist was deployed to investigate and evaluate mentally handicapped individuals referred (Eldred 1945). In 1948 this counselor became the clinical psychologist for Vermont State Hospital; he began to refer a number of patients to the Vocational Rehabilitation Division "for assistance in vocational planning to be put into effect after leaving the hospital and for various services to implement that planning once they had left" (Eldred 1957, p. 3). By 1957, when Vermont State Hospital was ready to inaugurate a research project in rehabilitation of chronic schizophrenic patients, including industrial therapy, both the hospital and the state vocational rehabilitation agency had had a decade of valuable experience (Black 1970).

The Colorado Division of Vocational Rehabilitation (DVR) established a different format in 1947 (Williams 1953). The position of supervisor of special services for the mentally and emotionally handicapped was established in Pueblo, and the office drew its clientele from the Colorado State Hospital located nearby. The supervisor was given complete access to the hospital staff and its patients. Referrals from hospital to the DVR were somewhat informal, so that patients could easily be called to the attention of the supervisor of special DVR services. No DVR services were actually given to hospital patients until just before or at the time discharge from the hospital was scheduled. The rehabilitation services consisted mainly of counseling and referral to jobs. Most of the patients served in this program returned to jobs that were similar or identical to those at which they had been employed before hospitalization. Little use was made of training programs, for the counselor noted that "we have just about concluded that the client stands a much better chance in making a permanent adjustment if he is capable of entering a vocation with the necessary knowledge upon his release rather than having to embark upon a training period of several months' duration and at the same time make an adjustment necessary to integrate himself into the community and learn a new occupation" (Williams 1953, p. 6).

It should be noted that the Vermont rehabilitation program dealt primarily with patients diagnosed psychoneurotic, and while the Colorado venture served a high proportion of patients in the psychotic categories, both state programs were dealing with a highly selective population among state hospital inmates of the time. These were people who had been employed, had a relatively short stay in the hospital, and had homes and family to return to. Most such persons would not be among the chronically mentally ill found in the public mental institutions or community mental health services today. There was obvious interest in a number of the state vocational rehabilitation programs in serving the "mentally restored," but the efforts to provide services were sparse and sporadic. The development of formal relationships with the field of psychiatry or mental health was yet to come.

In the early 1950s changes in the treatment patterns for mental illness had aroused a worldwide interest in rehabilitation. State mental hospitals were becoming more "open" with the advent of the "therapeutic community" concept (see Jones 1953), and the newly discovered neuroleptic chemicals were coming into wide use. Large numbers of patients were adjudged to be eligible for discharge after shorter hospitalizations. The World Health Organization asked Dr. Maxwell Jones, of England, and Dr. Allen Stoller, of Australia, to undertake an assessment of rehabilitation in psychiatry across the world. Their report (Jones and Stoller 1952) described attempts at industrial therapy and halfway houses in Europe, Africa, Australia, and New Zealand. They also visited the United States, but took note of only two facilities, both in New York City: the Fountain House and the Rehabilitation Center of the American Rehabilitation Committee, Inc., both described later. Their description of the developments in Great Britain aroused great interest among psychiatrists facing the problems in giving services in hospitals which were increasingly adopting the policy of the "open door." The Milbank Fund and federal and state governments made it possible for groups of psychiatrists to visit the British and some of the Dutch programs, and they returned with glowing reports about what was possible in community psychiatry, and particularly about developments in sheltered work or industrial therapy.

Except for the "curative workshop" of the American Rehabilitation Committee, no other community-based rehabilitation program specifically admitted mental patients discharged from hospitals. In 1946 this agency added a psychiatrist to its staff and began to accept neuropsychiatric patients for training in clerical work, printing, messenger service, and machine shop practice. The American Rehabilitation Committee had been established in 1924 by a prominent orthopedic surgeon with the cooperation of the then district manager of the New York State Division of Vocational Rehabilitation, which had its primary interest in serving the physically handicapped (Elton 1948). The industrial or real work aspects of the committee program never developed; however, the work-therapy philosophy of this rehabilitation center had significant impact on developing attitudes toward sheltered workshops for the physically disabled.

Special Workshops for the Mentally Disabled

Although over the years such community agencies as the Salvation Army, Goodwill Industries, and the Volunteers of America accepted "emotionally disturbed " among their clients, there was no clear commitment to serving the mentally ill as a specific category of handicap and no attempt to link the vocational training or experience with ongoing psychiatric treatment. The first program with these intents in the United States was a collaborative one between a voluntary psychiatric hospital, Hillside Hospital, in Queens, New York, and Altro Work Shops, Bronx, New York, the sheltered workshop of Altro Health and Rehabilitation Services, Inc. (Bellak et al. 1956). Patients discharged from Hillside Hospital were referred to Altro Work Shops, and after rehabilitation returned to the workaday world in the community. Altro and Hillside Hospital were very satisfied with the results, and Altro decided to extend the program to patients discharged from the public mental hospitals. The use of psychiatric drugs was taking hold, increasing numbers of patients were being discharged from the state hospitals, and New York's Department of Mental Hygiene had just opened aftercare clinics to provide follow-up of medication. The Bronx Aftercare Clinic was organized not far from Altro Work Shops to serve all patients discharged from mental hospitals who lived in the borough of the Bronx. With the assistance of the Russell Sage Foundation, Altro joined in an experimental-control design evaluation of the efficacy of the service (Meyer and Borgatta 1959).

Altro Health and Rehabilitation Services, and its Altro Work Shops, had had forty years of experience in the rehabilitation of such relapsing, exacerbating illnesses as tuberculosis and heart disease. It was a logical next step for it to turn to service for the psychiatrically disabled. The Work Shops (which will be described more fully later) had no difficulty in assimilating the psychiatrically ill among its other handicapped clientele. The results of the evaluative study suggested, but did not prove, the value of the transitional rehabilitation program provided by Altro Work Shops. The problem with the randomization of discharged mental patients to experimental and control groups was that too few of the experimental sample followed up on referral to the rehabilitation program. What became clear was that patients, once discharged from the hospital, and their families and friends, were inclined to consider themselves cured and not in need of further therapy or rehabilitation. The rate of relapse was very great, however, and by the time the patient realized that all was not going well, his symptoms had exacerbated to the extent that readmission to the hospital (which in those days was very rapid) ended any opportunity for community rehabilitation (Black, Meyer, and Borgatta 1960).

Two laws passed by Congress—one in 1954 amending the Federal Vocational Rehabilitation Act and another in 1956 establishing Title V in the Health Amendments Act—provided impetus for developing sheltered work and other vocational rehabilitation programs for the mentally ill (P.L. 83-565 and P.L. 84-911). The first made it possible for Altro Health and Rehabilitation Services to diversify the kinds of work utilized in its Work Shops and made possible an array of demonstration projects to offer sheltered work to the mentally ill and handicapped in a number of agencies across the country. The second law provided support for vocational rehabilitation programs, along with other community mental health experiments. Altro received support under the Title V provisions to move the base of its work with public mental hospital patients back into Rockland State Mental Hospital, from which the patients to the Bronx Aftercare Clinic were coming. This mental health project grant made it possible to place a team consisting of a psychiatrist, a psychologist, and a vocational rehabilitation counselor full time at the hospital and to set up a cooperative program with an assigned representative of the New York State Division of Vocational Rehabilitation.

The results of that cooperative program were reported in *Guides to Psychiatric Rehabilitation* (Black 1963). The findings of the Rockland State Hospital project are as sound today as they were then in guiding vocational rehabilitation in mental institutions. In brief, they stated (pp. 69–70):

1. Our experience in adapting our services to the needs of patients and staff at Rockland State Hospital and in continuing post-hospital contact with discharged psychotics clearly identified a group of patients without adequate help to bridge the gap to the community. Some patients recover so completely that they require no help; for others, the family, Aftercare Clinic, D.V.R., private psychiatrist, employment agency, casework agency, or financial assistance may alone provide the decisive method of help. In contrast, the very introduction of our comprehensive rehabilitation service stimulated the identification of patients with multiple needs and liabilities who require a variety of services coordinated into a unified program of help.

2. The needs of the psychotic patient clearly go beyond his protection and maintenance during the acute phase of his illness. His requirements in every one of the multiple facets of living must be examined and assessed, and provisions must be made for meeting those in which he may be lacking. These encompass the problems of dwelling, supervision, employment,

job placement, social relations, family relations, and medical and psychiatric care.

3. Undertaking rehabilitation with a specific patient requires a comprehensive and thorough assessment of him. It is necessary to identify the patient's assets and strengths that can be further strengthened and that provide a basis for his life in the community. The assessment must also identify the weaknesses of the patient that will require bulwarking, watching, and care.

4. Identification and assessment of needs are meaningless activities unless resources are available to fulfill resulting plans.

5. The validity of assessment of a patient in the hospital or in the community depends upon the breadth of informational sources. In the hospital this means that everyone who knows the patient—the physician, psychiatrist, ward attendant, work supervisor, occupational therapist, social worker, D.V.R. counselor—must share or contribute information. In the community these sources will include the family, the employment agency, sometimes the employer, other social agencies, occasionally the police, and the psychotherapist.

6. In a psychotic's rehabilitation the process of assessment and implementation is ongoing. The complex variables in the patient, the hospital, and the community make predictions incomplete at best. Moreover, the unfolding experiences in the life of the patient after his discharge from the hospital involve him in unforeseen situations and with unpredictable stimuli that require the rehabilitation agency to be ready at all times for reassessment and reimplementation.

7. When the multiple needs of many post-psychotic patients must be met to assure their return to the community, rehabilitation services unquestionably assume an important role. There is no mystery about the methods or concepts of the rehabilitation process. We are strongly impressed with the fact that the services and the personnel for modern rehabilitation programs already exist within the state hospital. What is required is a kind of administrative catalyst to activate hospital staff toward an interdisciplinary approach to the patient's needs, provide the apparatus for communication, and stimulate communication between disciplines in order to integrate the hospital with the community.

8. Successful rehabilitation is crucially dependent upon a close cooperative relationship between hospital and community. No single service can be considered rehabilitation. Hospitalization, psychiatry, casework or vocational counseling, recreational services, employment agencies, sheltered workshops, residential arrangements, and financial support are not in themselves rehabilitation. Rehabilitation is all of these—not necessarily all working together with the same individual but all integrated into a program in which any, some, or all of them are available for an individual.

One effect of the federal acts was to provide financial stimulation for a number of experiments and demonstrations in work therapy and in sheltered work both in mental hospitals and in community agencies. In the decade between 1956 and 1966 quite a number of such programs were developed, most of them following the traditional pattern of the sheltered workshops serving the physically disabled. Two demonstrations, however, sought different models: the transitional work program of the Fountain House Foundation, New York, and the peer-group support system developed by Dr. George Fairweather at the Palo Alto Veterans Hospital in California. Both of these will be described in later chapters. Some interesting modifications of the sheltered work model were also demonstrated with federal grants, among the more notable being a program for geriatric persons by the Federation Employment and Guidance Service of New York and a program designed to serve family members of psychiatric patients, by the Community Mental Health Center of Lincoln Hospital, in the Bronx. Neither of these played much part, however, in the furtherance of sheltered work for the mentally ill.

The organization of new sheltered workshops specifically for the mentally ill and/or the mentally handicapped (mentally retarded or developmentally disabled) followed a similar pattern, whether started in a mental hospital or as part of a community agency. Space was set aside or acquired to allow for benches and chairs, room for storage of materials, and for pickup and delivery of merchandise, and office space for supervisory employees. Frequently, unused ward space or an unused building on the hospital grounds was put to such use. Arrangements were made to solicit work from business or industry, most usually requiring simple processes of assembly, packaging, or elementary fabrication—what one workshop manager referred to as "gosinter" operations, meaning "this goes into that." The contract with the business that provided the work to be done customarily specified the rate of production expected and the quality desired and set a price per so many completed items of satisfactory quality. In the beginning the prices set provided little than enough more income to pay the wages of the patients/employees. In the mental hospitals, as well as in a number of the community agencies, space, furnishings, and the cost of supervision were met by the mental health facility out of its regular budget. As time went on, successful workshops raised the cost factors upon which payment for work was made by business customers. Three factors contributed to these moves toward more "businesslike" practice. First, questions began to be raised about the unfair undercutting of prices competitive with normal business. Second, these sheltered workshops were included as subject to the provisions of the wage and hour regulations of the U.S. Department of Labor, and the federal minimum wage law (special minima for the handicapped) and state labor laws, in several instances, became applicable. This raised the costs of doing business.

Third, some hospital and mental health administrators began to insist that the sheltered workshops meet a larger proportion of their costs from income for their contract work, including the costs of space and supervision.

Two somewhat parallel advances in the use of sheltered work for the mentally ill took place in the mental hospitals and in community agencies under the stimulation of the federal grants. For the most part, sheltered workshops in hospitals were funded by the National Institute of Mental Health, while those in community agencies were supported through the Federal Office of Vocational Rehabilitation. The U.S. Veterans Administration also supported some sheltered workshop services, notably in Bedford and Brockton, Massachusetts, and in Palo Alto, California.

Workshops in the Mental Hospitals

A look at some of these earlier state mental hospital ventures illustrates quite clearly the purposes for which they organized and the problems they faced.

MANHATTAN STATE HOSPITAL

The first workshop in a mental hospital was opened by Dr. Herman Denber at Manhattan State Hospital, on Wards Island, New York City. Dr. Denber had been among the psychiatrists who visited European mental hospitals in 1954. He was in charge of research with the new ataractic drugs. He and his associates "were struck by the lack of appreciation of the schizophrenic psychopathology in structuring the daily life on the ward; the absence of individual attention to specific details of each patient's symptoms and a non-recognition of the rehabilitative potential during the hospital stay" (Denber and Rajotte 1962, p. 31). It was not until 1958 that he was able to obtain permission, through an act of the New York State Legislature, to open a sheltered workshop performing contract work directly from the community. He conceived the workshop as a research undertaking and received a grant from the National Institute of Mental Health.

Denber first used occupational therapists to supervise the patients' work and make clinical observations. Later, he turned to the use of the nursing aide staff. These attendants saw their role in the workshop as much more satisfying and helpful to patients than their traditional one. It seemed that the aides saw the workshop as a tool uniquely available to them for therapeutic purposes (Black 1970).

The Manhattan State Hospital sheltered workshop solicited very simple bench assembly, packaging novelties and colored construction paper. In an old, unused building on the hospital grounds, away from the wards, long workbenches were set up in a light, airy room. The project suffered from a typical problem of mental hospital workshops, and indeed, of many of those set up in the community: there was not a constant flow of contract work to be had. The problem of work procurement was one to which hospital staff were not accustomed, nor had they the time to devote to it nor often the right to perform it within their job requirements.

Another problem usual to hospital workshops was that there was no program continuity for patients who became functionally able to leave the hospital. For some time Denber "graduated" some of his better workers to Altro Work Shops. At that time, however, Altro's major occupation was machine sewing, which was of great interest to the women patients, but only a limited number were willing to make the trip to the Bronx from Wards Island. These were mostly patients who had been in the mental institution for years, and it was significant that Altro reported high success in training and placing these women in industry. The Manhattan State Hospital sheltered workshop lasted only as long as Dr. Denber and Dr. Rajotte, his assistant, continued their research under grant funding. It then closed down, and not until new rehabilitation center programs were established in the New York State mental hospitals in the early 1970s was a sheltered work type of program reestablished.

MIDDLETOWN STATE HOSPITAL

The director of Middletown State Hospital, New York State, had also been among the psychiatrists sent by the Milbank Fund to visit programs in England and Holland. Dr. Hyman Pleasure took advantage of the legislative permission to open a sheltered workshop in 1963, utilizing space in hospital buildings and in locations close to the wards. Dr. Pleasure combined the subcontract work he obtained from local industry with some work in hospital occupations, thus predating by many years manpower training programs for the mentally handicapped in hospitals. Occupational therapists were assigned to instruct and supervise patients in folding shopping bags, cutting and baling cloth remnants, lacing leather pieces for shoes, hand weaving, and other simple bench work. The hospital woodworking shop was used for training, and the hospital furniture refinishing shop was allowed to accept orders from private individuals along with its work for the hospital.

A hospital staff member was given the responsibility of soliciting contract work from businesses and industry in the Middletown area. A cadre of long-term patients served to insure the flow of work done. Even though the mental hospitals did not have to report to the Wage and

Hours Division of the U.S. Department of Labor until a Supreme Court decision of 1968, Dr. Pleasure was meticulous in insisting that pricing of work be predicated upon the minimum wage paid by the customer in his own plant for similar work. The orders received were translated into piecework rates for payment to the patients according to their production. Eighty percent of the income from production was used for wages to patients; 20 percent was retained by the workshop to supply items not included in the hospital budget, such as radios for the working areas and small luxuries not available to the patients.

As the years went on, greater use was made of a community workshop strongly supported by the state Division of Vocational Rehabilitation. The hospital workshop has become much more of a "work activity center," about which more will be said later.

MEDFIELD STATE HOSPITAL

Two early programs in Massachusetts mental hospitals were important in the development of concepts in the use of sheltered work. In 1962, under a grant from the National Institute of Mental Health, a research demonstration project in rehabilitation for chronic schizophrenic patients was opened at Medfield State Hospital. About 300 schizophrenic patients, out of a total hospital population of 1,200, who were 60 years of age or under and hospitalized for at least one year were randomly assigned to experimental and control groups. For the experimental group a quite extensive array of services were provided. For the control group no change was made in the usual array of hospital services.

In its report to the National Institute of Mental Health (Lee 1963), the project listed the components of the experimental program as including

1. An in-hospital and extra-hospital work program for patients under the supervision of a vocational counselor;
2. An evening activity program under the direction of an occupational therapist;
3. A discussion group program under the direction of a psychologist;
4. Intensive search for relatives and other sources of family and community support for the patients by the social worker;
5. Special training classes in groups;
6. A sheltered workshop providing training in factory-type work and with payment for it;
7. Involving ward and work area personnel in the assessment of and planning for patients;
8. Recruitment of volunteers for specialized jobs with activity groups and as assistants to the regular staff members;
9. The use of a ward building in a manner similar to that of a half-way house in which emphasis was given to the patient's own responsibilities in managing;

10. A standardized rating system under which each patient was evaluated at work and on the ward and was given previously-announced privileges on the basis of his ratings (known as the *step system*). (Pp. 5–6)

The vocational counselor attached to the experimental group of 140 chronic schizophrenic patients developed work placements appropriate to their interests and abilities. In-hospital work areas used by the project were more varied than those in most state hospitals, and included the bakery, beauty parlor, kitchen, electrician's shop, elevator operation, garage, laundry, library, housekeeping, furniture repair and refinishing, lawns and outdoor maintenance, power house, storeroom, record room, reception, and work with the mason, plumber, electrician and painter, and work on the farm. The sheltered workshop had contract work in the making of strings of Christmas-tree lights; stringing key-chains; engraving Bakelite dials; cutting flowers, ribbons, and other millinery articles; and assembling and packaging jewelry and novelties. Those patients who reached the highest level of capability were able to go out to work in the community while still living in the hospital or in the "halfway house" set up in a building on grounds (Paquette and Lafave 1964). Outside work was obtained in a local hat factory; as chambermaids, kitchen help, or caretakers and maintenance personnel in a hotel; in repair work on lawns and houses; in nursing homes; and in a bakery and a cleaners. These are all typical of the employment opportunities used in the more recent community programs, to be described later.

It is significant to current understanding of the needs of the chronically mentally ill that this program considered sheltered work alone as insufficient. "It was the firm belief of those who originated the project that for the chronic schizophrenic patients to be served, the program must be concerned with their living arrangements, recreational and diversional activities, their family life and socialization, as well as the work they would be doing" (Black 1970, p. 75). Three aspects of the Medfield State Hospital program are particularly relevant in work with chronic patients. First, there was a frank recognition that motivation on the part of schizophrenic patients for rehabilitation would be very low. Second, the use of a "step system" allowed for a structured and measured progression with rewards for increasing functional abilities. Third, the project was able to demonstrate the feasibility of using operant conditioning in increasing performance on the job, in areas of speed of work, accuracy, punctuality, personal appearance, ability to work with others, and acceptance of authority.

BOSTON STATE HOSPITAL

The second mental hospital program in Massachusetts germane to the development of sheltered work was developed at Boston State Hospital in 1963. At the time this hospital was at the forefront of developments in community psychiatry. Drawing upon the experience of Dr. Querido of Amsterdam in introducing crisis intervention services, open hospital wards, and day-and-night hospital service, Boston State Hospital had been opening such programs on an experimental basis. The hospital also organized a patient-employee program paying those patients selected for assignment to hospital jobs at the rate of $16.00 a week (Black 1970). The newly established rehabilitation department decided to complement the patient-employee program with a sheltered workshop.

The sheltered workshop in the hospital was not successful. Contracts were difficult to obtain, and the hospital personnel were not knowledgeable about the business procedures and the right kinds of equipment to perform satisfactory assembly or manufacturing. The hospital director turned to a local businessman for advice, and he recommended their setting up a nonprofit corporation, with representation on its governing board from industry in the community. A state-chartered corporation was organized, called PROP (Patients' Rehabilitation Occupational Program, Inc.). PROP negotiated with manufacturers for work, obtained a certificate as a sheltered workshop from the U.S. Department of Labor, and met the wage and hour requirements of the federal government and the state.

PROP was able to advertise its services to businesses. It claimed advantages in its ability to pay wages below the costs in outside industry and free the customer of the costs of fringe benefits and in its exemption from federal employer taxes, state unemployment compensation, and workmen's compensation costs. It advertised that the state hospital would furnish space; light, heat, and power; and supervisory personnel. It pointed out that the customer would be freed of the costs of recruiting, training, and labor turnover. While true, and of real value to businesses subcontracting out assembly or fabrication work, in another context many of these can be considered disadvantages. As will be discussed later, some in the business world considered these unwarranted subsidies by the state and productive of unfair competition.

OTHER MENTAL HOSPITALS

Two other states that invested rather heavily in developing sheltered workshops in their mental hospitals were California and Illinois. The first workshop in a California state mental hospital opened in Napa

State Hospital, at Imola, in 1960. Nelson (1971) described this shop and subsequent ones at Porterville and at Agnews state hospitals as "bootleg," for there was no budgetary or administrative authorization for such enterprises until 1962, when the legislature made an appropriation to add sheltered work services at Patton and DeWitt state hospitals. Soon after the legality of sheltered workshops was established in California in 1963, there were forty-two workshops in the then existing state hospitals. California has to all practical purposes closed most of its state institutions, so that today little remains of what was a fairly comprehensive demonstration.

In Illinois the emphasis was upon sheltered work programs in the hospital wards (Nelson 1971). The aim of these work programs was to evaluate the ability of patients to move to a central workshop or out to the community. Concern was with the development of work habits and behavior, and the shops were thought of as components of the patients' therapy. While certain hospitals put great stock in ward workshops (Chicago State Hospital had fifteen ward workshops in 1968), there were complications to their management that limited their expansion. Sufficient space could not always be kept inviolate for work activities, necessitating storing work in progress and taking it out again during work hours. Materials and equipment had to be moved and delivered between a number of locations, adding to the cost in time and transport of raw material and finished goods.

WORKSHOPS IN THE VETERANS ADMINISTRATION HOSPITALS

Soon after World War II the Veterans Administration hospitals began to develop work-related rehabilitation programs in an effort to prepare patients for return to community living. This effort was independent of the amendments to the Social Security Act and the vocational rehabilitation amendments (Knudson 1959). Concern was raised that the use of patients in the usual hospital occupations might be considered exploitation, so the manager of the hospital at Perry Point, Maryland, designed what he called the Member Employee Program. This called for the work assignments to be coordinated with the vocational counseling service. The idea was to relate hospital work experience with the veteran's expected work experience after discharge. The Member Employee Program was carried to the Brockton, Massachusetts, Veterans Administration Hospital with the transfer of the Perry Point manager and was enlarged to become the Continued Opportunity for Productive Endeavors (COPE). Shortly, the Member Employee Program became a recommended rehabilitation plan for VA hospitals.

COPE and its facsimiles (e.g., the VIP—vocational industrial placement—at North Little Rock Hospital) could not meet the needs of many patients. Dr. William Winick, director of the Brockton Hospital, was one of the psychiatrists influenced by the developments in England and Holland. He set about seeing whether the industrial therapy model (called sheltered workshops in the United States) could be used to rehabilitate the long-term chronic patient. Brockton Veterans Administration Hospital was entirely a psychiatric hospital. A sheltered workshop was set up in quarters apart from the wards, requiring that patients who went to work had to leave their living areas, thus normalizing one aspect of working.

Earl S. Frost, coordinator of the physical medicine and rehabilitation services at the hospital, was put in charge of what came to be known as CHIRP (Community Hospital Industry Rehabilitation Program) (*SK&F Psychiatric Reporter* 1962). Frost, assisted by staff from his department and from manual arts therapy, developed one of the most successful sheltered work programs in a mental hospital in the United States. Brockton was located in an area of small industry, and by actively soliciting contacts with key people in those firms Frost was able to obtain quite an array of work for the patients to do. In addition to the simple bench assembly and packaging familiar to most hospitals, CHIRP took on industrial work requiring the use of tools and equipment supplied by the manufacturers. This included inspecting and testing electrical components, grinding and soldering jewelry, buffing and polishing copper bowls, and small drilling assemblies. The businesses seemed highly satisfied with the quality and rate of production, and expressed satisfaction in contributing to the rehabilitation of hospitalized veterans (Frost 1965a, 1965b).

Two characteristics of the CHIRP experience have great relevance to the progress of sheltered work. First, the contacts between the business firms and the sheltered workshop were carried on by a hospital staff member who had himself had factory work experience prior to professional training. This, as we shall see, took a page out of the European experience with workshop management. Second, the work setting was made to look as much as possible like a real work environment, including the use of time clocks and insistence upon acceptable deportment. Production requirements were comparable to those in industry, and the federal minimum wage was paid. The earnings were credited to an account for each patient; the amount actually made available to the patient was determined medically.

The business standards and practices had much to recommend them to other hospital sheltered workshops. Visitors from state mental hospitals and from European sheltered work programs were not so impressed, however. They noted, in discussions with me, that the patients in CHIRP were much younger and seemed more highly selected for functional capacity than the long-term chronic patients in the public mental hospitals.

One other Veterans Administration hospital should be mentioned at this time—the VA Hospital at Palo Alto, California—not for its sheltered workshop, which resembled that at Brockton, but as the setting in which a different form of work rehabilitation was developed—what has come to be known as the Fairweather Group Program. This will be described in a later chapter.

Changes in the Mental Hospital System

At first, the pioneering workshops just discussed and the results of a federal judicial decision had the effect of stimulating the establishment of sheltered workshops in the state mental hospitals. Complaints had been made about the use of patients as workers in the hospitals on menial jobs with little or inadequate remuneration. A class action suit against the U.S. Department of Labor resulted in a ruling that fair wages must be paid to patients performing work of economic benefit to institutions even if the work was labeled as therapy (*Souder vs. Brennan* 1973). While this ended the use of patients in the long-standing system of peonage, it also ended the use of hospital occupations as part of a therapeutic process, for the states did not have the means to pay such regular wages. A number of the state hospitals then sought certificates to operate sheltered workshops, either directly for the hospital or by organizing nonprofit corporations for the purpose. A few years later another Supreme Court decision ruled that the minimum wage and overtime provisions of the Fair Labor Standards Act could not be constitutionally applied to state and local government employees engaged in activities which are an integral part of traditional governmental functions (*National League of Cities vs. Usery* 1976). Since it was not clear whether patient-workers in hospital sheltered workshops were really state employees, and it was not established that sheltered workshops were engaged in "traditional governmental functions," the U.S. Department of Labor removed public hospital sheltered workshops from wage and hour jurisdiction. Some states (e.g., New York) continued the regulations under state mandate, but in most instances the workshops were left without standard-setting oversight. It was not until 1985 that the U.S. Department of Labor, beset by complaints from community-based sheltered workshops of unwarranted competition and urged on by a report of the comptroller general of the United States (Comptroller General 1981) reinstated publicly operated sheltered workshops under the wage and hour regulations.

During the period that sheltered work programs were being established in the mental hospitals there occurred what has been referred to as a "revolution" in the care and treatment of the major mental illnesses. First there came the opening of closed wards, the inauguration of the "therapeutic community," the humanizing of treatment, and the speeding up of discharge from state institutions. The use of the major tranquilizers made the behavior of many patients more tractable, and there was increased concern for the civil liberties of patients and for treatment in "the least restrictive environment." The expectation by funding bodies and the state legislatures that there could be economic savings in the cost of public care if more patients could be discharged sooner resulted in an increasing flow of dischargees, in a process now referred to as "deinstitutionalization."

The movement of such large numbers of still very dysfunctional people into their communities put extra pressure upon the comprehensive community mental health centers, which had been authorized in federal legislation in the 1960s (P.L. 88-164, the Community Mental Health Centers Act of 1963). Later, community support systems were developed as well as provisions for alternative living arrangements for ex-patients who could not return to their family homes. These will be discussed in a later section.

Just as the sheltered workshops in the hospitals were beginning to flourish, the discharge of the most functionally capable of the patients began to affect their operation. Sheltered work has been defined as "any vocationally oriented rehabilitation facility which provides (1) training, including structured employment, for handicapped workers who have potential for competitive employment or (2) full-time employment for severely handicapped persons who cannot move from sheltered into competitive employment" (Comptroller General 1981, p. 1). In the mental hospital system of the United States, however, sheltered work was seen almost entirely as transitional, as a means of preparing patients for return to community living and to normal employment. In fact, it was not until after the 1967 amendments to the federal Vocational Rehabilitation Act established the concept of "extended employment" that thought was given to the possibility of using sheltered work environments as places of permanent employment. By then, deinstitutionalization was well under way, and the hospitals found it increasingly difficult to maintain workshops capable of meeting customers' requirements in production and quality.

The Work Activity Center

A new category of service—the work activity center—was developed in the 1974 amendments to the U.S. Fair Labor Standards Act.

These centers were established to meet the needs of those patients or clients unable to produce work at more than 50 percent of regular minimum wage. Certificates for work activity centers are issued by the U.S. Department of Labor with the approval of the state agency for vocational rehabilitation. The rules applying to work activity centers require that such facilities be entirely separate from any regular sheltered workshop. Patients in a work activity center must be paid for their production at the same rate but can earn less than the 50 percent of federal minimum wage required as a base in the regular sheltered workshop. It is possible for a sheltered workshop to obtain an individual exemption to the 50 percent by obtaining individual certificates for severely handicapped patients, but this involves a lot of paperwork, and does not fit the needs of the part-time worker.

Work activity centers turned out to be particularly valuable as part of the treatment services for the mentally ill. They allow for the linking of recreation and socialization programs and of psychotherapeutic services with part-time work. This was of great value to the mental hospitals left increasingly with residual populations of severely disabled and elderly patients. Part of a day of work could be joined with occupational therapy, creative arts, and skills training to provide a more rounded rehabilitation program. A recent analysis shows that nearly 50 percent of all workshop certificates issued by the U.S. Department of Labor are now for work activity centers, and over 70 percent of all handicapped workers are in these programs (*NARF Rehabilitation Review,* December 23, 1985).

There are two distinct disadvantages to the work activity center for mental patients. One of these is a business structural problem, the other clinical-programmatic. Generating a flow of work to be done by the patients requires the same attention to subcontracting of work, quality control, delivery schedules, and other business matters as for a regular sheltered workshop (Black 1965). The amount of production possible in a work activity center, since it operates on a part-day basis, is usually too low to interest business contractors. Therefore, many such centers are combined with or linked to larger sheltered workshops serving a more diversified clientele. The other disadvantage is that there is an inclination on the part of many professionals to keep patients for long periods in these partial work programs on the surmise that serious mental illness is directly correlated with inability to be productive at work. Frequently such patients are able to raise their functional levels to be able to participate in sheltered work or even in regular competitive employment, and to keep them in a work activity center is a disservice.

Early Sheltered Workshops in Community Agencies

Following World War II community rehabilitation agencies began to note a change in the clientele they had been serving. Modern rehabilitation medicine and an expanded economy made it possible for many of the physically handicapped (primarily orthopedically disabled) to return to the community and to obtain employment after treatment and physical therapy, without the need for a period in a sheltered workshop. The rehabilitation services found they were dealing with an increasing number of multiply handicapped people, in which the barriers to employability appeared to be in the psychological sphere. In 1955 the Federal Office of Vocational Rehabilitation awarded one of the new research and demonstration grants to the Jewish Vocational Service of Chicago to test out ways of dealing with emotionally disturbed clientele (Gellman et al. 1955).

This agency, under the direction of Dr. William Gellman, a psychologist and social worker, had a long history of bringing work therapy to a wide array of physically handicapped people. It had opened a small sheltered workshop, obtaining simple bench assembly and packaging work from local business and industry. In this shop it had pioneered techniques for serving the more severely disabled, the younger handicapped entering the labor market for the first time, the older worker with job placement difficulties, and the emotionally disturbed and mentally handicapped. Gellman advanced six assumptions for his study of work adjustment of the emotionally handicapped. These were

1. Job turnover is more often due to inadequate vocational adjustment than to lack of job skill, and the majority of unskilled and semi-skilled positions require a 'work personality' rather than specific skill experience.
2. When the work done acquires a positive value for an individual, his job performance, his job satisfaction and even his job seeking efforts will increase.
3. A successful work experience which leads to job satisfaction will help the person to attain the 'work personality' which is admired in our culture.
4. If a person has a satisfying work experience and therefore develops the desire to work, his confidence in his ability to work will be enhanced, and he will be enabled to accept more realistic vocational goals and a vocational attitude consonant with his abilities.
5. A satisfying and successful work experience will stimulate the development of an adequate work personality, this in spite of cultural resistances to working.
6. Even where the resistance to entering the world of work is primarily the result of personality adjustment, a guided work experience will help the individual to reach vocational adjustment. (Gellman 1956, p. 113)

These principles hold fairly well in today's work with the mentally ill, except that Gellman did not give much attention to the lack of motivation which is so much a part of the character of the schizophrenic illnesses. The Chicago Jewish Vocational Service introduced only the simplest kind of bench assembly work into its workshop in order that supervision could be done by psychologically trained staff without their having to acquire the special skills of industrial production. Patients/clients remained in the workshop a limited time, eight or twelve weeks, and elaborate rating devices were applied on a number of diagnostic, remedial, or restorative objectives. It became clear by the end of the demonstration that while the program was quite successful for many with emotional difficulties, it was not meeting the needs of those diagnosed in the major psychiatric classifications who came to the workshop after a stay in the state mental hospitals.

The Chicago Jewish Vocational Service then followed the lead of the Altro Work Shops and set up a study cooperatively with the state mental hospital, Chicago State Hospital. A sheltered workshop was established in a remodeled factory building three miles from the hospital. At first, patients were bused from the hospital to the workshop, but after a few months most of the patients were traveling by public transportation. A very tight research design in assignment of patients to the sheltered workshop program, with urging from the project and hospital personnel, avoided the dropouts and refusal to participate experienced by the earlier Russell Sage Foundation study at Altro Workshops.

Three sample groups were utilized. One was the experimental group at the workshop; one has provided only the services routinely offered to all patients; and the third group was provided with recreational therapy outside the hospital, at the Chicago Mental Health Center. In this study the results were statistically significant in successful outcome of the experimental group compared to the controls. Evaluation was in terms of parameters on obtaining competitive employment and length of time remaining in the community. Interestingly, the group receiving recreational services was also significantly more successful than the group provided only the normal hospital services (Soloff 1968).

As was generally true of sheltered workshops in the United States at the time, the Chicago Jewish Vocational Service considered its program a transitional phase toward community integration. The experience with Chicago State Hospital raised questions that foresaw the nature of rehabilitative efforts after deinstitutionalization. The vocational service said: "Continued support appears necessary for many clients to implement new roles and to learn still other roles. All aspects of the program are still necessary parts of the rehabilitation process, of the major goals of community living, social functioning and productive roles. The staff of the program will often need to remain a major resource to clients making the last stage of a long effort to achieve these goals" (Soloff 1968, p. 7).

Jewish vocational services in other cities followed the prototype of the Chicago agency and obtained federal funding to demonstrate work adjustment programs. The Jewish Employment Services of Philadelphia modified its existing workshop in 1958 to "promote the employability of disabled individuals with emotional and mental problems by strengthening work attitudes and behavior and by stimulating the formation of an adequate work personality" (Jewish Employment and Vocational Service 1962). This project assigned a professional counselor to each client, who assisted in placement in outside industry. There were group sessions of clients where a number had problems of a similar nature, a system that predated the "job clubs" used by a number of rehabilitation agencies today. In placement in jobs after the work adjustment center the project reported its greatest success with the group of clients labeled psychotic, amounting to 40 percent of its total clientele. The Jewish Employment Services of Philadelphia is remembered today for a later development, that of a widely used vocational evaluation procedure referred to as the JEVS program.

The Jewish vocational services of Cincinnati, Milwaukee, Los Angeles, and Essex County, New Jersey, followed suit. Each made modifications in the prototype, but each found it necessary to establish closer working relations with the hospital of referral, to gradually extend the time limits of the work adjustment program, and to add counseling and recreation services. Other community agency programs cooperative with mental hospitals developed about the same time, as demonstrations supported by the Federal Office of Vocational Rehabilitation. Most notable were that of the Goodwill Industries of Fort Worth, Texas, in cooperation with the U.S. Public Health Service Hospital, and that of the Handcraft Industries of Hollywood, California, with Camarillo State Hospital.

The Goodwill Industries program was the first of a number of later programs in the various Goodwill Industries that were set up to give special attention to the "mentally restored." Some of these members of the national Goodwill Industries network now offer more than one of the kinds of work programs described in this volume. A more detailed description of one of them, in Orange County, California, is given in the last section of this chapter.

One of the few original community demonstration projects to continue its services to the mentally ill uninterruptedly over the years (another being Altro Work Shops) has been that of Handcraft Industries, of the Jewish Vocational Service of Los Angeles in Hollywood, California. Set up originally as a sheltered workshop for German Jewish immigrants following World War II, the workshop soon opened its doors to a variety of handicapped persons. Its demonstration of services to the mentally ill was inaugurated in 1963 in cooperation with Camarillo State Hospital (Goertzel et al. 1967). This project used the bakery of the hospital as the initial testing station in preparation of work adjustment from which the patients could move on to work at Handcraft Industries. The patients were all schizophrenic men, 18 to 45 years of age, whose home location was within easy commuting distance to the sheltered workshop. The program at Handcraft Industries followed the prototype of the Chicago demonstration.

The results of the Handcraft project were threefold. On the negative side, when the federal funding ended, the hospital bakery lost interest in taking in these generally low-functioning patients and returned to its usual selection of long-term, more productive people, until the *Souder vs. Brennan* decision in 1973 ended the use of unpaid labor by patients. As to positive results, the project demonstrated the efficacy of a continuum of services from hospital out into the community; the outcome figures for the 146 patients served were impressive. It also resulted in a cooperative agreement between the California Department of Rehabilitation and the California Department of Mental Hygiene that a comprehensive vocational rehabilitation program at Camarillo State Hospital be established under the direction of the project's supervisor.

Changes in the Community Mental Health Picture

Before we turn to Handcraft Industries and other sheltered work programs as they now exist, it is necessary to account for some major changes that have occurred in the community mental health systems. First, the federal demonstrations did have the effect of interesting the vocational rehabilitation agencies in the possibilities of serving the mentally ill. The amendments to the Vocational Rehabilitation Act opened the door for demonstrations, and the controlling regulations were modified to include the mentally ill among the "severely handicapped" to be covered under the expanded mandate. The result was, as in the Handcraft-Camarillo project, greater willingness by the state vocational rehabilitation agencies to enter into cooperative compacts with the mental hospitals.

In New York State, for example, new rehabilitation buildings and facilities were constructed on the grounds of a number of the state hospitals, and a cooperative rehabilitation services was established in which the local or regional DVR staff were to function as a unit with the hospital rehabilitation personnel. For a few years some of these functioned quite well. Then the changing mental health system and the effect of deinstitutionalization broke the cooperation asunder. The DVRs complained, with a good deal of justification, that the patients left in the hospital were not prepared nor ready for vocational rehabilitation counseling, never mind job placement, and that the DVR relationships should be with community agencies rather than with the hospitals.

Even before deinstitutionalization became recognized as the trend, the Community Mental Health Centers Act had stimulated the building and operation of scores of community-based facilities across the country for treatment and aftercare of the mentally ill. These "comprehensive community mental health centers" were expected to deal with two great problems, the recently recognized public mental health need for psychiatric services among the general population, as depicted in the Midtown Study (Srole 1962) and other epidemiological findings, and the increasing need for aftercare services for patients discharged from the mental hospitals. In the regulations for the establishment of these centers there was attention to the necessary liaison with the mental hospital, as well as to day hospital and crisis intervention and other elements of a psychiatric treatment program, but no mention was made of rehabilitation services of any sort. When questioned, federal officials insisted that the need for rehabilitation was obvious, but as one who reviewed many applications for federal and state grants for establishing such centers I rarely found any reference to including rehabilitation services, and never to the organization of a sheltered work program.

By the early 1970s the regulations had been modified to require a larger number of "basic" services, and these did include reference to rehabilitation. A few centers began to form cooperative programs with sheltered workshops and other types of rehabilitative services, mainly for housing. However, the full number of comprehensive community mental health centers planned across the country were never established, leaving vast areas where there were little or no community services. In the mid-1970s the mental health center movement was charged with not having met the second of its expected obligations, that of services to the discharged mentally ill, specifically the chronically mentally ill population (Comptroller General 1977). The National Institute of Mental Health then inaugurated a new national initiative entitled Community Support Program to help the states organize integrated aftercare, outpatient services to the dischargees from the public mental hospitals. The community support programs were to be required to include demonstrations in continuity of social and psychiatric care for the chronically mentally ill, including transitional housing and vocational rehabilitation (see Turner and TenHoor 1978).

A review of sheltered and other types of work programs for the mentally ill reveals that most of the relatively few such facilities included with the community support program agencies are work activity centers rather than full-fledged sheltered workshops. Some have opted for other kinds of work-related services, such as transitional or supported work, but most have formed cooperative relations for referral to a community-based rehabilitation agency willing to accept mental patients. Examples will appear in later chapters.

A complicating factor to the use of community vocational agencies in rehabilitation of the mentally ill has been the differing requirements for funding by the mental health and vocational rehabilitation agencies of the states. Notwithstanding cooperative agreements at the federal and state levels between these human service agencies, there have been sharp differences in practice. The federal-state vocational rehabilitation system is bound by legislation that expects its funds to be expended primarily towards return to or reestablishment in a job in the open labor force. The mental health field has utilized funding from Medicaid (Title 19) and public social services (Title 20) funds of the Social Security Act which have been interpreted to be mainly for health services. Unhappy distinctions are frequently made between what is called "treatment" and "training." Good vocational rehabilitation programs for the mentally ill have been closed because the state DVR would not grant funds to a mental health facility for what it considered to be "therapy" or because the mental health authority would not make a subsidy available to a community rehabilitation agency for what it considered to be "training." In reading the definitions for the two approaches in New York State regulations, for example, it is impossible to understand the distinction between "treatment" or "training" in a mental health agency.

Contemporary Sheltered Workshops

A better understanding of what sheltered workshops look like today and appreciation of the range of their services can be derived from a description of some examples. I have selected three workshops from among the many I have known and visited, ones I consider to be typical of the various approaches in use. Discussion of the therapeutic systems used, and business practices and issues, will be reserved for a later chapter, after presentation of alternatives to the sheltered workshop have been described. Matters of therapy and of business are common to all of the different types of work programs used in therapy and rehabilitation of the mentally ill. At any rate, the classification distinctions I am making are purely subjective; many programs carry on more than one approach, and some combine parts of two or more into modifications of their own. The sheltered workshops I have selected for illustration are (1) Altro Workshops, of the Altro Health and Rehabilitation Services, New York, New York, illustrating a program almost entirely dedicated to rehabilitation of the mentally ill; (2) Goodwill Industries of Orange County, Santa Ana, California, one of the largest of the Goodwill Industries, in the process of shifting most of its services to the mentally ill and the mentally handicapped; and (3) South Shore Rehabilitation Center, a division of Work, Inc., of North Quincy, Massachusetts, a sheltered workshop for all handicapped which has been experimenting with special programs for the mentally ill.

ALTRO WORKSHOPS

I have already described the origins of the program at Altro for the mentally ill. Altro's background evolved more within the framework of public health than of vocational rehabilitation services. In fact, the sheltered workshop was considered the ancillary program in the era of dealing with the handicap of tuberculosis. It was a way station on the road to encapsulation of the tubercle bacillus, in which "work hardening" was considered necessary between leaving the sanitorium and returning to the long factory days of the first three decades of this century. From the beginning, then, the rehabilitation team consisted of physician, nurse, social worker, and workshop supervisor. Much later, when cardiac rehabilitation was added and when it was recognized that there were psychological difficulties for some of the tuberculous patients, psychologist and psychiatrist were added to the team.

The day at the workshop had been regulated, on prescription of doctor and nurse, into periods of work and periods of rest. The concept was one of returning the patient to a normal work setting, but "conditioning" the work pressures to the needs of the patient. This concept, with modifications, was carried over into work with the psychiatrically handicapped. Another concept, still adhered to, was that while the patient was at work, the demands of the workplace would take precedence, a principle to be discussed in the chapter on the balance between therapy and employment.

Altro Workshops today is located in a good-sized factory-type building originally used for automotive sales and repairs. There are two floors above ground and a full, well-lighted, and airy basement. The lowest level is occupied by its workshops for machine tool operations and mechanical assembly. The first floor houses business offices, the garment manufacturing plant, and the nursing and medical offices. The upper floor has workshops for packaging and direct mail, printing, and food services. There are also rooms for vocational evaluation, group sessions, social workers and other professional staff, and a lunchroom and lounge. On any one day there are some 360 clients in the workshops of Altro. In addition, the parent agency serves over 300 clients in two "proprietary homes for adults" (group residential homes for discharged mental hospital patients), providing case management services and a work activities center (the Bench Assembly Workshop). In its Manhattan offices and in other community residences run by the agency another couple of hundred clients are provided with programs. All in all, Altro Health and Rehabilitation Services helps some 1,700 psychiatric clients a year. Altro also has been developing a transitional employment program, using the businesses of some of the members of its board of directors, and is planning a supportive work program.

Clients are referred to the Altro program from a variety of sources. The two large state mental hospitals within commuting distance—Bronx and Manhattan Psychiatric Centers—account for a sizeable group, as do the community mental health centers in the Bronx, upper Manhattan, and lower Westchester County. Schizophrenic disorders account for 52 percent of the handicapping diagnoses of the clients, personality disorders for 19 percent, affective disorders for 8 percent, anxiety disorders for 4 percent, and organic brain disorders for another 4 percent. About 13 percent fall into other diagnostic categories. Altro claims to place some 35 percent of its clients in competitive employment in the open labor market; another 21 percent go on to school or return to homemaking or settle into volunteer work. Less than 6 percent are rehospitalized.

In keeping with its treatment-oriented focus, Altro bases admission to its programs on a complete psychosocial evaluation, which includes a medical examination, a psychiatric evaluation, psychological testing, and social history. A team consideration of the findings, to which the referring agency is invited, leads to a decision as to acceptance and as to which of the various work programs the applicant will be assigned. There is participation by the patient in this decision-making, an important principle of rehabilitation programming these days. Concern that this process unnecessarily delayed admission to the workshop and produced a high rate of dropouts between referral and admission has speeded up the procedure, and some of the admission assessment is now completed after the patient is tentatively assigned to a work or work-evaluation setting.

Although Altro is proud of the fact that 56 percent of its "graduates" are successfully placed in jobs, school, volunteer work, or homemaking—a fairly high rate for agencies dealing with the chronically mentally ill—and proud of its very low rate of hospitalization, it believes it could do better. For this reason it seeks to augment its workshops with other approaches to using work in therapy and rehabilitation. It is proud, too, that it has modified its work programs to keep up with the changes in the employment market and has shifted in its admission policy to try to meet the needs of changing clientele. Thus, as data processing gave way to computerized operations in the commercial fields Altro shifted to computer services; as machine lathe work decreased, Altro moved to machine stamping; as the service fields have increased, Altro has added food services; and so on. Recognizing some years ago that the clientele being referred were more seriously disabled, Altro moved to add services such as case management, work activity, and skills training to its armamentarium at the workshops. It has developed special services in residential care under the state's Community Support Program and is turning its attention to the increasing public mental health problems of the homeless mentally ill and the young chronically mentally ill.

The budget under which Altro functioned in 1984–85 totaled over $11 million. Over 60 percent of the income supporting this expenditure came from workshop sales and services. Nearly 33 percent came from governmental grants and fees, the largest amount from the mental health authorities of New York State and New York City. Contributions of various sorts made up the rest.

For nearly sixty years the garment manufacturing plant at Altro was engaged in direct manufacture of hospital garments, which it sold directly to hospitals in the open competitive market. In the mid-1970s it sold this business to a commercial competitor but has continued this work area (of significance to the New York job scene) by subcontracts for the manufacture of garments for the Veterans Administration hospitals and the Army. These have become available through "set-asides" of government contracts under the Javits, Wagner, O'Day Act of 1971. These contracts constitute a resource much in use by sheltered workshops and transitional work programs, and will be discussed in a later chapter. Altro now also has such governmental contracts for machine stamping of tent pegs and for sending out housing violation notices.

It is important to note that Altro is seeking the array of service integration and continuity of care that mental health professionals keep asserting is so necessary to keep the chronically mentally ill functioning in community living. Thus the array of work opportunities with training, the search for alternatives for those who do not take to the sheltered workshop, the introduction of work activity, residential programs, case management, the closer work with the parents of the younger clientele. At the same time some homilies of an earlier era in rehabilitation are not lost sight of, such as the concept of supportive care and the concept of "a stitch in time," or what Dr. Howard Rusk used to call "the umbilical thread" (Black 1959).

Two characteristics of Altro Workshops are present in every successful sheltered workshop that has engaged in any work beyond the simplest of bench and assembly operations. Direction of the industrial or service procedures, and often of the job procurement and marketing and sales tasks, is by personnel having backgrounds in the occupational field in which the work is undertaken. As in any small business, there has to be know-how along with interest and zeal. From its inception Altro competed with open employment in hiring department heads and senior work supervisors who were familiar with the field. At the same time, the agency's board of directors is made up of a combination of persons of charitable interests including leaders in the work fields in which Altro is engaged. It has always had board members who were engaged in garment manufacture. When it added work programs in office skills, data processing and use of computers, the machine shop, and printing, it also added to its board of directors successful business people who could advise upon and recommend methods to keep these programs up-to-date and competitive in the workaday world. Visitors to Altro Workshops from the business world, as well as from the fields of professional services, are impressed with the business look of the various shops, the use of time clocks, and other appurtenances of quality control and personnel management.

GOODWILL INDUSTRIES OF ORANGE COUNTY

Goodwill Industries is a network of 175 autonomous facilities in the United States and 43 in other countries affiliated through statewide councils and the Goodwill Industries of America, Inc. The origin of Goodwill was the establishment during the depression of 1902 of a program for the poor by Rev. Dr. Edgar J. Helms. He was searching for a dignified way to make donated clothing and other articles available to those in need. What he did was collect cast-off clothing, furniture, and other articles for poor people to refurbish and repair, selling the products for small sums and using the income to pay wages to the destitute (Plume 1965). Other missions and churches followed suit, also following Helms's principle of recruiting influential businessmen to assist in insuring that the programs followed sound management procedures.

As the years passed, an increasing proportion of Goodwill's clientele were from among the disadvantaged and handicapped populations. Various of the Goodwill Industries began to turn their attention to providing a greater variety of occupational choices and job-training opportunities, using professional help in designing services and available public funds to augment and expand what they were doing. One of these was the Goodwill Industries of Orange County, south of Los Angeles. This agency was established in 1924; it was incorporated in 1932 and at that time became a member of the national program. Goodwill

Industries of Orange County is now one of the largest members of the national network, operating on an annual budget of over $4 million and serving more than 500 clients a year, some 220 of whom are employed in its sheltered workshops. Some 100 clients are in a work activity program.

Goodwill Industries of Orange County today describes itself as "a comprehensive approach to Vocational Rehabilitation. Our rehabilitation department includes a highly skilled selection of professionals with extensive backgrounds in Evaluation and Assessment, Behavior Management, Training and Counseling Services" (Goodwill 1985). It states its mission as "to provide (1) Vocational Evaluation, Training, Work Experience, and Placement, and (2) Personal Social and Career Counseling for individuals desiring to overcome disabilities, both physical and mental, to achieve their highest degree of economic and personal independence." The disability categories represented among its clientele are 38 percent physical, medical, and sensory; 24 percent psychological (mostly the mentally ill); and 39 percent mentally retarded and developmentally disabled.

The sheltered workshop building is located on a busy thoroughfare just off the center of the Santa Ana business district. The two-story building was designed and built for the agency in 1957. It has large workshop spaces on the ground floor and an array of professional service and business management offices on the second floor. Its arrangement and decor are pleasant; its corridors, doors and elevator are accessible to the handicapped. Its workshop has more than the usual amount of space for storage of goods and parts, but never enough when work is plentiful.

As would be expected, the largest workshop is for the refurbishing and repair of donated clothing, textiles, electrical appliances, radios, television sets, wheel toys, furniture, shoes, dishes, pots, pans, and bric-a-brac. Revenue from the sale of these is Goodwill's primary source of operational income. Sales are conducted in twelve Goodwill shops scattered all over Orange County; the largest shop is in a one-story building next to the main building. Although Orange County is considered one of the counties with the highest average incomes in the United States, there are pockets of poverty, and the Goodwill shops are very popular among low- and middle-income families. Just before my visit there had been an annual Christmas sale of repaired dolls, and these had literally sold out.

Goodwill Industries lists among its services to the handicapped the following: vocational evaluation services, work activity center services, extended work program services, personal work adjustment services, placement services, technical-trade training and on-the-job training, and support services. The vocational evaluation service is an intensive program that assesses the client's vocational potential using a general medical exam, psychological testing, work sample testing, and situational assessment. Much use is made of a vocational rehabilitation evaluation procedure known as VALPAR, but the vocational evaluator emphasized that total behavior rather than testing scores alone are used in his assessment.

The Goodwill's technical-trade and on-the-job training is at present a curriculum offered by the Rancho Santiago Community College for course credit. It is given at the Goodwill Industries for twelve to fifteen weeks at a time and includes the fundamentals of electronics assembly. While it is a popular course, it is limited in that there is no accompanying factory work as part of the training, and such experience is a requirement for placement in the industry. The telephone company has granted funds for IBM personal computing equipment so that Goodwill can now offer training in word processing. Goodwill will provide a teacher and the community college will grant course credit.

In its support services Goodwill Industries provides instruction in English as a second language, employment preparation, instruction in human growth and development, and group counseling.

The work activity center, serving some sixty persons, most of whom seem to be developmentally disabled, is engaged in the traditional sheltered work contracts. Simple packaging and mailing, shrink wrapping, sorting parts, and the like depend upon Goodwill's ability to obtain work from local businesses. In its contract work processes Goodwill cooperates in a Projects With Industry program in which a PWI Project Council brings business people (generally middle-management technicians) together with organizations giving vocational rehabilitation to the handicapped. The Projects With Industry approach will be discussed in Chapter 4.

In cooperation with the Orange County Health Care Agency, Goodwill has proposed a special service for chronically mentally ill individuals with little or no work history. This they are calling "A Supported Life Integration Program: Non-Slip Vocational Services." The proposal is to offer the services enumerated above to an increasing number of persons with chronic mental illness until a maximum of seventy-five persons per day are receiving services. In this program the work adjustment services will immediately follow acceptance and orientation, with the formal vocational evaluation postponed until the participant demonstrates a consistent work pattern over a four- to six-hour day. A case manager will be out-stationed at Goodwill by the referring agency. The project will have greater monitoring and follow-up than do the usual services, and an outside panel of evaluators will examine the results quarterly and recommend modifications and enhancements.

Except for the "Non-Slip" project there is little participation in the Goodwill services by the mental health system. In contrast to Altro, where the major part of governmental support comes from the state and local departments of mental health, Goodwill receives its major governmental funding through the California Department of Rehabilitation. Comments by professional staff at Goodwill indicate that there is little contact between the county vocational rehabilitation and mental health staffs. This is not uncommon across the country.

In addition to the help and advice that it receives from a board of directors and an advisory board of influential business leaders, Goodwill Industries has organized an active volunteer group called the Helmsmen whose members contribute money and time to assist the organization in many ways.

SOUTH SHORE REHABILITATION CENTER

The South Shore Rehabilitation Center, located in North Quincy, Massachusetts, a few miles south of Boston, is a sheltered work program in transition to expanding other types of work experiences for the handicapped. Its program began twenty-five years ago as a small workshop for the mentally retarded. It then merged with a small general service to the physically handicapped known as Work, Inc., to form the South Shore Rehabilitation Center. About 40 percent of its present clientele are mentally ill; the majority caseload is of the mentally retarded or developmentally disabled. In addition to sheltered work programs, South Shore operates two "prevocational" workshops, one for the mentally ill and one for the developmentally disabled. A major program is what it calls CREWS, a transitional work program which will be described in the next chapter. There is also a special service for the hearing impaired and multiply disabled, a "Career Education Services" that offers subcontract work to forty-four schools throughout New England for handicapped young people 14–20 years of age, and four group homes and cooperative apartments for developmentally disabled adults. In all, South Shore serves some 600 persons, of whom it claims 40 percent are mentally ill.

South Shore Rehabilitation Center is housed in a two-story factory building in an industrial complex. Its workshop space, which once employed 330 clients, has been divided for some of its different programs. The prevocational unit for the mentally ill is at a different location. The sheltered workshop has been reduced to a work force of about ninety, and the intent of the center is to further increase its use of CREWS, as well as promote a small industry it is developing for the manufacture of hospital items (such as cooling pads and urinary bags). The goal is to have the workshop strictly for work adjustment, prevocational activities, and extended employment for the very dysfunctional.

The director of South Shore is a psychologist. He and his program director, who is trained in vocational rehabilitation counseling, have been impressed with how functionally capable at work many seriously mentally ill are, provided there is proper prevocational preparation before placement in the workshop or in a transitional work program. It is for this reason that South Shore has expanded its prevocational services for the mentally ill. This program offers more intensive supervision than does the usual vocational program. The vocational sequence then followed is the traditional one of assessment, work adjustment and training, and placement.

Three characteristics are common to all four of the sheltered work programs herein described. Each has no hesitation about accepting the mentally ill among its clientele. Except for some special programs that are funded separately by mental health authorities, there is no question raised about admixture of handicapping conditions. Each is concerned about good business management and ensures it by employing work foremen and managers who are experienced in the industrial and business world. Each is sufficiently concerned about high quality of rehabilitation and therapeutic services to have obtained accreditation from the Commission on Accreditation of Rehabilitation Facilities, the standard-setting agency for the field. Because of its health agency status, Altro Health and Rehabilitation Services is accredited additionally by the Joint Commission on Accreditation of Hospitals and Health Agencies. The issue of accreditation will be discussed further in Chapter 9.

3
Transitional Employment Programs

A number of forms of work programs for the rehabilitation of the handicapped and disabled have developed in this country during the past two decades, many of them now utilized for the mentally ill. They are all seen as alternatives to the sheltered workshop, although in a number of instances the providing facility does link the new program to an ongoing sheltered workshop.

An early analysis of work-related programs by the Massachusetts Rehabilitation Commission (McCann 1963) arrived at a classification of six types: (1) general services workshops; (2) training centers (primarily for the mentally retarded); (3) specialized evaluation centers; (4) mental hospital industrial workshops; (5) transitional sheltered workshops (for salvage and repair); and (6) extended employment in sheltered workshops. A decade later the Massachusetts Rehabilitation Commission (1974) grouped the activities of these programs as (1) vocational evaluation, (2) vocational training, (3) job placement, (4) transitional workshop employment, (5) extended workshop employment, and (6) work activities. The commission did recognize that most of the rehabilitation facilities it supported offered more than one, or all, of the programs in the listing. The New York Association of Rehabilitation Facilities (1980) decided that there are only three types of programs serving the mentally ill—(1) preparatory exit programs, (2) community prevocational programs, and (3) transitional and supportive employment programs—a classification agreeing with that of a study by the ICD Research Utilization Laboratory (Robinault and Weisinger 1978). There is, of course, no strict division among such programs, for there is much admixture of methods and techniques. Simply for the purpose of making clear the origins of these programs and their differences and similarities in principles and philosophies, I have chosen to divide the programs into these groupings:

1. Sheltered workshops and work activity centers, discussed in Chapter 2;
2. Transitional employment programs, the concern of this chapter;
3. Fairweather lodges, taken up in Chapter 4;
4. Supported work and projects with industry, also discussed in Chapter 4; and
5. Affirmative industries and open employment, discussed in Chapter 5.

Again, there is no greater value of one classification over the other. My discussion of various specific program makes clear how much overlapping there really is.

The Psychosocial Club Development: The Fountain House Model

Transitional employment programs owe their origins to an extension of the sheltered workshops of the British Industrial Therapy Organisations (ITOs) and, in the United States, to adaptations provided by the psychosocial club developments. In the early sixties ITO–Bristol had experimented with arrangements with local industries to allow patients from the mental hospital to fill entry-level jobs in a factory manufacturing drinking straws, and later with having a group of patients accompanied by a nurse work as an "enclave" on simple packaging tasks there and in a shoe factory. The hospital was delighted with the results, and the factories were satisfied with the production. Visitors to the ITO in Bristol were proudly shown these "add-ons" to the industrial therapy program. One of the visitors from the United States was John Beard, director of an ex-mental-patient club in New York known as Fountain House Foundation.

Fountain House was founded as a social club by a group of former mental patients of Rockland State Hospital, about thirty miles north of New York City, which in the 1940s was the mental hospital serving residents of Manhattan. Aided by community volunteers the group called itself the WANA Society (We Are Not Alone) and "held in common the belief that many of the obstacles which confront patients in leaving the hospital and in rebuilding their lives in the community could be overcome or at least alleviated, if the patients themselves could come together, share their problems and be encouraged to provide each other with mutual help and assistance" (Beard 1976, p. 393). The membership of WANA grew, as did professional and philanthropic support, and in 1948 the club members were able to purchase a brownstone building on the edge of mid-Manhattan to serve as a permanent clubhouse. A small fountain in the patio of the building suggested the present name of Fountain House Foundation. The members incorporated and set up a board of directors, to which they added business leaders, philanthropists, and prominent psychiatrists. By 1954 the membership of the club had so grown that the board employed a young social worker, John Beard, who had experience in working with "back-ward" patients in a large mental hospital in the Midwest.

Beard brought to Fountain House a firm and intense conviction that persons with chronic mental illness have much more functional capacity than was realized or accepted by the citizenry or professionals and that they should have every possible opportunity to participate in developing their capacities for community living. He began to work with the club members and the volunteer community leaders to establish the program that has come to be known as the "psychosocial club." Shortly thereafter similar types of clubs came into being in other parts of the country—Horizon House in Philadelphia, Thresholds in Chicago, and Portals House in Los Angeles, among others. After a long hiatus in which only a few psychosocial clubs opened in the larger cities, the movement has taken off in recent years. In 1984 there were over 100 psychosocial club programs in the United States and Canada, and through training programs and dissemination of ideas, the number of such clubs is increasing rapidly (Rutman and Armstrong 1985). Over the years the Fountain House Foundation has been transformed from a mutual self-help club of former mental patients to a structured nonprofit agency serving the mentally ill, who are called "members." The other psychosocial clubs mentioned above began as rehabilitation agencies without ever having gone through the WANA Society phase.

Beard described succinctly the underlying principles of a psychosocial club at a meeting of these organizations in New York State (Doughty and Hayes 1979):

> Psychosocial Club Model programs are designed in such a way as to convey four profoundly important messages to each of their clients:
> *a.* Every person is called a *member* . . . each person coming into the program develops a keen sense of membership, i.e. of *belonging* to a vital and significant social and vocational community.
> *b.* Every member is made to feel that he is *expected* . . . that his coming makes a *difference* to someone, indeed to everyone in the program.
> *c.* . . . the program is intentionally set up to ensure that it *will not work* without the cooperation of the members.
> *d.* It follows that members come to feel that *they are needed in the program.*

The principal components of the psychosocial club program were listed as (*a*) a prevocational day program, (*b*) a transitional employment program (TEP), (*c*) evening and weekend programs (seven days a week), (*d*) an in-hospital and in-community outreach program, (*e*) a cooperative apartment program, (*f*) the thrift shop program, (*g*) a club newsletter, and (*h*) a club name (signifying identity and independence). Only the first two components have significance for this book, and I will restrict discussion to them. Those interested in more complete descriptions of the psychosocial club program, including the cooperative apartment houses, the evening and weekend activities, and "reach-out" services, should refer to Beard 1976; Doughty and Hayes 1979; and Beard, Schmidt, and Smith 1963.

THE PREVOCATIONAL DAY PROGRAM

Fountain House had close referral ties with Altro Workshops and with other sheltered workshops in the New York City area, and a number of its members spent all or part of their days in workshop training. However, most of the members did not seem capable of the travel involved, nor did they function well in the structured environment, nor did they even have an interest in sheltered workshops. Initial training in what has come to be known as "competency skills" had to take place in the clubhouse. Ninety percent of the members of Fountain House are diagnosed as schizophrenic, are quite dysfunctional when first seen, and are quite unmotivated to participate in any form of structured classroom training in daily living skills. Whatever abilities they demonstrate in the hospital that lead to the decision to discharge them rarely carry over into the after-hospital period. The necessity of keeping the clubhouse operating offers a way whereby the members can learn daily activities by doing. The program is not designed to find "chores." It creates a setting, according to its proponents, "where the chronically mentally ill can be seen at their best."

Such activities as cleaning and household tasks, maintaining the furnishings and the library, clerical tasks, and working in the music room, beauty parlor, intake-reception areas, TV room, administrative areas, game room, and snack bar are shared by members and staff. The members man the switchboard, buy and prepare food for 250 noonday meals, write and produce a daily newspaper and a monthly magazine, handle correspondence, operate a thrift shop, keep attendance records, assist with bookkeeping and research functions, and take responsibility for showing visitors around and helping in inaugurating new members.

> Both staff and members become engaged in a process where important shifts begin to occur with respect to their concepts of disability. Staff become more aware of the social and vocational potential of the disabled psychiatric patient, while the individual member discovers personal abilities and talents which lead to greater social effectiveness and more meaningful

work productivity . . . In summary, the activities performed in the day program are done by members and staff working together. They have selected activities which have a clear relationship to the basic operations and functions of the clubhouse. Members are encouraged to explore and choose the activity area which is of interest to them and to assume a level of responsibility which can be successfully handled. In most instances, members view their participation at Fountain House as a natural process. They are members of a club, and as members they voluntarily provide help and assistance. They do not usually view themselves as undergoing an organized, consciously directed rehabilitation process. For many, Fountain House assumes the role of an extended or substitute family. (Beard 1976, p. 399)

Strict adherence to these principles—and Beard and his staff were quite evangelical in their practice—is not without its complications. Members quite often were not capable or effective until they had learned how to do their tasks, and it takes a particular kind of staff to be willing to accept the inefficiencies of daily living in the clubhouse. I can well remember the difficulties of reaching John Beard by telephone or of having messages properly delivered because the member assigned to reception or the switchboard at the time was new to the duties. The response to complaints was always "He (or she) will learn."

THE TRANSITIONAL EMPLOYMENT PROGRAM

It should be easy to understand, with the foregoing principles in mind, why Beard was not anxious to establish a sheltered workshop at Fountain House. The very organizational structure and the requirement for a hierarchical administration are at odds with the clubhouse concept. He saw in the British experience a way of providing the next step for members who had demonstrated their capacities by volunteer work in the club and appeared ready to try their wings in the outside workaday world. Aided by a grant from the Social and Rehabilitation Service, U.S. Department of Health, Education and Welfare, the Transitional Employment Program (TEP) began in 1964.

The essence of the TEP is an agreement between a business or industrial establishment to allow one or more entry-level jobs to be used for the training of clubhouse members. Fountain House first approached Alexander's, a New York department store chain selling low- to medium-priced merchandise. The wife of the president of the stores had a Ph.D. in sociology and a long interest in services to the handicapped and the elderly. For some years before Sunday openings became a pattern, Alexander's had made its stores available on Sundays to residents of homes for the aged so that they could shop in comfort and not have to contend with the usual shopping crowds. In the Fountain House pattern full-time stock clerk jobs were held open to be filled morning and afternoon by two members selected by the rehabilitation center. The job was rotated among the members every four to six months. Fountain House guaranteed that the work would be done to the satisfaction of the employer, even if this meant that a member of the staff would have to do it when no club member was available. The staff person working with a group of members was expected to become familiar with a TEP placement before assigning members to it, and the business would have to be assured that there was a staff member who could do the work satisfactorily.

Payment to the member was by the business at the going rate for temporary workers. The agency bore the costs of staff involvement and the counseling and other services available from the House. Fountain House requires that members in the TEP program continue their association with the clubhouse and participate in its activities during the time they are not at the work station. By the end of the 1970s Fountain House reported that some forty-four different firms were providing TEP job slots for over 200 members. In addition to small establishments such as stationery stores and messenger services, the program included well-known businesses such as Macy's, Sears, Manufacturers Hanover Bank, Chemical and Chase Manhattan Banks, major life insurance companies, and advertising and publishing houses.

An extension of the TEP at Fountain House was inaugurated in 1972 with another grant from the federal government under what was called Projects with Industry (described in the next chapter). This allowed for developing group placements in factories and businesses. In these work enclaves, as they are sometimes known, groups of six to ten members are transported by van to the place of employment. The group placements include factory assembly and work in warehouses, restaurants, and cafeterias. For some years Fountain House managed and staffed one of the Chock Full O'Nuts fast-food outlets in mid-Manhattan. The principles of payment, supervision, and so on are the same as for individual placements.

When, after three or five years, the federal grants for TEP expired, the state Office of Vocational Rehabilitation agreed to include the costs of staff and club services in its fees for services. In more recent years funding for elements acceptable to the Community Support Services program have been included in grants from the New York State Office of Mental Health.

The Fountain House Model, as it has come to be known, has been widely disseminated. In 1967, the van Ameringen Foundation, in honor of its late president, helped to establish at Fountain House the van Ameringen Center for Education and Research. The National Institute of Mental Health awarded Fountain House a special five-year training grant in 1976 to allow it to offer a series of three-week sessions to colleagues from all over the country. In these cycles the trainees were given the opportunity of working side by side with members and staff in the various programs. There were visits to Fountain House apartments and participation in members' meetings, in the dinner meetings for members in TEP, and in independent employment. Audiovisual presentations were reviewed and daily seminars conducted. In the first three years of this training venture, 66 new psychosocial club programs were established, with transitional employment programs serving 900 members in 350 businesses (Doughty and Hayes 1979). Visitors from elsewhere in the world came to observe, and Fountain Houses have since been opened in Lahore, Pakistan; Cairo, Egypt; and Stockholm, Sweden. In other countries existing rehabilitation services have been modified along Fountain House lines. After the NIMH grant expired, Fountain House has continued to provide similar training to staff members sent by and supported by their agencies. Also, until funding dried up, New York State's Office of Mental Health used special monies from the Public Health Services Act and Title XX of the Social Security Act to send groups of staff from hospitals and community agencies in the state of New York to observe and have "hands-on" experience at Fountain House.

A Fountain House survey in June 1984 produced a list of 117 agencies with TEPs, serving 1,420 clients in 586 places of employment and producing wages of close to $5.3 million (Fountain House Foundation 1984). I have reason to believe that a number of other agencies serving the handicapped in the United States have inaugurated types of transitional employment programs, often using this title (Black 1986). A recent evaluative study of transitional employment programs agrees (Rutman and Armstrong 1985).

> Beard assessed the role of TEP as follows: Transitional employment is an extremely important part of the Fountain House model. It is very difficult to tell whether or not a person will succeed at a job, but the difficulty in assessment should not deprive the person of the opportunity to try the job. What has been done at Fountain House is to remove the barriers that prevent members from learning whether they can successfully perform a job . . . Through the transitional employment program, members can avoid all the usual barriers (e.g., job interview, past job history, references, motivation to seek work) that face the chronically mentally ill in trying to obtain employment. (Doughty and Hayes 1979, p. 13)

Modifications of the Fountain House Model

While the basic principles remain the same, there has arisen a variety of modifications to the Fountain House model. These may be summarized as follows:

1. Some agencies vary the time per day spent by the client member on the TEP job slot. A few make assignments for a full day only; a number supply flexibility from two hours per day to full time, according to the needs and abilities of the clients.
2. A number of agencies report that they prefer to have the employer pay the agency for work performed; the agency, in turn, pays the members.
3. A few programs report that they allow a member or client who is successful in the TEP placement to be hired in that job slot permanently. The agency then has to negotiate another TEP slot with the employer or seek another source of transitional work.
4. Quite a number of institutional agencies—for instance, hospitals, rehabilitation centers, and large mental hospitals—are establishing forms of transitional employment using job slots in their own establishments.

Examples of these and other modifications are best illustrated by reference to existing programs described in the literature and to programs I have visited.

THRESHOLDS, CHICAGO

One of the largest of the psychosocial club programs in the United States is Thresholds in Chicago. It was formed under the aegis of a countrywide demonstration in the 1950s of services to former psychiatric patients by the National Council of Jewish Women. Other such centers were formed in Cleveland (Hill House), Pittsburgh (Council House), and Louisville (Bridge Haven). While the basic principles of Threshold follow closely those promulgated by Fountain House, its practices differ in significant ways. The emphases from the beginning were in reducing recidivism to the mental hospital, assisting reentry to the workaday world, increasing social functioning and independent living, and improving academic achievement. Thresholds has limited its intake to patients in the major working-age range, 16–50 years old.

The headquarters and main clubhouse activities are centered in a fine old house, refurbished and quite comfortable in its atmosphere. There are now two additional such buildings serving other areas of Chicago. The clientele are considered and referred to as "members," and a members' council does set daily policy in the clubhouse. However, staff direction and a fairly large number of volunteers provide a much more structured environment than is found at Fountain House.

The vocational rehabilitation sequence is also more structured. Members are grouped into "work crews" for assignment to duties within the clubhouse. Those who show or develop abilities on their crew assignments may progress to volunteer work. The next step is to the transitional employment program, and finally to help in placement in outside regular employment. This "step system," while not rigidly applied, is a departure from the very flexible approach of Fountain House. The procedures for the TEP are similar to those of Fountain House. A number of prestigious Chicago firms participate in the TEP. Threshold had a sheltered workshop, but Dr. Jerry Dincin, Threshold's executive director, has found the TEP approach much more feasible for the present Threshold program (Dincin 1975; Robinault and Weisinger 1978; Lamb et al. 1971; Bond et al. 1985).

The Thresholds approach has become more structured as time has gone on. In the beginning socialization activities were relatively unstructured, but it was found that a number of members failed to participate. Gradually the idea evolved of grouping members with the addition of staff and volunteers. Specific activities could be planned, such as preparing a newspaper, arts and crafts, or folk dancing. Volunteers could be assigned to members on a one-to-one basis, in a relationship that is friend to friend rather than staff to client. While the members are free to join the groups that interest them, there is an atmosphere of high expectations in the social and vocational programs. One very important group, especially for new members, has to do with medication. In this group, members learn about the reasons for continuing treatment, and there is staff supervision to see that prescribed medication is taken. Other special groups include a "spinning wheel" group for frequent recidivists, a group program designed for older adolescents and young adults, a group for members who are mothers with babies, a parents' group, and a women's awareness group. A remedial education program is certified by the educational authorities to carry credits toward high school graduation and preparation for college.

Thresholds has experimented with these and other groups and modifications in its program in an effort to reduce what is normally a very high dropout rate from psychosocial club programs. In addition to the special groups just listed, Dincin has tried lowering expectations, particularly with the young adults and with a new venture called the "Bridge" for the most recidivist of the members (Bond et al. 1985). The Bridge program, which involves the use of "assertive case management" as developed in a training-in-community-living program in Mendota, Wisconsin, is built around home visits to help with members' crises. Thresholds undertook an experimental-control design and reports a significant reduction in rehospitalizations. There is much in the Bridge program that resembles the French sector crisis team approach.

Thresholds serves more than 800 members a year. It spends well over $2 million annually on its programs, of which more than half comes from the state Department of Mental Health and Developmental Disabilities and the Department of Rehabilitation Services.

HORIZON HOUSE, PHILADELPHIA

Horizon House represents an admixture of the flexibility of the Fountain House philosophy, friendly and supportive and comfortable, with some of the structure of Thresholds. It describes its program as an educational behavioral modification model. It follows a three-phase process, although members may enter at the phase they can handle. The first phase stresses vocational orientation, individual and group counseling, and a didactic training program in basic interpersonal skills and community functioning. Horizon House operates a sheltered workshop, which it uses for this phase. In the second phase these instructions are continued, there is greater time spent in the sheltered workshop, or assignment is made to one of the work placements in the club building. The final phase places the member almost full time in the vocational program. The total expected time in the Horizon House program is expected to be no more than a year, although in individual cases this can be flexible. Horizon House has made little use of transitional employment outside its own walls.

OTHER PSYCHOSOCIAL CLUBS

Council House, Pittsburgh

The Council House program—which, like Thresholds, makes heavy use of volunteers—uses its building for administration, intake, and some counseling. Its direct programming is conducted in community facilities such as community centers, Y's, schools, churches, and civic agencies. In place of paid work, Council House uses volunteer "personal adjustment" placements in educational institutions, insurance firms, and health and other nonprofit agencies. It also operates a plant nursery for prevocational training.

Friendship House, Hackensack, New Jersey

Located in the "inner city," Friendship House has a sheltered workshop, a thrift shop, and substantial TEP and work crews programs. Friendship House also provides a partial hospitalization service, which it finds valuable for its younger, more volatile members.

Portals House, Los Angeles

One of the older and larger psychosocial rehabilitation agencies, Portals House serves 350 persons per year. It is housed in a large old residence next door to what was a church, which it has taken over to enlarge its facilities. Another house on its grounds has been converted into a residence for members. Portals House has the usual array of club programs, including vocational services in clerical work, maintenance, and food preparation. In addition to preparing lunches for the members it does catering for organizations that would like to have box lunches prepared for their employees and clients. The experience of this agency with transitional employment has not been good, and in recent years Portals House has given it up entirely. The agency has continued unpaid volunteer transitional experience at a nonprofit organization in the community, and uses this for vocational evaluation and personal adjustment training. Portals' explanation for ceasing TEP is that it has had a hard time finding interested employers and difficulty in finding clientele who are sufficiently stable workers to satisfy employers. In California there is no financing for TEP by the Department of Rehabilitation, as there is in New York and other states. This makes it difficult to supply the staff supervision needed. Portals House is considering developing a "supported work" program or an independent business enterprise. It has had a study made and recommendations from a group of business school students from the local university.

In passing, it is interesting to note that the director of Portals House described his program as much more flexible than what he called "the rigidity" of the Fountain House model. Such a comment was made in a number of instances on my visits to psychosocial clubs, but never by anyone who had spent time at Fountain House. In part, it seems that this comparison had more to do with protecting deviations from the Fountain House array of services than with the quality of services to the members.

Community Mental Health Centers

A number of community mental health centers have built transitional employment programs into their catalogue of services. Most usually this has been in connection with the development of a community support program (CSP), which will be described later.

BAYAUD INDUSTRIES, INC., DENVER

Bayaud Industries is a branch of the Fort Logan Mental Health Center, Denver, Colorado, founded in 1969, and incorporated as a private, nonprofit corporation in 1972. Bayaud Industries has established a range of work programs in the Denver metropolitan area. It operates two sheltered workshops, work activity centers, a work-study program for adolescents cooperatively with public school districts, a large TEP with group placements in industry, and a placement service to open competitive employment. Over 470 people were served per year according to the last report (brochures and literature from Fort Logan Community Mental Health Center). The average length of stay in the TEP program is three months. Fifteen percent of the clients who successfully complete a first TEP are placed in a second. An average of 45 percent of those who complete TEP enter the competitive labor market. There is strong support for Bayaud from the Colorado Division of Vocational Rehabilitation, the Colorado Division of Mental Health, other community mental health centers, and the business community.

One interesting facet of the Bayaud services is the "Patient Worker Program," inaugurated in 1982, in which a group of job slots in the Mental Health Center are utilized as TEP placement. Clients assigned here include those who are unproductive in the work therapy program and experiencing long-term hospitalization, nonrehab fundable. They are paid one-half of the prevailing minimum wage. Many state mental hospitals across the country have established similar patient-employee programs, usually in conjunction with their work-activity or sheltered workshop program. Some of these were made possible under federal manpower training programs, such as the Comprehensive Employment and Training Act (CETA), no longer in force.

INDEPENDENCE HOUSE, DALLAS

Independence House is a unit of the Dallas County Mental Health and Mental Retardation Services. Housed in an old two-story residence in a run-down area of Dallas, it is both a psychosocial club and the headquarters of the Community Support Program of the Dallas County Mental Health and Mental Retardation Services, a nonprofit agency under contract with the Texas Department of Mental Health and Mental Retardation. The parent agency offers the traditional services of a community mental health center. It took advantage of funding made available for establishing community support program (CSP) networks to open Independence House to give services to the very chronically mentally ill people that the regular program did not reach. The CSP Network of Independence House has four divisions: residential, occupational, psychosocial, and screening–case management.

The residential division operates twenty-six apartments for group living, with four residents in each. It also has four Fairweather groups (to be described in the next chapter). The occupational division provides a number of transitional employment programs. Some six to eight jobs slots (two half time in each) are reserved in the parent agency in clerical work, food services, and housekeeping. These provide payment at the federal minimum wage and are seen primarily as useful for client training. About ten people at a time are in contract employment in hotels and restaurants in food preparation; another fifteen to twenty are engaged in housework and cleaning. A work enclave of twenty to thirty persons are involved in packaging and distributing samples for advertising. While many sheltered workshops are planning to shift to TEP and other nonworkshop forms, this agency is thinking of parlaying its work enclave program into a sheltered workshop, probably in cooperation with one of the shops for the mentally retarded.

The psychosocial services division is responsible for the work programs in Independence House, the food services, clerical jobs, maintenance (including a greenhouse of which they are justifiably proud), and social activities. These are considered prevocational, and no pay is provided. In fact, these services were described by participants much in the same terms as members of psychosocial clubs are wont to use. The screening–case management division has introduced what is fast becoming one of the hallmarks of the community support programs across the country.

Community Support Programs

It is the community support program concept that has linked the use of work in therapy and rehabilitation to the community mental health centers. A decade ago, in January 1976, the National Institute of Mental Health called a "founding conference" to consider what should be done to meet the problem of an increasing number of adults with chronically disabling mental or emotional disorders being discharged from mental hospitals to their home communities. The existing conditions were listed as follows (Turner 1976; Turner and TenHoor 1978):

- Recent court decisions have established the right to freedom for thousands of mentally or emotionally disabled people. So far however, no judicial means have been found to require public agencies to assist those with severe functional impairments in taking full advantage of their rights and privileges as citizens.
- Thousands of these people remain confined in unnecessarily costly and restrictive settings, such as mental hospitals and nursing homes; additional thousand reside in substandard foster homes, boarding homes, single-room-occupancy hotels, and other such environments offering few or no incentives or opportunities for meaningful and productive participation in community life. Others may

be found simply wandering from place to place, virtually homeless, rootless, and unwanted.

- Despite the dramatic decline in recent years in reliance on state hospitals as the locus of long-term care for such people, a new system of services adequate to their needs has yet to be conceptualized and developed.

At this conference the idea of the community support program was born. Congressional budget allocations allowed the National Institute of Mental Health to assist the states in developing community support programs on a project-by-project basis. After small demonstratins with this federal funding, a number of states began to augment the establishment of such programs using other federal monies, such as Title 20 of the Social Security Act and public health block grants to the state.

The community support program concept included an array of services, with strong emphasis upon housing, work, supportive programs, socialization, advocacy, medical and health services, and the forging of individual social networks. Since the majority of these services were already components of the psychosocial club movement, the community support effort had the effect of stimulating that development, along with the training venture of Fountain House Foundation previously referred to. The emphasis upon work programs was in marked contrast to the guidelines for the establishment of the community mental health centers. While the CSP literature often mentioned sheltered workshops as the form of work program recommended, most centers found it easier to follow the psychosocial club model into TEP. The primary goal of most CSP programs for some time was to set up alternative housing for their clients, and it has only been in the past few years that concerted attention has been paid to remunerative work programs. The CSP approach has allowed for greater flexibility in the array of services made available to the chronically mentally ill, and in fact, to many formerly mentally ill people who have need of more than psychiatric-medical followup. It is seen increasingly, however, as distinct from formal psychiatric care and ineligible for financial support out of medical and health funding. Even the community mental health centers which use CSP seem loath to give it complete status as a core function of the center program. (For a discussion of the future of CSP see Mosher 1986.)

One example of a community support program is the Community Support Center, Inc., a division of the Midtown Community Mental Health Center of Indianapolis. The Mental Health Center serves a catchment area of 350,000 people in the central city of Indianapolis and operates through six satellite clinics. The Community Support Center (CSC), independent of the clinics, is available to clientele from all of them. Those who come to the Community Support Center are primarily chronically mentally ill, mostly schizophrenics. About 60 percent are men, with 40 percent women; 47 percent are white, and 53 percent black. CSC serves persons 18 years of age and over, 18 percent of whom are 18–24 years of age, a population that the director reports is increasing. One-third of the clientele is in the age range 25–44. The most dysfunctional clients from the clinics seem to be sent to the CSC.

The Community Support Center is located in the Central Avenue United Methodist Church, a solid, finely constructed building in what was at one time the residential center of the city. Maintenance of the building for both church use and CSC provides some of the therapeutic work and skills learning; however, minimum wage is paid those who participate. There is a strong emphasis upon volunteer work by the members, and this work is used as the base for vocational testing (evaluation) and in preparation for jobs. The overall program of the Support Center seems to be a composite of a psychosocial club and a day center. The center has available many structured programs, including educational, social, and recreational activities. Emphasis is placed on developing skills in such daily activities as money management, cooking, shopping, meal planning, doing laundry, and taking the bus. Recently, remedial classes have been added in reading, math, spelling, and writing.

Two years ago the CSC set up a nonprofit corporation called the Community Involvement Center, Inc., to undertake contract jobs, mostly cleaning, maintenance, and gardening. The work force wears blue coveralls with a CIC emblem. The clients I observed looked like well-dressed blue-collar workers and seemed proud of their uniforms. There has been no difficulty in obtaining sufficient work. Pay is at minimum wage. Job supervision is by CSC staff members, though at least one job is supervised by a client member. New work comes by way of word of mouth; the CIC has had no problem with unions or with commercial competition.

The Community Involvement Center employs one staff member, a bookkeeper. The entire CSC has a small staff of about ten, including three nurses, a social worker, a psychologist, a recreational therapist, and a part-time psychiatrist. The CSC is used for internship training for nursing students from DePauw University and by student social workers and psychologists from the University of Indiana at Indianapolis. Each staff member carries a caseload as a primary therapist. There are weekly therapeutic community meetings; the one in progress on my visit had about forty clients (members) in attendance.

A very interesting fiscal analysis supplied by the team member in charge of the CSC, Joyce Berner, R.N., compared the costs of service in CSC with that in other units of the Mental Health Center. The cost per visit to CSC in the year ending June 30, 1984, was a little over $25, compared to a clinic cost of $50–$99 and a daily inpatient cost of $189. Staff members complained that the CSC receives little help from the state Division of Vocational Rehabilitation. The DVR has little understanding of mental illness, and, like its counterparts in other states, considers this kind of clientele as having little potential for entering the world of remunerative employment and the work programs of a mental health agency as not relevant to rehabilitation.

Rehabilitation Centers

A number of rehabilitation centers serving the mentally ill and other disabled persons have shifted to or added transitional employment programs. Three good examples are from California and Massachusetts.

RUBICON PROGRAMS, INC., RICHMOND, CALIFORNIA

Rubicon Programs was established in 1973 as a nonprofit corporation to provide day treatment, vocational rehabilitation, independent living, housing, and advocacy services to disabled residents of western Contra Costa County in the San Francisco Bay area. It started with volunteer staff in an old storefront in downtown Richmond and has grown to include seven program components throughout the county (literature, brochures, and personal visit). Its initial clientele, and still its largest population, are the mentally ill. In recent years it has opened its programs to the mentally retarded/developmentally disabled and to other disabilities.

In its Rubicon Day Center the organization provides counseling, resocialization, and prevocational and independent living skills training for clients in the age range of 18–44. In its Synthesis Day Center it carries on day activities and skills training for an older group of clients who come mostly from board and care homes. Over one hundred clients, about evenly divided between men and women, are served in the day centers each year. Whites account for over half of the clientele, blacks for about 30 percent, and Hispanics and Asians for the rest.

The Rubicon Housing Services comprise thirty-six units, including a six-unit apartment complex for the elderly and disabled, a ten-unit apartment complex housing eight clients and two community residents, a ten-unit complex designed as a demonstration project for twelve chronically mentally disabled clients, and an Independent Living Housing Assistance Program providing ten units of subsidized housing. In the housing programs blacks outnumber whites two to one, females outnumber males, and the population is fairly evenly divided between those under 25 and those 25 and over.

The major vocational service program is the Rubicon Garden Center, founded in 1979 through funding from the Contra Costa County Mental Health Department and the California State Department of Vocational Rehabilitation. Not only is gardening and horticulture an important work area in the northern California region, but the agency also aimed at using horticulture as a therapeutic, healing, and learning medium in restoring work-handicapped individuals recovering from psychiatric hospitalization. There are two elements to the Garden Center: a comprehensive nursery selling nursery stock and gardening supplies and offering expert horticultural advice, and a transitional employment program supplying contract work crews for landscape and yard work.

The Garden Center is located across from a major BART (subway) station in Richmond. It has all the look and feel of a well-stocked commercial nursery. The TEP work includes contracts for landscape maintenance at the Alameda Federal Building, the San Francisco Court of Appeals, and elsewhere. Work at the two governmental buildings was obtained through NISH, the National Industries for the Severely Handicapped, which will be described more fully in Chapter 9.

A division of Unemployed Support Services was established in 1983 under a grant from the West Contra Costa County Community Health Corporation, using federal funding under Public Law 98-8 (the 1983 jobs bill). This was for the purpose of providing counseling and rehabilitation to persons who had been unemployed during the past two years or who had exhausted their unemployment insurance. Known as the Rubicon Employment Assistance Program (REAP) it offered support group activities, a form of "job club," individual counseling and family counseling, and temporary job placement during the intensive job-seeking period, "frequently seen as the most traumatic period of unemployment when many workers choose to exit the job market."

Plans are under way to add a component of food service training. Rubicon has employed as developer someone experienced in restaurant management. It intends to start with food preparation and serving in a center for senior citizens, and hopes to develop a catering business.

The total operating budget of Rubicon is just under a million dollars a year. Mona Reeva, a licensed social worker with a master's degree in public health, spoke of there being eleven sources of funding; this is but one of the complicating factors in operating services for the mentally ill that involve a combination of therapeutic and vocational programs. Rubicon (whose name comes from the historic river that Julius Caesar was forbidden to cross with troops and had to cross to start on his successful campaign for the leadership of the Roman Empire) has been able to forge a working relationship between the mental health and vocational rehabilitation authorities in its area in support of its program.

SOUTH SHORE REHABILITATION CENTER, QUINCY, MASSACHUSETTS

At its peak the South Shore Rehabilitation Center employed 330 persons in its sheltered workshop, most of whom were mentally retarded/developmentally disabled. Gradually the agency has moved in the direction of increasing its mentally ill population and of developing transitional, and now supported, employment programs. It has reduced the sheltered workshop population to ninety persons, and, as explained in the last chapter, expects to reduce it to sixty or fewer. Now the majority of the clientele are employed in a program called CREWS (Community Rehabilitation Employment Work Sites).

CREWS began as a janitorial contract in a Boston federal building obtained through NISH. This has expanded to a number of work groups, ranging from six to fifteen or twenty persons, doing janitorial work, packaging in publishing houses and import firms, small motor assembly, and the like. A few of the groups are engaged in what I will describe in a later chapter as "supported work." In one work enclave in industry the agency has arranged with the firm to keep its CREW unit there even when there are seasonal or other unexpected drops in work to be done. In this event South Shore may bring other work into the plant for its clients to do. The appeal for businesses is that this work force will be maintained for the firm's work when work again becomes available.

Janitorial work is a large part of the jobs of CREWS. South Shore has just contracted for the janitorial services in the federal court building in Boston. This CREW unit will use some fifty to sixty clients and require sixteen staff members. Relations with the union of janitorial and building maintenance workers is maintained by hiring only union members for the staff positions and by keeping lines of communication open.

South Shore considers the mentally ill among its most productive workers. It has found that it can serve quite a number of chronically mentally ill persons by introducing them gradually to a CREW group set up initially with the most productive and least behaviorally deviant clients. This has been found to be a particularly good way of introducing CREWS to new employers. When they see that productivity is maintained even though the work group absorbs apparently lower-functioning clients, employers become more tolerant of deviant behavior. The program director describes this as a valid trade-off.

South Shore Rehabilitation Center does assign staff members as case managers for its clients, but it insists that any supportive therapy and medication control come from the referring agency and not in any way interfere with the work. While there are high expectations, South Shore sees itself as quite flexible in its approach. It is not concerned that a client can do only two hours of work a day; it is concerned that a schedule be adhered to and that the client can be depended upon to adhere to it. South Shore publishers a well-organized and appealing quarterly newsletter, widely distributed in its region, that keeps its readers regularly informed about its many programs. The agency is accredited by the Commission on Accreditation of Rehabilitation Facilities.

INCENTIVE COMMUNITY ENTERPRISES, INC., NORTHAMPTON, MASSACHUSETTS

Incentive Community Enterprises (ICE) is a rehabilitation agency that has moved into transitional employment programs with a vengeance. Its executive director, Joseph T. Campbell, joined the agency in 1980 and immediately, with the assistance of an active, business-oriented board of directors, set about replacing three sheltered workshops with TEPs. Headquartered in Northampton, the agency serves a large catchment area in western Massachusetts. It now serves over 400 clients a year, about 250 daily, most of whom are placed in an array of work sites in industries and service establishments (literature, brochures, and correspondence).

Campbell questions the value of sheltered workshops as regards their efficiency "especially for bringing handicapped clients into the world of work as active producers and serious wage earners." Two of the workshops are now phased out and the third is gradually being diminished.

ICE operates in a "step system" of five levels, and under the philosophy of "normalization" with high expectations. In brief, the levels into which the work sites are classified are as follows:

Level I: Entry-level work, with maximum support and an emphasis on work habits and quality. Uses identified industry-based work sites and ICE business ventures and service crews.

Level II: Supervised production work, with emphasis on work and production. Places groups in industry, with preferably not more than five workers in each group under the supervision of ICE staff.

Level III: Unsupervised work in industry. Places three or fewer clients in a normal industrial setting, with supervision by employer company.

Level IV: Transitional employment. Places one client for a maximum of six months in an individual slot.

Level V: Competitive employment.

If a geographical region offers a large array of work settings which allows for classification of slots according to such a step system and if there is sufficient flexibility of movement between levels, then this can be a very powerful rehabilitation model. However, sheltered workshop directors with whom I have discussed this approach question their ability in many regions of the country to obtain such a variety of job slots.

Comments

It can be seen that the various forms of transitional employment offer serious alternatives to the sheltered workshop. About all that can be accomplished in a sheltered workshop can be replicated in one or the other of the TEPs. The advantages of TEPs to agencies serving the mentally ill appear obvious. The facility does not have to wrestle with the many problems of running a small business: the structural setting, supplying equipment, dealing with marketing, sales, deliveries, and so on. On the other hand, the TEP requires a higher ratio of staff to clients. The employing unit is unlikely to pay towards the cost of supervision by the agency, and in many instances the human service agencies have not been cooperative. A different kind of marketing, to obtain job slots rather than work to do, is required, and it is sometimes difficult to find professionals or paraprofessionals with the skills or interest.

There is no question but that the use of transitional employment is growing in the rehabilitation of handicapped persons, and particularly of the mentally ill. A question that has not been resolved, however, is whether the various programs that offer TEP are serving the same populations. The philosophies under which they operate range from recognition that they are dealing with seriously dysfunctional people who need support and nudging towards competence, to expectations that by providing a "normal" setting for work trial all clients will "rise to the occasion." There is a world of difference between a Fountain House or a Thresholds, where there is a great deal of social support, and a community mental health center with a clinical orientation. And there is certainly a difference between these and a South Shore or an ICE, in which the unproductive clients must fall by the wayside. Since we have found no way of predicting in advance which patients or clients will be successful in any setting, analyses of client characteristics may be less than useful. The prevalence of serious mental illness is so great, and the numbers of rehabilitative resources so small, that at this time it may be sufficient to provide as wide a variety of programs as is possible.

4
Fairweather Lodges, Projects with Industry, and Supported Work

I mentioned earlier that along with transitional employment programs only one other alternative to the sheltered workshop evolved from the demonstrations supported by the federal agencies in the late 1950s and early 1960s. This was what has come to be known as the Fairweather Lodges.

Fairweather Groups

During the 1950s Dr. George W. Fairweather, a psychologist with the Veterans Administration hospital in Palo Alto, California, had been studying the factors that made for success and failure in discharge to community living by patients with tuberculosis. He was struck with parallel failures exhibited by patients with psychiatric diagnoses, interestingly a similar but totally independent concern that had earlier led Altro Workshops into shifting from tuberculosis rehabilitation to opening its doors to the mentally ill. Fairweather and his associates noted that the longer a patient remained in the hospital the more likely it became that his future stay would be lengthened. They reported that the differences in community living outcome between patients who received intensive individual and/or group therapies and those who received none disappeared by eighteen months after discharge. They "began to consider the notion that perhaps a subsystem could be created that would protect individuals from this typical [negative] community reaction [from those who considered their behavior deviant] while at the same time providing them the opportunity to work and live with some autonomy and security" (Fairweather 1980, p. 5). Building upon what was then known about the psychology of small groups, they set about seeing whether, starting with patients who were still in the hospital, they could organize them into self-functioning small societies, capable of coping autonomously with the problems that arose in daily living. Each group of patients was then aided to move as a unit out into the community.

The concept was derived not only from research on the behavior of small groups. Fairweather and his associates pointed out that the notion of special groups had been a norm of "our society's historically diversified experience." New immigrants to the United States kept to themselves in social enclaves where they could "be themselves, or adhere to the old social norms of their country. At the same time this small social enclave . . . served to interface with the larger society where the immigrants worked to provide the living to support their families" (Fairweather, 1980, p. 5). Fairweather and his associates set about to determine whether, in the same way, former patients of a mental hospital could be formed into such small societies, and whether such a process could enhance the possibilities of their integration into the larger community.

Detailed descriptions of the Palo Alto research are in the literature (see Fairweather 1964, 1980; Fairweather and Simon 1963; Fairweather et al. 1960, 1969). It is sufficient here to outline the differences between the handling of the experimental group and what is usually the case in the mental hospital. On the traditional ward the new patient is interviewed by staff, is given assignments by staff, may make appointments to discuss problems with a staff member, attends individual or group therapeutic sessions as set in the ward roster, and must make requests for passes or money.

On the experimental ward the new patient, after a brief interview by a professional staff member, was told that he was now a member of a task group, and this group took the responsibility of orienting him to the ward and explaining the program to him. Communication between the group and the hospital professional staff was through formal notes. Each patient was expected to progress through four steps, and the group was responsible for monitoring the progress. On four days of the week the task groups met without staff members present, evaluated each other, and prepared recommendations for the staff when they met with them on the fifth day. After this meeting with the staff, at which the group presented its recommendations about how the group could better its performance as well as what should be done about each member's privileges, job assignments, and problems, the staff adjourned and made decisions as to the merit of the group's recommendations. While in this group process the staff still kept responsibility for final decision-making, the role of the patient changed from a completely subordinate one in an individual-to-individual relationship to that of a participant in group discussion and recommendations.

The step levels through which each member of the group was expected to progress were as follows:

1. Responsible personal care; punctuality on assignments; orientation of new members. At this level the member received ten dollars and a one-day pass per week.
2. Adequate performance in step 1 and qualitatively acceptable work on the job assignment. Members at this level received fifteen dollars a week and an overnight pass every other week.
3. Adequate performance in steps 1 and 2. Members at this level could recommend their own money and pass allowances. They became eligible for up to twenty dollars per week and for three overnight passes during the weekends of the month.
4. Continuing performance at the earlier levels. At this level members were given greater flexibility in passes and withdrawal of money from their accounts and became responsible for recommending departure plans.

This system of preparing groups of patients for the Fairweather Lodge Program has become the standard preparatory methodology. In almost every case the procedure is followed within the mental hospital before discharge of the group of patients. Originally, Fairweather had hoped to perform the preparatory training in the community after discharge, but this was not possible within the constraints of the Veterans Administration hospital. The results of the experiment were highly successful. "Perhaps the most important finding of this study was that small groups of patients—many of them considered to be chronically hospitalized for mental illness—could learn to solve problems and take care of one another if certain procedures were followed. The study determined that in order for problem-solving groups to be effective the patient participants had to function autonomously without staff present; the participants would only function well as a group when there was both a group and an individual reward system in which the rewards were considered meaningful by the group" (Fairweather 1980, p. 9). When most of the members of the group were functioning at level 4, it became time to arrange to move the group out into the community.

An extremely important element in the forming of the Fairweather groups is the makeup of the group. The aim is for heterogeneity, a mixture of more highly functioning and less well functioning patients. The inclusion of too many potential leaders poses problems as to how the group can remain intact; too many "schlemiels" will produce a nonoperating group. While staff members play a large part in the initial selecting or suggesting (for the patients are given the opportunity of volunteering), some adjusting and "shakedown" occurs after the group begins its tasks. During the experimental phase in Palo Alto, one of the most interesting and intriguing aspects of the groups was the inclusion of one or two such "schlemiels" among the groups' members. It seemed to me, in the days before deinstitutionalization, that here was a possible way to move some of the back-ward patients out into community living—people who were most unlikely to be even considered for the traditional treatment or even rehabilitation programs. Even today, this and similar methods of forming small special groups lends itself to preparing a variety of patients, including some apparently very dysfunctional persons, for movement out into community living (see, for example, Carpenter 1978 and Carpenter and Black 1983).

Fairweather Lodges

The Palo Alto researchers recognized from the beginning that their plans for community settlement of their special group must include work for the members to do as well as a place to live. They decided against organizing or utilizing a sheltered workshop. They explained, "As the situation appears to be at present for the returning chronic patient in America, participation in the sheltered workshop is most likely to enmesh him in a system of dependency upon professional aid and advice which consistently reinforces his patient status" (Fairweather et al. 1969, p. 14). They were also cognizant that sheltered workshops in the United States at that time were expected to be transitional to competitive employment and therefore did not seem to lend themselves to the needs of persons requiring long-term regular employment.

The traditional aftercare programs also did not fit the needs of the special group, for "full citizenship status comes *after* departure from the system, not *before* [a patient's] entrance into it as a discharged hospital patient" (Fairweather et al. 1969, p. 14). The solution devised by the research team was to move the group *in toto* into a rented building as a "family" and to organize a small business to be run by and worked in by all members of the group. Through the affiliated university a community corporation was established, which then set about contracting for housecleaning and yard-keeping jobs. The program was referred to as "the Lodge."

At first the coordinating and business-management functions were performed by a psychologist from the hospital research staff. In time the group became more autonomous, with staffers performing only in a consulting role. Coordination was then undertaken by a lay person chosen by the group. In a few of today's groups this task is performed by one of the members. The entire description of the development of the Lodge is beautifully detailed in Fairweather and associates 1969 and in Fairweather 1980. The research included comparisons with traditional aftercare and with group formation in which the work element was not included. The studies concluded that "the autonomous Lodge society drastically reduced recidivism, greatly improved employment and did so at a remarkably reduced cost—one-third of traditional hospital treatment at the outset of the project with the Lodge members eventually becoming totally self-supporting over a five-year period." Both the predischarge research and the Lodge establishment were supported with grants from the National Institute of Mental Health.

It is important to keep in mind the principles upon which the Lodge movement is based. Briefly, these are (Fairweather 1980, pp. 21–31):

- Managing and controlling their own enterprise gives ex-patients a sense of personal success in terms of the social values of their culture. The amount of ego involvement of the participants must be great. The feeling of identification with the success of the Lodge was greatly enhanced by their ownership of the business.
- The system must give as much autonomy to the members as possible, consistent with their performance.
- The Lodge should have a vertical organization so that a division of labor is possible and so that a meaningful role can be found for all the members.
- The subsystem must be compatible with the broader society of which it is part. Such requirements as adequate bookkeeping and financial records, a monitoring system to deal with behavior unacceptable outside the Lodge, and locating in a neighborhood in transition from lower economic residential to commercial can insure that some deviant behavior will be ignored or tolerated.
- The internal norms of the Lodge must be tolerant of the behavior that is typical of the mentally ill population. However, the leaders of the Lodge must be able to differentiate between the behavior norms of the outside society and the subsystem.
- There must be a communications system that insures a continuous feedback about the performance of members. In the original Lodge this was accomplished through the use of an "executive committee" and through informal exchanges of information in the dining room.
- Entry and exit from the Lodge should be possible to the individual without penalty. Free access to the outside community should be available; training for living in the larger community should be one

of the primary aims. However, no penalty should be attached to a person's remaining in the Lodge if he is incapable of completely independent living.

- Members should perform as groups wherever possible. Studies have shown that membership in a reference group is important in maintaining the chronically mentally ill person in the community.
- Only a limited number of people should participate in such a subsystem. Close interpersonal contact must be maintained for the members to promote identification with the subsystem and its goals.
- The subsystem must not be dependent upon the goodwill of the immediate community for its very existence. It is important that it be financed and supported by agencies or groups who are not directly dependent upon the immediate neighborhood for their financial support.
- The social organization of the Lodge must be so arranged that individuals may substitute for one another when required. This is particularly important in respect to the work undertaken.
- There should be emphasis upon both rehabilitative and work norms.
- There must be appropriate mechanism for handling medication.

State hospitals in Arkansas and Colorado replicated the group and Lodge formation. The follow-up from these showed very similar outcomes to those for the first Lodge. There was a marked reduction in recidivism, improved satisfaction with living arrangements, improved employment record, and lower costs. However, it was not until the National Institute of Mental Health supported a "dissemination and implementation" project that the findings of the first studies were called to the attention of hospitals across the country and there began to be interest in organizing Fairweather Lodges. At the present time there are Fairweather Lodges in sixteen states. Texas alone had forty-seven lodges as of June 1985. Dr. George Fairweather is the director of the Ecological Psychology Program at Michigan State University and remains available for consultation to the Lodge movement. A picture of some of the presently operating Lodges will describe their use of and modifications to the original design.

HOUSTON LODGE, MENTAL HEALTH AND MENTAL RETARDATION AUTHORITY OF HARRIS COUNTY, TEXAS

Texas, through its state authorities for mental health and for rehabilitation of the handicapped, joined the Fairweather Lodge movement in 1975. Preparation for Lodges began in three state hospitals—San Antonio, Austin, and Terrell—with the primary specialized training program for the Houston area (Harris County) located in Capitol Lodge, connected with the state hospital at Austin. Patients volunteer for the program, and when ten to fifteen are available to form a group they are transferred to Capitol Lodge. Apart from evidenced interest, those selected must have had three or more hospitalizations and not be considered eligible for a transitional employment program or direct competitive employment.

Once at Capitol Lodge, patients undergo a two-week evaluation period. Classes and meals are provided at the Lodge, on the hospital grounds. Some 80 percent stick out the evaluation period, with an average of six to eight patients then completing six months of training and becoming a group ready to move to one of the community Lodges established in Harris County. The procedures during the training period follow those of the original experiment. There are five steps, or levels, for the patients to achieve, each level providing greater autonomy and rewards. Patients receive payments of eight dollars at level 1 and twenty-five dollars at level 5. The members are encouraged to save; the group should have savings of $4,000—and the usual group saves $8,000—by the time of "graduation." During the six-month training periods, patients attend classes in janitorial training, budgeting, bookkeeping, cooking, survival skills, public transportation, first aid, and fire training. The formalized note system is used for communication between the group and the hospital staff. The group decides upon assignments as "crew chief," assistant "crew chief," bookkeeper, fire marshal, and medical chairman (to be responsible in seeing that medications are taken). If the group is functioning by the end of six months, there is a formal "graduation."

The hospital staff coordinator (one of whom is assigned to every two Fairweather groups) assists the new group in searching for and choosing housing. The Houston system has had a private housing speculator interested in holding houses available to newly formed Lodge groups. The staff coordinator helps the group to register at the county courthouse as a small business and to take out liability insurance. There is now a Texas State Fairweather Lodge Association, which has a volunteer CPA available for consultation on business organizing matters. The staff coordinator in each hospital also arranges for a monthly evaluation of the medical status of the group members. The group itself monitors medication-taking by its members and develops its own household rules.

Since the group's savings, even if they amount to $8,000, are insufficient to get the Lodge going and the business under way, there is funding assistance from the Texas Rehabilitation Commission for room and board and work adjustment, and some start-up money from Austin State Hospital. According to the director of Houston Lodge, Tom

Mitchell, who verbally supplied most of this information, the people who enter the Lodge program want to work. They are willing to give up dependence on Social Security Disability payments or Supplementary Social Insurance to join the Lodge. The program offers classes to the groups in how to obtain contracts. The coordinators supply consultants on janitorial services, cooking and nutrition, business methods, and so on. Most of the work obtained is janitorial or building maintenance or yard or garden work. The businesses set up in Harris County include Astro Cleaning Technicians and Stardust Company.

The Fairweather Lodges in the Houston program have done quite well. There has been no problem in finding suitable housing in transitional neighborhoods, and there has been an abundance of the kinds of work the groups can do best. Earnings have been at minimum wage or better. The crew chief, who carries more responsibility than other members, earns more, but all others in the group are paid the same amount of wages.

The makeup of the membership has been 60 percent male and 40 percent female. The best result has been with long-term chronically mentally ill. Some people have used the Lodge as a stepping stone to the outside community. Recidivism, as measured by a return to hospital care, has been very low, 8 percent. Seventy-five percent of those who enter the program complete the training. The longest-lived group in the Houston program has been functioning for five years; the youngest, six months. The program is set up to produce one or two new Lodge groups a year. A "mini-feeder" training program is maintained in Houston for filling in vacancies in the existing Lodges. On-the-job training is utilized in operating Lodges. Mitchell notes that the "fill-ins" seem to be higher-functioning people. The state association of Lodges is working on a health-care package to be made available to members. Thirty-two of the Lodges which carry on cleaning businesses have formed a Cleaners Cooperative, which meets monthly, bills customers, and distributes income to the member Lodges. Mitchell expects that the co-op will become a for-profit corporation.

OPPORTUNITY HOUSE, FORT WORTH

Another Texas facility illustrates some of the problems that beset the Fairweather Lodge system. Opportunity House is a division of the Tarrant County Mental Health and Mental Retardation Services, Fort Worth. It is the focal point for the Community Support Services program (CSS), and embraces the residential units, the prevocational program, the psychosocial club, and the Fairweather Lodges. A thrift shop is also located in Opportunity House. The House occupies a one-story former elementary school building, refurbished for the agency's use. It is located in a section of town that is in transition; many one-family homes have been converted to group and apartment use. I saw a number for rent on a recent visit. Small apartment dwellings, two-story, two to four apartment complexes, are used by the agency as alternative housing, with three patients per apartment.

As a psychosocial club Opportunity House follows many of the principles of the Fountain House model. The prevocational unit uses duties in the management of the House, janitorial, maintenance, clerical, reception. The vocational unit uses a transitional employment program, with individual and work-crew placements. Janitorial and yard work contracted for the work crews includes kitchen work at the Hilton Hotel and low-level cleaning work at the local Air Force base. Contract payments are very low in the Fort Worth area and do not cover the costs of supervision. The agency is presently negotiating with the Texas Department of Rehabilitation for fees to cover "work adjustment" as a way to cover the costs of staff.

The Fairweather Lodge program was initiated in 1979 under a grant from the National Institute of Mental Health. There are now five Lodges in Fort Worth. Opportunity House has depended upon Witchita Falls State Hospital to select and train groups for Lodge living. This arrangement is about to be eliminated as the result of a Texas court decision that has mandated a larger staff-to-patient ratio in the state hospitals. Witchita Falls State Hospital has decided that preparation of patients for Fairweather Lodges is not really its responsibility. Tarrant County Mental Health and Mental Retardation Services (Community Support Program) is looking for resources to allow it to set up training in the community. The question is whether it will be possible to select and keep groups of former patients together for training and evaluation without the structure of the hospital.

The Fort Worth experience has differed in a number of ways from the procedures which were proposed as a result of the original Fairweather experiment and which are followed in the Houston program (agency literature and visit). In summary, these differences are

1. There is no board of directors for the Fairweather Lodges. The Tarrant County Mental Health and Mental Retardation Services' own board of directors looks unkindly upon a policy-setting body for a subsidiary unit.
2. The Lodges are not incorporated units. Each group of Lodge members is considered a partnership. One staff member ruefully admitted that the Lodges cannot raise the $600 it takes for incorporation, even though they recognize its value.
3. The principle of autonomy is violated in that there are no meetings of

Lodge members independent of staff, although there are independent staff meetings. It would appear that the agency is not entirely comfortable with giving hospital dischargees that amount of autonomy.

4. The communication procedures designed to reduce the superior-inferior relationship between staff and members did not follow beyond the training in the hospital.
5. The staff has found it hard to deal with the decisions of Lodge members on replacements of group members. Staffers believe that the members generally make very poor selections.

When a member leaves the Lodge he or she usually leaves the work force too. Opportunity House allows members of other residential programs to fill vacant work slots in the Lodges on a temporary basis. Social Security Supplemental Security Income (SSI) has only recently become available in Texas for the chronically mentally ill. At first the Tarrant County agency was loath to have patients who were being considered for vocational programs apply for SSI. It considered SSI a disincentive to rehabilitation. Economic need, however, has led to applications by patients. While some people *are* afraid that by doing any kind of work they may lose their benefits, most have not been concerned. Nevertheless, the agency is now careful to plan the early stages of vocational rehabilitation so as to protect these and other benefits for clients.

The Community Support Services program has gradually won support from the parent agency by virtue of its willingness to accept clientele no other division wants to deal with; its ability to develop new resources, such as a crisis stabilization unit, a respite program, special clinical relationships with the psychiatric emergency service of the local general hospital, and the Fairweather Lodges; and its ability to organize an integration of psychosocial, vocational, and residential services.

FAIRWEATHER TRAINING PROGRAM, SAN ANTONIO STATE HOSPITAL

San Antonio State Hospital initiated a Fairweather group training program as one of the services of its Transitional Living Unit in 1977. The Transitional Living Unit is a complex of six cottages on the hospital grounds, providing what the hospital calls its "Quarterway" and "Outreach" services as well as its Fairweather program. The intent of the transitional living program is to "provide an alternative to continued hospitalization on an active treatment ward for those patients who, with an appropriate transitional, home-like environment, might be restored sooner to their family, friends, and community" (literature from the hospital). Except for the Fairweather training program the cottages are used as a short-term transitional environment for patients being prepared for restoration to community living. The average stay in the Quarterway program, behaviorally oriented with a primary goal of restoring independent functioning, is from thirty to forty-five days. Outreach evaluations, respite care, and provision for boarding family members who travel long distances to visit patients are of even shorter duration. The Fairweather training program averages eight to ten months in length. One or two Fairweather groups are trained each year.

The cottage used for training houses six to eight patients. These are referred to the Transitional Unit by the treatment teams on the hospital wards, and are screened by an Admissions and Dispositions Committee composed of a psychiatrist, a social worker, a psychologist, and a rehabilitation specialist. Admission criteria for the Fairweather Program include:

- Primary diagnosis of major mental illness, with history of psychotic onset;
- Adult history of chronic dependency and/or institutionalization, the "revolving-door" pattern;
- Poor or no job history;
- History of failure in other training or placement programs;
- Ability to function in a hospital client work program (these are TEP-type occupations using placements in the hospital);
- Willingness to participate in the program;
- No interested relatives, no relatives at all, or a destructive family relationship making return to family undesirable;
- Age 18 or older;
- Willingness to work to some extent;
- Willingness to take supervision.

The training program follows procedures similar to those of the original Fairweather Lodge. There are the same communication arrangements through the use of notes, and a point system is used in evaluation to determine movement from level to level. The group is held responsible for the behavior of its members. When the group members have completed the training phase, the Transitional Unit alerts the San Antonio, Texas, Urban Council, a nonprofit agency which coordinates and operates community services. In cooperation with the community mental health centers serving Bexar and Nueces counties the Urban Council helps to obtain housing, job contracts, and a coordinator for the Lodge.

The director of the Urban Council described the organizational efforts of the first Lodge (Fairweather 1980). The group had saved $4,000 to be used for start-up costs. The Urban Council, however, was skeptical about this being sufficient and wanted the group to leave a balance to help if there were financial problems later on. A fund-raising campaign among local churches, using auction sales and donations of furnishings, and gifts of janitorial equipment from local businessmen allowed the group to retain most of their initial investment. The Texas Rehabilitation Commission supplied $300 per member for each of six months, ostensibly for "work adjustment training," and this gave the Lodge the leeway it needed to obtain contracts. The Lodge, operating as the Jitney Janitorial Cooperative Association, had no difficulty in getting work. Churches, in particular, had been having problems in finding custodians or part-time cleaning help, and the Lodge work force met their needs ably. As was true in the Houston experience, applications at first were not made for SSI, food stamps, or other governmental aid such as Section 8 housing aid from the U.S. Department of Housing and Urban Development. Later, it became obvious that the group needed some supplementation of income, for the surplus on their contracts did not always meet their living costs. After applications and turndowns and appeals, the rights to SSI were established, adding somewhat over $100 a month per member to the household income.

The coordinator is supplied under contract with the mental health center and proves a stabilizing element in the continuation of the Lodges. This program has not had the experience of one or two others in having the coordinator emerge from among the ranks of the members or be employed by the group from entirely outside the mental health system. It is possible that the original Lodge and the early ones following it had available for membership some much more highly functioning individuals than are now being referred for Fairweather training. Certainly, the criteria for admission to the San Antonio program just enumerated would effectively rule out persons capable of serving as coordinator.

PANTA RHEI, INC., CLEVELAND

One of the earlier Fairweather Lodge programs began in Cleveland State Hospital in 1969. The hospital had received one of the Hospital Improvement Program grants from the National Institute of Mental Health, and the staff decided to try the small-group approach in one of the cottages on the hospital grounds. They followed the principles and procedures of the prototype program, but moved the members of the group up the levels only when all of the members had achieved the step. They felt that this "was a very effective way of making the members of the group responsible for each other's behavior, and it developed group cohesion and group support in a very short time" (Fairweather 1980). Some other Fairweather Lodge programs have followed this process since.

With help from the county Mental Health and Retardation Board, the Cleveland Foundation, and the Bureau of Vocational Rehabilitation, the Fairweather program acquired a building on a street with older houses that had been converted to use as fraternity and sorority houses, university offices, and the like. A corporation was formed, called Panta Rhei, according to agency literature a Greek phrase which means "everything flows" or "nothing stays the same," referring "to our goal of promoting movement, change, and growth for people who have been stagnated by institutionalization." The corporation established an office-cleaning business. When Cleveland State Hospital was closed in 1974, Panta Rhei became a contract agency of the Cuyahoga County Community Mental Health Board.

At the present time, Panta Rhei offers a more comprehensive program of vocational and social rehabilitation for people who have had long-term stays in mental hospitals. In addition to the three Fairweather Lodges it operates a sheltered workshop (Near West Works) engaged in furniture manufacturing, furniture refinishing, and venetian blind cleaning. The office-cleaning business has contracts to provide janitorial service to a number of large office buildings, community centers, and day care programs. Panta Rhei has also added a satellite apartment house. These facilities are treated as an integrated service. Persons who live in the satellite housing or who have left the Lodges may continue to be employed in Panta Rhei Office Cleaning or the Near West Works. All clients are paid the federal minimum hourly wage.

The agency describes its major features in these terms: "Provides immediate gainful employment, rather than only the promise of a job after training. Work is structured to minimize the chance of failure, so that people who have not worked in many years can start on a job immediately on a task they can do. All work is done in small groups which become a source of emotional support and practical help. There is initial tolerance of deviant behavior which does not interfere with job performance. Clients participate in the structuring of work and training activities. There are paths of upward mobility in responsibility and job complexity" (literature from Panta Rhei).

Since the closing of the state mental hospital a dozen years ago, Panta Rhei has been able to set up group training for Fairweather Lodges in the community. Its former executive director, William Mateer, has written of three "survival threats" which the program has thus far been able to manage. One is the danger of growing so big that it loses its emphasis upon self-help and its ability to leave decision-making to the clients. Another is the continuing need, in response to staff turnover, to provide in-service training and orientation so that new staff members learn quickly the principles upon which the Fairweather group approach is predicated. A third threat is the necessity of becoming accredited so as to continue to receive funding from the Bureau of Vocational Rehabilitation, when the orientation of the standards set by the Commission on Accreditation of Rehabilitation Facilities is toward professionalism rather than toward client control (Fairweather 1980). Mateer pointed out, too, that the original expectation that the Fairweather Lodges would become financially independent through their business incomes has not held true in practice. Subsidization through governmental fees or contracts and through payments by clients from their Social Security or welfare benefits is a continual requirement. This, too, brings the threat of controls that may hamper flexibility and experimentation.

With all the doubts that Mateer raised, the Panta Rhei program seems to be a continuing one. Now that the locus of care of the long-term chronically mentally ill has indeed moved from the mental hospitals out into the communities the prototype of future Fairweather Lodge programs will be that of using the community rather than the hospital as the base for training. How to involve prospective members in the training process becomes an issue, particularly since so many of the chronically mentally ill are unlikely to volunteer for such programs. Fairweather pointed out the dilemma in describing experience with the prototype Lodge:

> This information raises the issue of the responsibility a society has to those who are relatively incapacitated but who do not volunteer to participate in community subsystems that are designed to benefit them. It can, of course, be argued that any such involuntary membership is a violation of the democratic ideals of this society. Thus, it would be argued that it is more important for the society to support in other ways those members who do not participate in such programs, even when the programs might benefit them, than to jeopardize the important principle of voluntary membership. On the other hand, it can also be argued that such citizens may be incapable of making a rational decision at the moment it is offered and that they therefore should participate in programs found to be beneficial to others like themselves . . . it is clear that in the near future our society will have to make this kind of moral determination as treatment programs are moved further and further into the community and away from the large mental hospital, and as new and innovative programs are created for the disadvantaged. (Fairweather et al. 1969, p. 341)

That "future" is now our present.

The Fairweather Lodge program is a distinctively American approach. I am not aware of the small-group methodology being attempted anywhere else in the world, not in rehabilitation of the mentally ill or, in fact, for any other handicapped population. Another

American development during the past decade has been that of supported work, which received its impetus from a plan promulgated in the 1978 amendments to the federal Vocational Rehabilitation Act as Projects with Industry (P.L. 95-602).

Projects with Industry

The concept of Projects with Industry (PWI) was originally written into the Vocational Rehabilitation Amendments of 1968 as a small demonstration program to try to provide more direct linkages between rehabilitation programs and the private business sector (P.L. 90-391). The initial concern was with the more seriously physically handicapped, and for some years only ten such projects were funded. More specific language was written into the 1978 amendments, and the level of funding increased from an initial $1 million to over $13 million by 1984. Agencies with services to the mentally retarded/developmentally disabled recognized PWI as an answer to their growing dissatisfaction with sheltered workshops and as a way of introducing many stabilized, low-functioning individuals directly into competitive employment. Gradually, services to the mentally ill are beginning to use PWI as an assist to transitional employment programs and to supported work as well.

The 1978 law states (p. B, sec. 621):

> The Commissioner, in consultation with the Secretaries of Labor and Commerce and with designated State units, may enter into agreements with individual employers and other entities to establish jointly financed projects which—
>
> (A) shall provide handicapped individuals with training and employment in a realistic work setting in order to prepare them for employment in the competitive market;
>
> (B) shall provide handicapped individuals with such supportive services as may be required to permit them to continue to engage in the employment for which they have received training under this section; and
>
> (C) shall, to the extent appropriate, expand job opportunities for handicapped individuals by providing for (i) the development and modification of jobs to accommodate the special needs of such individuals, (ii) the distribution of special aids, appliances, or adapted equipment to such individuals, (iii) the establishment of appropriate job placement services, and (iv) the modification of any facilities or equipment of the employer which are to be used primarily by handicapped individuals.

The law further required that compensation paid to handicapped employees under this program be at least the applicable minimum wage. The total of grants made to any project may not exceed 80 percent of the cost of the project. Regulations required the setting up of Industry-Rehabilitation Advisory Councils to assist and monitor the projects. Four models were developed, although a specific program might incorporate more than one of them. In brief, these models are

1. Job placement model: Places work-ready clients in competitive employment. Uses a "job coach" and a placement counselor. The Business Advisory Council does job development and monitors the job-seeking program.
2. Work adjustment model: Uses transitional worksites under the supervision of a rehabilitation counselor or "job coach." PWI staff maintain contact with the client after placement to improve job-retention rates. The Business Advisory Council assists in the job placement of clients.
3. Skills training model: Uses classroom-instruction format for training at the rehabilitation facility or in industry. The Business Advisory Council oversees curriculum and job development, and helps in job placement after skills training.
4. Linkage model: Organizations in a geographical area work together in a network to expedite referrals matching clients to jobs. There is a local advisory board of all participating businesses and rehabilitation facilities. Job openings within participating companies are listed at the project office, which notifies the rehabilitation agencies.

The National Association of Rehabilitation Facilities (NARF) listed eighty-four federally funded PWI projects in its most recent directory (NARF 1984b). Many more rehabilitation agencies participated, however, for a number of project grants were made to regional or national organizations which in turn made part of their grants available to members or affiliates. Among such "umbrella" organizations were NARF itself, which provided PWI support for some fifty rehabilitation facilities; Goodwill Industries of America; the Florida Association of Rehabilitation Facilities; the International Association of Machinists and Aerospace Workers; the Human Resources Development Institute of the AFL/CIO; the National Restaurant Association; Electronics Industries Foundation; IBM Corporation; and Control Data Corporation.

Examples of programs developed through such umbrella agencies are the two PWI programs operated by Goodwill Industries of Western Connecticut and Sheltered Workshop, Inc., and the National Restaurant Association's Eden Express in Hayward, California.

Goodwill Industries operates one of its PWI programs in food services and the other in clerical trades, using the work adjustment and job placement models outlined above. The job-training sites are in the facility. Topics covered in the food services training include food preparation, short-order cooking, main-dish cooking, counter attending, kitchen cleaning, dishwasher operation, nutrition, menu planning, shopping, cafeteria set-up, cash register operation, and hygiene. In the clerical fields the training covers typing, filing, office practices, introductory bookkeeping, telephone use, transcription, and introductory computer terminal use. The two curricula take three months and six months, respectively, to complete.

The food services training advisory committee consists of representatives from two commercial food services companies and from the Bridgeport Hospital Department of Dietetics. The clerical training advisory committee includes representatives from Sikorsky Aircraft, banks, the high school, two local industries, and a department store. The advisory committees assist with job placement of trainees who have completed the courses. This Goodwill Industries reports that 60 percent of its clientele "have an emotional disability" (data from correspondence and agency brochures).

Eden Express is a nonprofit agency that owns a restaurant in downtown Hayward, California. Job counselors work alongside the trainees; training is "on-the-job." Assistance in learning "survival skills" is given on an individual basis. The National Restaurant Association claims that the clientele are well trained and reports that 98 percent of the eighty graduates each year find jobs in competitive employment. The clientele have a wide array of handicaps, including mental illness (Kennedy 1985).

A number of mental health agencies also make use of Projects with Industry. These include Fountain House Foundation in New York; Harbor House in Paterson, New Jersey; and the Menninger Foundation in Topeka.

Fountain House Foundation uses the PWI assistance for support of group placements in transitional employment. Transportation is supplied by Fountain House. The work settings are carefully structured to provide peer-group support, and job-coach supervision and follow-up are part of the program. A council of employers from the business world develops new training sites, and participates in fund-raising and in the Fountain House staff-training program previously referred to (NARF 1984b).

Harbor House, Paterson, operates a county-wide PWI program involving a network of five agencies in Passaic County serving the mentally ill. The funds are provided through St. Joseph Medical Center, the parent body for Harbor House. The business participants include restaurants and a local retail warehouse. Services include counseling, on-the-job training, placement, and follow-up. An advisory council of business representatives keeps the agencies abreast of hiring trends and assists in placement of those who successfully complete the transitional employment (NARF 1984b).

The internationally known Menninger Foundation has long had consulting services with a number of industries. It has taken advantage of the PWI program to set up a number of transitional work slots in offices, hotels, hospitals, and micrographics companies. Under the auspices of the Center for Applied Behavioral Sciences of the Menninger Foundation, clients are provided with counseling, community education, job-seeking skills training, and lifetime "follow-along" for clients placed after training. There is an advisory council in Topeka and others for satellite programs elsewhere in the state. Represented on the advisory councils are officers from banks, the hospitality industry, manufacturers, insurance companies, and hospitals (NARF 1984b).

In response to a request of Congress the Rehabilitation Services Administration evaluated the Projects with Industry program and reported on February 20, 1986 (*NARF Rehabilitation Review,* March 10, 1986). The findings were quite positive. Some 16,000 persons had been served during the preceding year. Of these, 61 percent were male; 78 percent were white. Most clients were severely disabled and undereducated. Twenty-four percent were mentally ill, 18 percent were orthopedically handicapped, and 15 percent were mentally retarded. The report stated that 50 percent of the participants were placed in competitive jobs, with rehabilitation agencies reporting the highest placement rates. Nearly 5,000 people served on advisory councils. Only 14 percent of the clients had required SSI supplementation during their participation in the program.

The parent agency for the Rehabilitation Services Administration, the Office of Special Education and Rehabilitative Services of the Department of Education, has proposed future priorities for the Projects with Industry program (*NARF Rehabilitation Review,* October 28, 1985):

1. Training sites should be at locations where trainees will be subsequently employed.
2. There should be formal agreements with businesses and labor unions that they provide training and employment for disabled persons.
3. There should be training and employment for older adolescents and young adults making the transition to the work world.
4. Training and support services should be provided to move disabled persons from segregated work into more competitive employment.

It should be noted that if these priorities are followed strictly, they would eliminate such programs as that of the Goodwill Industries of Western Connecticut described above.

Supported Work

A term that is coming into general use in the rehabilitation field, and serving as a generic concept for many of the alternatives to sheltered workshops already discussed, is *supported work.* It has been generated most specifically by leaders in the field of rehabilitation of the mentally retarded/developmentally disabled as they experimented with programs that would open more doors to competitive employment for their clientele. Both the Administration on Developmental Disabilities, of the U.S. Department of Health and Human Services, and the Office of Special Education and Rehabilitative Services, of the U.S. Department of Education, have now made the term and the concept official in their initiatives and regulations.

In two excellent guides the National Association of Rehabilitation Facilities summarizes the concept and outlines the steps to follow in development of supported work (NARF 1985a, 1985b). Supported work is defined as

> a combination of employment and ongoing services utilized primarily to place retarded individuals into competitive employment. It requires intensive involvement of the rehabilitation staff throughout job placement, job-site training, ongoing assessment and long-term follow-up. Important aspects include active training involvement at the job site both for teaching the client job skills and work behaviors; and assisting employers and co-workers to work with and adjust to the client . . . Supported work does not supplant existing vocational services; it has a role as a complementary service within a full vocational process. (NARF 1985b, p. 2)

The Rehabilitation Services Administration (RSA), Office of Special Education and Rehabilitative Services, proposed extending the supported work idea to all severely handicapped groups. The definition it proposed was

> Supported employment . . . means paid work in a variety of settings, particularly regular work sites, especially designed for severely handicapped individuals, irrespective of age or vocational potential—
> (1) For whom competitive employment at or above the minimum wage is unlikely; and
> (2) Who, because of their disability, need intensive ongoing post-employment support to perform in a work setting. (*Federal Register* 1985)

The proposed rules explain what is meant by the "supported employment services" intended:

> (i) Job training to prepare and enable the handicapped individual to perform work;

(ii) Ongoing supervision of the handicapped individual on the job;
(iii) Ongoing behavior management; and
(iv) Case management including assistance to coordinate services from various sources.

After receiving responses from across the country to these proposed regulations, the RSA made the following changes: (1) The word "integrated" was added to the phrase "variety of settings " to "clarify that the employment outcome should provide some contact with non-handicapped individuals." (2) The focus of the program was "clarified" to ensure that it "is to provide severely handicapped individuals with an opportunity to earn substantially more than the traditional wage paid in other settings, such as work activity centers." (3) The RSA made clear that training should take place at the potential job site rather than in the form of prework or preparatory training at another place prior to placement.

These definitions have great significance for agencies serving the mentally ill. While many of the programs I have described under transitional employment and Fairweather Groups and Projects with Industry would easily qualify as supported work, a number of the supporting agencies would not agree with limiting training to business sites for many patients and clients. The RSA definitions not only carry a leadership imprimatur, but they also greatly influence the availability of funding through the federal-state vocational rehabilitation system and the availability of "set-aside" contracts through the National Industries for the Severely Handicapped (NISH). At a "Town Meeting" of the California Association of Rehabilitation Facilities last year with officials of the federal government a number of pertinent issues were raised (*NARF Management Review,* April 1985): (1) There has been no evaluation data on the long-term effects of supported work. (2) Retention rates for lower-functioning clients have only been 40–50 percent. Program leaders use terms like "severely handicapped" to describe clients whom many facilities categorize as "higher functioning." (3) There is general confusion about the federal initiatives on supported work and transitional employment services. There is too much focus on the mentally retarded/developmentally disabled populations to the exclusion of much larger groups of and more severely disabled groups of the handicapped.

Establishing a concept leads to the promulgation of "models." The step system used by Incentive Community Enterprises, Northampton, Massachusetts (described in Chapter 3 above) is often used as such a model. G. Thomas Bellamy and his associates at the University of Oregon have developed what they call the "Supported Jobs Model," the "Electronics Industry Enclave Model," the "Mobile Crew Model," and the "Benchwork Model" (see NARF 1985a). These are all another categorization of programs I have already described. A slightly earlier promulgation of the supported work idea was referred to as "work stations in industry," also developed for the mentally retarded by organizations disenchanted with sheltered workshops. Two excellent manuals are available from University of Wisconsin—Stout (Hagner and Como 1982) and the University of Nebraska Medical Center (Rood 1983).

Dr. Paul Wehman, of the Rehabilitation Research and Training Center, Virginia Commonwealth University, justified the use of supported work in a speech at the 1985 Annual Conference of NARF (*NARF Rehabilitation Review,* July 15, 1985). Referring to the "inability of many persons with severe disabilities to carry over or transfer those skills learned in special centers to real jobs," he pointed out that most persons with severe disabilities will not be able to obtain real jobs without professional help. He believes that supported competitive employment maximizes the use of limited case-service dollars, the fees paid a rehabilitation facility by the state vocational rehabilitation agency. He stated that supported work programs are more cost-effective than day centers or vocational skills, vocational evaluation, or work adjustment programs, since the cost is the same for job coaching on a real job as on pre-employment preparation activity. Wehman is credited with developing a model referred to as "fading," in which the trainer (job coach) gradually withdraws or "fades" supervision, finally leaving the client under normal industrial supervision. How this would work with chronically mentally ill clients, subject to exacerbation of symptoms, is not clear.

It is difficult to give examples of programs which could be considered "pure" supported work, for so many of the alternatives to the sheltered workshop already given do meet the definition. What is important is to keep in mind these primary elements:

- Supported Work should be given in real work settings where the client has the opportunity to associate with fellow employees who are not handicapped, preferably in the competitive work world.
- The client (trainee) should be paid by the employer for whom he or she works at the going rate commensurate with production.
- A staff member of the rehabilitation agency should perform the services of "job coach" to assist the client in understanding and learning the work tasks and to help the employer understand any special needs or behavior of the trainee.
- The referring agency must take responsibility, after the work training, for helping the client find a permanent job (job placement services).
- The rehabilitation agency must provide follow-up, often now referred to as "follow along," to insure stability in the work setting.

Actually, all of these elements are present to some degree in the better mental health rehabilitation enterprises. What the supported work concept does is provide a focus for integrating them into a comprehensive approach.

Three supported-work programs that do not quite fit the other classifications are those of Rise, Inc.; Career Services for the Handicapped; and Altro Health and Rehabilitation Services.

RISE, INC., SPRING LAKE, MINNESOTA

Rise is a community rehabilitation agency, a private not-for-profit corporation, which provides vocational evaluation, prevocational and vocational training, sheltered workshop employment, counseling, and job placement services to adults in the working-age range with physical, mental, and emotional disabilities. The agency was founded in 1971 and now serves over 350 persons per day in its various programs, over 25 percent of whom have "mental health disorders" as the primary disability.

Rise established its "Community-Based Training and Employment Model" in October 1984 with a grant from the United Way of Minneapolis Area. Now, twelve business host sites are used in a "partnership" for supported work training. As of the end of 1985, sixty-eight persons had been served in this program; on a daily basis about 11 percent of the rehabilitees are in supported work. Rise uses this program as another step in an array of vocationally oriented programs leading to permanent employment, either in sheltered or competitive employment. Clients may be referred to community supported employment after successfully completing any number of the other programs. Supported work is available to individuals who have been able to work at a minimum of 50 percent of competitive work capacity and have demonstrated stability in work production, job quality, daily attendance, and work deportment (*Rise Reporter,* December 1985, and agency literature).

In contrast to some of the agencies serving the mentally retarded and/or developmentally disabled that are utilizing supported work as their primary or only model of service, Rise uses this program as a valuable addition to an already rich assortment of vocational services.

CAREER SERVICES FOR THE HANDICAPPED, ALBUQUERQUE, NEW MEXICO

Another agency that follows the pattern just described of linking supported work to an already established array of vocational and prevocational services is Career Services for the Handicapped. The program is called "Supervised Employment," and the job slots sought are for the most part entry-level clerical or maintenance. Wages range from the federal minimum of $3.35 an hour to $5.00 an hour, plus such benefits as sick leave, health insurance, and paid vacation. This program differs, however, from the true maxim in that the trainees are treated by the businesses as temporary workers, with payment made by the business to Career Services, which in turn pays the employee. Career Services does supply supported assistance by a rehabilitation counselor. Clients can work full- or part-time, and the length of employment can be from a few days to a few years. The agency reports that most clients are ready for competitive employment within six months (correspondence from agency).

ALTRO HEALTH AND REHABILITATION SERVICES, NEW YORK

Altro is about to engage in a supported work experiment that has a variation not found in the examples I have given thus far. With the support of a foundation grant, the agency is seeking a business or industrial firm willing to lease space in its plant for an enclave of Altro clients. This group would be available to perform work for the business in the tradition of transitional employment, but Altro Workshops would supply work to the enclave during periods when the employer did not have work available. This could be looked upon as simply transposing a sheltered workshop to a competitive business location, but as Altro has designed it, all of the principles of supported work would be built in. In addition, the advantage to the business participant would be the availability of a supplementary work force when needed. Altro expects that the atmosphere of a regular business establishment will have great beneficial effect on clients placed there.

The philosophy of supported work, as well as that of any of the work programs for the disabled placed in the competitive work world, is predicated upon two well-known rehabilitation principles: (1) an old maxim from the field of physical rehabilitation that rehabilitation should begin as close to the onset of the disability as possible and in as normal a setting as the handicap allows; and (2) the concept of "normalization," developed in relation to services to the mentally retarded, that the normal world is the best place to train handicapped persons for living in it.

At this writing, provisions for supported work programs have been included in the 1986 amendments to the Rehabilitation Act of 1973 (P.L. 99–506). The definitions are essentially those described above, with the additions that the term supported work applies also to part-time work and "includes transitional employment for individuals with chronic mental illness" (sec. 103i). While the regulations upon which practice will be based have not yet been written, the opportunities for vocational rehabilitation services for the mentally ill appear to have broadened.

5
Other Work Programs: Manpower Training, Businesses for the Handicapped, Volunteer Services

It would not be fair to the variety of work programs that have been or are being tried in this country for the mentally ill and handicapped to leave out the roles played by the public manpower-training programs, the limited number of businesses (sometimes referred to as "affirmative industries") that supply employment without governmental subsidy, or the volunteer work activities.

Manpower-Training Programs

Programs for the alleviation of poverty have been of major domestic concern for Congress and the president since the Roosevelt administration of the 1930s. Ideas for linking training and education to breaking the cycle of poverty came into focus during the Kennedy and Johnson administrations, resulting in the Manpower Development and Training Act of 1962 (U.S. Department of Labor 1963). Johnson used that act in connection with the Office of Economic Opportunity in his "War on Poverty," which saw the development of Labor Department Youth Opportunity Centers, Community Action Manpower Programs, a Neighborhood Youth Corps, a Job Corps, and a number of vocational education programs. Some of these provided on-the-job training in public service employment, and a few were located in private business and industry (see Levitan and Magnum 1969).

In the formation of these programs not much thought was given to the physically and mentally handicapped as trainees or as recipients of services. A few of the federally financed demonstration projects for dealing with juvenile delinquency or with the community-based mentally ill, such as Mobilization for Youth, in New York City, did utilize funding from the Manpower Development and Training Act to set up what today we would call transitional employment or supported work, but these programs ceased with the end of budget authorizations. Not only was it difficult to organize training under an act that made no reference to coverage of the handicapped (even though the case could be made that disabled persons were subsumed under the poor, unemployed, and socially disadvantaged for whom the legislation was intended), but the U.S. Department of Labor and the Congress also kept changing the program every year or so, and what was acceptable in the regulations in one year was invalid the next. I remember, for example, running a highly acclaimed machine-shop training program for mentally ill young adults in a sheltered workshop under U.S. Department of Labor piecework rates when a revised program required that all participants be paid one dollar an hour without regard to production. This not only removed the incentive built into our program but was illegal under our workshop certificate. The opportunities for job placement in the private sector were thus denied to clients who required the supportive services of the rehabilitation agency.

The Comprehensive Employment and Training Act (CETA) was enacted in 1973 to take over the federally funded manpower and training programs (P.L. 93–203). The primary distinction of this act was the establishment of a network of state and local administrative units for service delivery, called "prime sponsors." Again, handicapped persons were eligible to participate in CETA programs by virtue of their being of low income, unemployed, or in need of training, but it was not until the CETA Amendments of 1978 (P.L. 95–524) that handicapped individuals were explicitly targeted for inclusion. *Handicapped* was defined in the amendments to mean "any individual who has a physical or mental disability which for such individual constitutes or results in a substantial handicap to employment." The act included handicapped persons living in institutions, receiving services in a sheltered workshop, prison, or hospital, as well as those living at home or in community care facilities (U.S. Department of Education 1980).

Through the U.S. Department of Labor, the state labor departments, and the prime sponsors (usually municipal or county governmental agencies) manpower-training funds became directly available to rehabilitation and social service agencies interested in training and transitional work ventures. CETA programs were widely used for the training of ward-level staff (ward aides and therapy aides) and of other entry-level personnel in mental hospitals. To a more limited extent CETA was used for the training of paraprofessional personnel for clinics and community agencies. Surprisingly, there was not a lot of use of CETA for work training of clientele. It may have been that the procedures of dealing with the labor field, the prime sponsors, and a whole set of jargon and nomenclature different from that of mental health services stood in the way of rapid utilization. Also, since CETA was in force only from 1978 until 1982, when the Job-Training Partnership Act was passed, there was not enough time for rehabilitation services for the mentally ill to catch on. Nevertheless, some examples of the use of CETA in services to the mentally ill are worth noting.

USING HOSPITAL OCCUPATIONS FOR TRAINING

A series of CETA projects at Bronx Psychiatric Center, in New York City, and at Rockland Psychiatric Center, in Orangeburg, New York, were set up to examine the feasibility of such manpower-training settings in the state hospitals (Black 1982; Black, Carpenter, and Robinson 1986). The intent was to use hospital occupations as training sites, with the model being that of the transitional employment program (TEP). Four major elements were provided for:

1. Real work in a real world. State Labor Department experts selected four job areas where it was judged there would be opportunity for employment after training. These were mailroom/clerical, housekeeping and minor building repairs, grounds maintenance, and garage and minor vehicle repair. The fourth area was not available at the Bronx hospital.
2. Training supervision. The founders of the program selected training sites where the regular job supervisor was willing to accept CETA trainees, who were paid at the federal minimum wage. At each site a "work counselor," paid by the CETA project, was made available to assist the regular work supervisor and help teach the trainees.
3. Guarantee that work would be done. The work counselors were selected from applicants with experience in the field to which they were assigned. They were therefore available to ensure that the work would be done if for any reason the trainee was absent or unable to perform.
4. A therapeutic/support structure. At each hospital a professional staff member was assigned as liaison with the treatment programs and served as a kind of "case manager" to link CETA to the aftercare or community mental health program that had referred the patient for training.

In terms of organization, the CETA projects employed a program coordinator at each hospital, the work counselors just referred to, and a "job developer." The responsibilities of the job developer included group instruction in how to seek a job as well as opening contacts with potential employers. Details of the project procedures are available in manual form (Black, Carpenter, and Robinson 1986).

Most of the successful clients (55%) among the 150 trainees were placed in jobs in public employment; a minority found work in the private sector. A separate research staff measured changes in attitudes toward work, performance ratings, supervisors' ratings, the work environment, and the social networks of the trainees. The most significant findings were that the attitudes of these mentally ill clients toward work did not differ from those of persons without mental illness, that the supervisors' ratings were early on the most sensitive to the eventual success or failure of the training, and that successful clients enjoyed not greater social networks but networks that had greater "density," that is, the people in them had greater communication with each other. Of significance, also, was that although trainees with diagnoses of schizophrenia or schizoaffective psychoses numbered most greatly among the failures, 42 percent of them *were* successful in making the transition to open employment.

The original plan for this demonstration was for random assignment of referrals from community clinics and mental health centers to the CETA program and to usually available vocational rehabilitation services. The administrative machinery for CETA approval, with long delays between steps, made this impossible. In fact, even consistency of services was hampered by a six-months' hiatus in receiving approval for continuing into the second year of the Bronx program, necessitating an almost complete change in the staff personnel. The shortness of time usually allocated to such a manpower-training project—usually not more than a year for each contract—makes difficult its application to serving the more seriously handicapped.

USING CETA TO AUGMENT A PROGRAM

Some services for the handicapped were able to contract with their local CETA prime sponsors to augment an already ongoing work-training program. Rise, Inc., of Spring Lake, Minnesota, was able to obtain a collaborative training agreement with the Anoka County CETA office. This allowed Rise to add fifteen training slots to its food services and custodial services. The food-service training was conducted at the local Area Vocational Training Institute; custodial services training was at the county courthouse and in a school district. Rise's work-activity trainer was assigned to the CETA program. He was responsible for intake procedures, establishing eligibility, adapting training curricula for the new sites, monitoring trainee progress, and maintaining liaison with the employers. The CETA contract added a vocational teacher who assisted by assuming training and supervisory responsibilities in the food services program.

Through this program the school district was enabled to keep its cafeteria open during the summer session. Trainees were supplied with funds by CETA for special uniforms and shoes, and an allowance for transportation. The trainees completing the program were assisted in permanent job seeking by Rise's job placement team and by a vocational counselor from CETA. Rise reported a job retention rate of 85 percent (*Rise Reporter* 1983).

Another rehabilitation agency that made satisfactory use of CETA was Dial Industries, Inc., of Cleveland. Dial was able to contract with its local prime sponsor to include its skill-training programs in housekeeping/custodial services and in retail sales within the CETA orbit, making it eligible for CETA funds to provide salaries at minimum wage for work time spent by twenty clients.

Vocational Industries of Elkhorn, Wisconsin, was able to arrange with CETA to provide a "Job Club" for its clientele. The Job Club provides intensive training in job-seeking skills. It is becoming of increasing interest to agencies serving the mentally ill, and will be described more fully in a later chapter. Pine Rest Christian Hospital and Rehabilitation Services, Grand Rapids, similarly used CETA for augmentation of its training and job-placement services. A one-week work-skills evaluation was provided, after which the client was placed in outside employment for training. Pine Rest offers an extensive skills-training and job-placement program, primarily for mentally ill and mentally handicapped clients, and in its CETA project it tried especially to have training lead to job hiring at the training site.

THE JOB TRAINING PARTNERSHIP ACT

Influenced by a new federal administration dedicated to decreasing governmental involvement in direct services and in lowering human service costs, the U.S. Congress in 1982 passed the Job Training Partnership Act (P.L. 97–300). JTPA replaced CETA in October 1983. It differed from CETA in the following ways:

- It prohibited or severely restricted training activities in public employment.
- It removed the work-experience-training provisions of CETA.
- It curtailed the amount of funds available for administrative costs to 15 percent of total expenditures.
- It placed severe restrictions on income support to trainees.
- It gave greater responsibility to state governments.
- It placed authority for local planning and management in the hands

of private industry councils instead of local or county government.

- It sharply reduced the toal federal allocation to JTPA from that allocated for CETA. In New York State, for example, the JTPA allocation was one-third the previous allocation for CETA.

The only reference to services to the handicapped in the act is in section 203(2): "Up to 10 percent of the participants in all programs in a service delivery area receiving assistance under this part may be individuals who are not economically disadvantaged if such individuals have encountered barriers to employment." The word "handicapped" is included in the list that follows.

The key to participation in the JTPA is the local private industry council. The governor of each state decides upon the service areas to have such councils, and their membership is determined by a public nomination and recommendation process culminating in certification by the governor. Business representatives are recommended by businesses in the service area, education officials recommend their representatives, and local community groups are expected to recommend their nominees. Over 8,000 business volunteers serve on the local private industry councils (PICs), public education is widely represented, but community-based organizations, including rehabilitation and mental health agencies, are only sparsely included: "The average PIC of 25 members has two CBO [community-based organization] representatives. Nearly one-fifth of the SDAs [service delivery areas] do not use CBOs to deliver any services, and nearly one of four SDAs used fewer CBOs to deliver services in 1984 than 1983" (National Council on Employment Policy 1985). One explanation for this decline is the use of "performance contracts" which defer payment until job placements are verified. Most community-based nonprofit agencies do not have the financial resources to cover costs in advance of payment.

The JTPA program is receiving mixed reviews. The administration seems pleased with the lessened costs and reports that the needs of the labor market are being filled. The General Accounting Office reported that while there are significant changes in clientele and program from CETA, most service-area officials believe the effect of such changes upon meeting the objectives of the JTPA have been negative (*NARF Rehabilitation Review*, Feb. 10, 1986). The changes, however, *are* significant for the mentally ill and "mentally restored" population. JTPA served a higher percentage of high school graduates, students, and unemployment compensation claimants and a lower percentage of dropouts, unemployed, and nonwhites than did CETA. There was a shift in training that doubled the use of on-the-job traineeships and a 66 percent drop in work-experience training. The National Council on Employment Policy judged that JTPA is a delivery system "less attuned to the needs of the disadvantaged and unemployed" (1985, p. 2). The New York State Commissioner of Labor labeled JTPA "merely a band-aid on a hemorrhage" (Job Training Legislative Transition Conference 1985 p. 3).

In spite of the reductions in the fiscal resources of JTPA from CETA and the negative repercussions for services to the handicapped, a few rehabilitation agencies have found participation in JTPA valuable. It is important to note this because others may also find it possible to use this manpower program and because if past practice is repeated, there can be modifications to law or regulations making the eligibility of the handicapped more feasible.

The Northern Rhode Island Community Mental Health Center, Inc., and the Community Counseling Center of Pawtucket, Rhode Island, have been able to set up a pilot job-training program under JTPA. The private industry council, on which the director of one of these agencies serves, has granted funds for the training of ten to twelve clients. The project provides a job developer, and the training is carried on in the agency's snack bar and restaurant unit. The private-industry-council representative expressed great satisfaction to me regarding the results so far, but he did explain that there was a hiatus in funding between the pilot program and the ongoing service because of the administrative procedures required. He reports that the Rhode Island Department of Mental Health has now requested applications for grants for supported work programs and that the private industry council has offered to match the grant should his agency win one.

Threshold Rehabilitation Services, Inc., of Reading, Pennsylvania, participates in what has become a most popular section of the JTPA, the School-to-Employment Program (STEP). (*Profile,* October 1985). STEP is school-based work-study program designed to develop the basic education and employability skills of pupils 14–17 years of age who are identified as potential school dropouts. It combines work training with academic instruction to upgrade achievement in reading, writing, and arithmetic, and to develop good attitudes toward work and good work habits. In addition to STEP, which Threshold has been operating since 1982, JTPA has granted the agency a youth employment preparation program (YEPP) in participating Berks County high schools. This provides preemployment skill training to eligible tenth- and eleventh-grade students in career exploration, job readiness and basic life skills, remedial education, and labor-market information. Students who successfully complete the course content will be given the opportunity of working in the Summer Youth Employment Program, also a JTPA venture. While many school districts now offer JTPA programs of this sort to disadvantaged youth, few are directed toward handicapped youngsters, and still fewer have developed the kind of cooperative program with a specialized agency that is exemplified in the Threshold–Berks County schools program.

Businesses for the Handicapped

Many a sheltered workshop manager has expressed the desire to have a commodity that could be manufactured directly by the shop and sold by the workshop. The dream is that direct manufacture would dispense with all of the problems inherent in finding subcontract work and in dealing with the periods when contracts do not overlap and work dries up, or when the prime contractor has problems that curtail deliveries of parts, and so on. The dream is also that income from sales of direct manufacture would be sufficient to generate "surpluses" (profits) such that writing applications for grants and other fund-raising activities would no longer be necessary. Over the years, quite a number of rehabilitation enterprises have tried direct manufacture and sales with varied success.

Among the earliest of what might be called "businesses for the handicapped" were those for the blind, for paraplegics (at Abilities, Inc., Albertson, New York), and for the tuberculous (at Altro Workshops). The Altro experience has analogies for the field of services to the mentally ill. Tuberculosis was a relapsing illness with great stigma attached to it by the outside community. The workshop developed a program of designing and manufacturing hospital garments and surgical gowns and of selling them directly to hospitals throughout the Eastern seaboard and the Midwest. It operated in the open competitive market and employed a sales force to visit its customers and develop others. About 20 percent of its work force were nonpatients, though a number of these were "graduates" who, though no longer infectious, were content to remain to provide stability and quality to the manufacture. Such a mix of handicapped and nonhandicapped workers was a characteristic of the other shops, and still is of the industries for the blind.

To a limited extent, rehabilitation services for the handicapped have been trying to organize manufacture or service businesses that could generate profits as well as meet the training and other rehabilitative needs of the clientele. The Fairweather Lodges might be thought of as such businesses, as could janitorial and food service programs of the psychosocial field. But such programs do not really operate in the open competitive market, for a goodly part of their overhead costs are borne by government grants and fees. The line between profit-making "businesses" that are set up specifically to serve the handicapped and not-for-profit agencies that operate units to manufacture products for direct sale to the public or to provide services in competition with regular business is a fine one.

An interesting new development comes from the field of services to the mentally retarded. Under the title "Affirmative Industry" Minnesota Diversified Industries, St. Paul, developed a format that seems very like the earlier patterns of Abilities and Altro. This involves organizing the business with a mix of clients and nonclients to ensure production and quality, and to arrange that the total costs of the business enterprise, both capital and operating, be met from business income. Either no supportive therapeutic or rehabilitative costs are met at all, with other agencies' providing such services, or these services are provided by a completely (legally) separate part of the parent organization.

Some examples of the various profit and not-for-profit agencies providing "businesses for the handicapped" will make clear the approaches being used and some of the problems dealt with.

BUSINESSES WITHOUT SUBSIDIES

Opportunity Workshop of Lexington, Inc.

Opportunity Workshop of Lexington, Kentucky (OWL), was established in 1962 by the Junior League of that city. This sheltered workshop program serves clients with a wide variety of disabilities, of whom about one-third are labeled as "emotionally disturbed." The clientele in its vocational rehabilitation programs number over 175 each day, in a range of services including vocational evaluation, work adjustment, work conditioning, skill training, sheltered employment, and assistance with job placement. OWL carries on a unique follow-up program by letters to its "graduates"; it pays for the return of a short questionnaire at the three and six months' periods and at the end of the first year.

The OWL production shop is involved in sales and service in assembling wheelchairs to meet individual requirements of the physically handicapped. It also assembles and installs hand controls on automobiles and converts vans for use by the handicapped by installing chairlifts, special seats, and various power controls. OWL Mobility Equipment, as it is called, functions as a profit-making enterprise. In a recent year, OWL reported over a million dollars of sales income, 46 percent of which went for wages to the trainees/employees. OWL paid over $70,000 in city, state, and federal taxes, even though the parent organization is a nonprofit corporation. The activities in the workshop afford training as an assembler in the fabrication, assembly, and repair of metal products; as a woodworking shop hand in the fabrication and repair of wood products; as a commercial or institutional cleaner; as a stock or inventory clerk; as a hydraulic chair assembler; and in a variety of clerical occupations. OWL has as a motto "Work . . . is good therapy. But, therapy is not work."

Beavercraft, Inc.

Beavercraft, Inc., is a nonprofit, tax-exempt corporation in Beaverton, Michigan, established in 1979 to provide rehabilitation services to handicapped adults. In addition to the usual subcontract work of a sheltered workshop the agency operates a shoe repair shop and is the prime manufacturer of a line of primitive, solid-wood furniture. In 1981 the agency received a loan from the U.S. Small Business Administration to cover the cost of a new building and the furnishings, equipment, and operating capital for a facility to serve eighty handicapped individuals.

The board of directors of Beavercraft set as a goal that the sale of goods and services should support all costs of the facility. No state or federal grants for operating costs are sought, though private contributions are solicited. The production management and supervision, as is true of OWL, is by personnel skilled and experienced in the work employed. Beavercraft is accredited by the Commission on Accreditation of Rehabilitation Services.

"AFFIRMATIVE" INDUSTRIES

In an effort to provide a longer time of employment for persons who while productive at work might not easily make the transition to normal work settings, some rehabilitation agencies are turning to client-operated business called "affirmative industries." The term is borrowed from the field of services to the mentally retarded/developmentally disabled. The "affirmative" designation is from the concept of civil rights for the handicapped. To the greatest extent possible these businesses are run as normal industry, without the support elements of supported or transitional employment. Only those clients who can be sufficiently productive to meet the quotas for a profit-making business are kept in the affirmative industry (DuRand and DuRand 1978). The lines of demarcation between affirmative industry and sheltered work are not always clear, however, and elements of all kinds of rehabilitative work, from sheltered to transitional, are to be found in what are referred to as affirmative industries. A few examples will make this clear.

South Shore Rehabilitation Center: Consolidated Products and Services

South Shore Rehabilitation Center, in Quincy, Massachusetts, as has already been described, operates a number of types of work programs. Among them is Consolidated Products and Services, Inc., a not-for-profit industry for the handicapped which manufactures medical and hospital items. It makes three different styles of drainage bags, a document pouch, an ice pack, a lanyard and drawstring pouch, and a round urinary drainage bag. Most of this work comes from the U.S. Veterans Administration under contracts obtained through NISH. In accord with the regulations binding NISH contracts ("set-aside" contracts with the federal government) at least 75 percent of the labor force must be handicapped, in this case mostly the mentally ill.

Consolidated Products is set up in its own rooms, which are made antiseptic and in which the employees wear white uniforms. At the time of my visit, in 1984, this industry was reported to be just on the verge of "making a profit." It had recently won an additional Veterans Administration contract for producing 120,000 round urinary bags, which would increase sales to the VA to almost a million dollars, insuring the fiscal viability of the business. It was necessary to add fifteen handicapped clients to the work force to meet production demands.

A picture of the variety of tasks available in the manufacture of the urinary bag is supplied by the agency:

> This urinary drainage bag is used in hospitals during surgery and post surgery. To produce the '6600' there are 11 steps in the manufacturing phase. This begins with one client die cutting strips of vinyl sheeting into the large round shape. Smaller interior valves and filters are separately cut. Next, the vinyl bag is silk screened with the CP&S logo, graduated markings and product identification information. One client operates the silk-screener. Using a machine called a perimeter sealer, the seal tube holder and filters are then secured to the bag. The next step requres the use of a perimeter sealing machine to seal the product's circumference. Three handicapped workers are responsible for this part of the process. In the final step, a mandrell sealing machine attaches the tubing to the bag. The product is then ready for assembly and packaging, which involves 15 separate steps . . . Each of the steps in the manufacture and assembly has been task analyzed and workers perform a single step until they gain proficiency, accuracy and speed. Client productivity ranges from 50% to over 100% of the industrial norm. (*SSRC News*, Spring 1984, p. 5)

It is easy to see how appealing to rehabilitation directors is direct manufacture, with its variety of job tasks, in contrast to subcontracted bench assembly and packaging, with its limited array of job operations.

Threshold Rehabilitation Services: Precision Micrographics

In 1985 the Pennsylvania Office of Mental Health made a grant to Threshold Rehabilitation Services in Reading, which specializes in services to the mentally ill and disabled, to enable it to upgrade its equipment in microfilming. A small business, Precision Micrographics, was then established for ten to twelve handicapped employees, along with two staff experienced in the business operations; the business opened its doors in September 1985. The work to be done, mainly for local businesses and industry, includes document preparation; the filming of documents onto reels, fiche, jackets, or aperture cards; and the processing and developing of the appropriate microfilms. Much assistance and guidance was given by the Bell and Howell Corporation, one of the main suppliers of equipment for the new business (*Profile,* May 1985 and January 1986).

Two affirmative industry attempts point to some of the problems facing development. One failed to get under way because of difficulties with raising capital; the other ran into roadblocks from the therapeutic establishment.

Marin Community Workshops, Inc.: The Bayport Project

In 1984 the Marin County Workshop (MCW), in Mill Valley, California, designed an integrated system of services to the mentally ill including an affirmative industry. Called the Bayport Project, it planned to employ over 200 disabled and nondisabled workers in a factory manufacturing disposable medical devices for markets in the United States and abroad. At least fifty full-time positions were to be earmarked for individuals with histories of mental illness. There was to be a preemployment training class for eighteen persons per month, contracted for with a mental health agency that would be a good source of workers; a transitional employment satellite with twenty slots would serve as an evaluation and selection instrument for the industry.

At the time of my visit, MCW had received foundation grants to enable it to launch the preemployment training class and the TEP and to purchase land for the industry. The foundation offered a $4.5 million loan, repayable in fifteen years at low interest, for construction and start-up operating costs. An agreement had been made with an East Coast biologics firm which would supply contracts for work and would market the products worldwide. This firm also contributed a matching grant of $1 million to finance acquisition of equipment and inventories.

The site for construction had been selected, it had been determined that the company would manufacture a number of types of intravenous infusion sets (IVs), and the training and TEP programs were under way. The MCW newsletter described a profile of the worker the Bayport Project would employ as follows: "male, unmarried, age 25–30, on medication, unemployed for two years, not violent, has some work history, receives public/family money, lives in a group home, can only work part-time, has been hospitalized, has had years of therapy, above average intelligence, legal problems, messy-unkempt appearance, inconsistent, uses public transportation, is lonely, Dept. of Rehabilitation case closed, not registered with Employment Development Department, will be referred by public/private mental health providers." It went on to say that "although Bayport's workforce will include other disability groups and non-disabled model workers, preference will be given to the mentally ill, and among that group, schizophrenia will be the most prevalent disabling condition" (*MCW News,* March 1984, p. 3). Staff for the Bayport Project were hired, including a project director with experience in the rehabilitation of the mentally retarded, along with production supervisors who were primarily vocational counselors.

When I inquired again in early 1986 as to the progress of the Bayport Project, I learned that the foundation had had second thoughts. It had decided to require an earlier paying off of the loan and to charge a higher rate of interest. The board of directors of MCW developed questions about the large scope of the plan, and there were doubts as to its feasibility. The directors decided to drop the affirmative industry component and to settle for a supported work program with a local industry; apparently the foundation is willing to provide this program with grant assistance.

It seems to me that there was an element of grandiosity in the Bayport Project, with its planners lacking sufficient expertise both in business development methods and with the disability it was intended to serve. I am reminded that some thirty-odd years ago a group of sheltered workshop directors of which I was a part met with the deans of a number of prestigious business schools to consider how we might stimulate education of the rehabilitation workshop managers of the future. The business school educators replied that they would not help in this task because the profit-making goal of the business world was inimical to the motives we were expressing on behalf of the handicapped. While I did not then, and still do not, believe the line is so clear-cut as did the deans, there is merit in recognizing that the real business world and that of rehabilitation of the handicapped are somewhat uneasy partners and that each requires an expertise of its own.

Isis: Ceramics and Woven Goods for Interior Design

In 1979 two occupational therapists with extensive experience in dealing with chronic mental patients opened Isis in a store in the Mission district of San Francisco. One of the therapists was skilled in producing ceramics for sale in the open, competitive market, the other in producing textiles. They both had been carrying on business activities part-time and decided to devote all of their time to commerce, putting it to use for mental patients. Isis functioned for about five years before being closed because of problems with financing and with unplanned turnover of clientele/employees.

Referrals to Isis were made by therapists and mental health agencies. Clients had to be interested in the creative work done in this "cottage industry." The specialties were hand-thrown ceramic lamp bases with fine handwoven shades, and a wide variety of handwoven scarves, shawls, and throws in mohair, silk, wool, rayon, and cotton. There was no problem in selling the products, for they were tastefully designed and beautifully crafted. Many custom-made pieces were commissioned.

Clients were scheduled to work a twelve-hour week. Their wages were based on productivity and a commission on the sale of items they made. One of the partners explained the concept of the program to me as follows: "I feel the Isis program captured the essence of what is needed for a chronic population: a stable, creative setting where people can go, earn some money, increase their functioning without the threat that the increased functioning means placement in a more demanding setting, and most of all, a small supportive environment that does not smack of the warehousing atmosphere common to so many 'sheltered workshops.' " That the program was financially valuable for the clients is attested to by the fact that after six months most of them were earning $150 to $200 a month for their production.

Various foundations made grants to Isis, and some local corporations donated materials and services. However, the total volume of business possible with the approximately twenty client/employees that could be accommodated during a year was not sufficient to generate income for costs of supervision and replacement of supplies and certainly not for the expansion required to put the enterprise on a cost-productive basis. No funds were made available from governmental sources. In addition, the therapeutic sources of referral made plans for the clients without regard to the work setting. Frequently, the referring therapist or agency peremptorily judged patients who were performing ably in Isis to be sufficiently improved to warrant their discharge from the therapeutic program, or to be transferred to another program. The problems of financing and employee turnover became too difficult for the two partners, and they closed the program. One of them has continued to operate a smaller business at the same location but without the component of service to the mentally ill.

Other Business Enterprises

Quite a number of mental health and mental retardation agencies have developed programs in baking, cooking, and gardening. For the most part, such programs have been used as evaluative and/or transitional employment settings, and no real attempt has been made to transform them into profit-making (or surplus-making) businesses. Exceptions that might be cited are the gardening and horticulture shop of

Rubicon Programs, Inc., in Richmond, California; Hearthstone Cafe and Catering, run by the West Side Community Mental Health Center, Cleveland, which specializes in chocolates, cakes, and box lunches; and two outlets established by the Rhode Island Department of Mental Health: Cookie Place, a retail and wholesale bakery, and New Leaf, a retail plant and garden-supply store. Altro Health and Rehabilitation Services, in New York, has opened Altro Cafe, which provides lunches and caters meals. As I have pointed out, the Altro Garment Factory, though most of its manufacture is now for the government through NISH contracts, is operated as a true "affirmative industry" and uses its surpluses for the support of other programs that have training or other rehabilitative focuses. Another businesslike venture that is within a more general rehabilitation agency is the manufacture of "Swish Rod" ice fishing poles and box spring frames by Handishop Industries, Inc., of Tomah, Wisconsin.

Volunteer Work

Many programs serving the mentally ill have used volunteer work to give clients something to occupy their time, as a means of retaining skills, as part of the process of evaluating work capacity, as work-adjustment training, as a first step towards transitional employment, or as some combination of these. All of the psychosocial clubs use volunteer services as a necessary part of maintenance of their programs, and most of the local chapters of the National Mental Health Association have provided volunteer placements to assist with clerical and fund-raising tasks. There are, however, some differences in opinion as to the place and value of volunteer work in rehabilitation of the mentally ill.

Some agencies, particularly those in the psychosocial center movement, consider volunteer work a necessary first step towards preparation for paid work, either transitional or regular. For example, the Tri-county Fountain Center of Lansdowne, Pennsylvania, has what it calls a "prevocational Day Work/Evaluation Program (DW/EP)" offering "clients an opportunity to develop and practice fundamental work habits and skills and to acquire the necessary stamina for successful pursuit of competitive employment, vocational training, or further academic education. Clients are assessed daily on categories ranging from attendance and punctuality to the development of self-confidence and performance of adequate quality and quantity of work" (correspondence with program director). This agency uses volunteer work in one of eight co-operating community agencies, such as the YMCA, the Red Cross, the public library, and local hospitals. The program is funded with state mental health monies through the County Mental Health/Mental Retardation Board.

Two other programs with the same name—Renaissance Center of Pittsburgh, Pennsylvania, and Renaissance Center, Inc., of Jacksonville, Florida—use volunteer work experience as a step towards job-seeking and job placement. The intent is to help "the member develop or redevelop skills applicable to most vocational situations, such as following directions, appropriate dress, punctuality, and dealing with co-workers and supervisors" (correspondence with Renaissance Center). The volunteer work stations include the usual array of clerical, food-service, landscaping (groundskeeping), and building maintenance tasks (including cleaning). Following satisfactory volunteer work experience, the member is placed in an "intensive Job Readiness program. This focuses on job-seeking skills, such as how to compile a resume, filling out a job application, interviewing techniques, etc." (ibid.). A placement specialist then assists the member in locating a job.

Some agencies have included volunteer work as an end point for certain patients. Goodwill Industries of Greater Grand Rapids, Michigan, has instituted a cooperative program with a group of community agencies. The idea here, shared by many mental health professionals, is that volunteer work is the extent of "productive participation" in society that many chronic patients can achieve.

In services to the young adult and older adolescent mental patients, volunteer work has also been put to use. The Y-East Center for Social Learning, Gresham, Oregon (near Portland), has found outdoor service in parks particularly helpful in interesting and motivating younger, and not so young, persons with long-term, severe psychiatric disabilities. Its Oxbow Park Program is a good example. One day a week, groups of clients under the supervision of a staff member with a background in parks and recreation build trails and do other forestry work in Oxbow Park in Portland. The work is linked with informal nature education. The crew members become friends, client leaders evolve, patients gain self-esteem, and community education is advanced by the contacts of regular park employees and the general public with well-functioning persons who happen to be mentally ill. This program, which is one of a number of vocationally oriented services of the Mt. Hood Community Mental Health Center, is very popular. It has run for over three years, and there are now plans to link it more closely to a prevocational training emphasis and to provide more formal feedback to the clients as to their performance.

Through the Vocational Education Act funding is available to the public schools to provide work-study programs for handicapped youngsters. One interesting form, using volunteer work assignments and incorporating some of the elements of supported work, is provided by the New York City Board of Education for handicapped high school students. It is called Vocational Instruction for Special Education Training Advancement, or VISTA. In 1985, 320 handicapped high school students, 18 years of age or older, were placed in groups of twelve and with a special education teacher were assigned to work in hospitals, nursing homes, and other public programs. The students perform a variety of tasks, usually two to three days per week, the other days being spent in classroom instruction in their high schools. The most usual occupations are clerical jobs, food services, building maintenance, stockroom or mailroom work, messenger services, and patient escort services. The teacher remains with the youngsters throughout their work periods and performs very much the same role as a "job coach" in a supported work setting. These teachers are vocational education teachers, capable of teaching the skills needed for the job assignment (information derived from personal visits and observations).

In the VISTA program student work performance is carefully rated both by the special education teacher and by the actual foreman or supervisor at the work station. Students receive school credit for participation; reports are that 20 to 25 percent of the students go on to earn high school diplomas. Most of the youngsters are classified as learning disabled, educationally mentally retarded, or emotionally disturbed. A few students who show great advancement in the Vista program are given the opportunity of a higher-level program in which there is no assigned teacher supervision and where there is some opportunity for wage payment by the employer. An interesting addition to the Vista program in the borough of the Bronx is role-playing instruction in job-seeking and a simulated job interview with the borough coordinator at high school headquarters.

The use of volunteer work for the mentally ill is much more extensive than these few examples would indicate. As one of the methods available for exposing patients or clients to the work-a-day world and for prevocational evaluation it has great merit. It may also be of intrinsic value for older persons unlikely to enter or reestablish themselves in paid employment or for persons whose ability to control disabling symptoms is very intermittant. The disadvantages of volunteer work are that it is not a substitute for the demands of the real work world and that there is a tendency for agencies who use volunteer work exclusively or mainly not to get the clients to try transitions to paid employment.

2
The Scene Abroad

6
Programs in Western Europe

When, twenty years ago, I wrote about the developing programs in sheltered work and industrial therapy for the mentally ill, it was necessary to look to the countries in northern Europe for the best examples of an incipient movement (Black 1970). Today, it is the American scene that provides the best picture of the variety of programs and their potential. Nevertheless, a survey of European programs and of those elsewhere in the world gives perspective to understanding our own developments and may suggest directions the services in the United States might want to take. It also throws light upon the effect of the American experience upon the rest of the world.

As has been true in the United States, vocational rehabilitation services for the handicapped in European countries originated out of concern for disabled war veterans. A sheltered work environment, Thermega, Ltd., was set up for "shell-shocked" veterans of World War I just outside of London by the British Ex-Service Mental Welfare Society. The Netherlands opened "Consultation Bureaux," with many aspects of aftercare and sociovocational therapies for the mentally ill, in the middle 1920s. Special vocational services were established in a number of settings in England for the tuberculous, many of whom were reported to have been emotionally disturbed (Black 1970). However, it was not until after World War II that Western European laws and regulations made explicit a range of services we can truly call vocational rehabilitation, which, though stimulated by the needs of disabled veterans, became available to all handicapped persons in the country.

Although European laws relating to disabled persons were usually general with regard to the handicapping conditions included (e.g., the British Disabled Persons Employment Act of 1944, the Netherlands Act of 1947, the 1953 act of the Federal Republic of Germany, the Belgian Special Aid Fund of 1956), the services available were mostly for the physically handicapped. It was not until the 1960s and 1970s that new legislation or amendments made clear the inclusion of the mentally handicapped and the mentally ill (Schulman 1981). In the United Kingdom (England, Scotland, and Northern Ireland) this was accomplished by the Mental Health Acts of 1959, 1960, and 1961, respectively. In the Netherlands the change was incorporated in the General Special Sickness Insurance Act of 1967. In West Germany an act of 1961 extended the scope of earlier legislation to include the mentally ill and psychologically handicapped. In Belgium it was the Rehabilitation Act of 1963; in 1972 Denmark expanded its nationwide program under the Rehabilitation Act of 1960 to all disabling conditions. Sweden's Royal Ordinance is dated 1963; the Norwegian Disabled Person's Act of 1958 added the psychiatrically disabled in 1961.

What appears to be significant from the viewpoint of sheltered and transitional work programs for the mentally ill is that these legal extensions of eligible categories of handicap and disablement came about in the same period that interest was rising in community approaches to psychiatric treatment. Even before the wide application of neuroleptic drugs in the mental hospitals, a number of European countries were experimenting with what we have come to call community mental health care. This was particularly true in the Netherlands, in Amsterdam and the Hague; in England, in Nottingham; out of the Karolinska Hospital in Stockholm, Sweden; and in such programs as Association L'Elan Retrouve, in Paris. Even though the term *sheltered work* was not used, references were widely made to "ergo therapy" and work adjustment. The European mental health programs gave much less emphasis to the psychotherapies and much more to what we now refer to as creative arts therapies (music, art, dance), occupational and recreational therapy, resocialization, and work activities. Attempts were made to utilize provisions for the disabled, particularly those for employment or preparation for employment, on behalf of mental patients. At first, success was quite limited.

Many of the European laws providing for the handicapped attempt three major areas of service. First of all they extend the general social insurance provisions to the disabled at whatever the age of disablement. They have set up programs that provide short-term sickness benefits preceding long-term or permanent disability benefits. Persons may be adjudged partially disabled and receive some portion of the total disability amount, in contrast to practice in the United States, where participants either receive full benefits or nothing at all (Berkowitz 1985).

Secondly, these European laws provide for special training and/or special work settings for those who are not able to return to open employment. This has been done "under the postwar conviction that government has a responsibility to create special jobs, not as a charity but as a right, under the commitment to full employment" (Reubens 1970, p. 41). Thirdly, they tried to make provision, usually through a quota system (about which more will be said), to hold jobs open for the handicapped in regular business and industry. The various disability insurance schemes are linked to the social welfare programs in their respective countries as well as to national health insurance provisions. Psychiatric care is an integral part of the health care system in the Western European countries, and all health care is a basic right of everyone under these nations' disability and social welfare schemes (Jansen 1986).

While these provisions ensure a basic economic underpinning for the disabled unemployed, many rehabilitation specialists believe that the all-embracing welfare schemes offer a significant disincentive for many handicapped persons to engage in work training or sheltered work. Nevertheless, even in a country such as Sweden, with as complete welfare insurance as could be designed, there is no dearth of interest by the disabled, including the psychiatrically disabled, in participating in rehabilitation enterprises.

Deinstitutionalization, which has had such a stimulating effect upon the development of community-based programs for the mentally ill in the United States, has progressed much more slowly in Europe than here. Most European countries have taken a conservative and cautious approach. They are more concerned than we have been about having community support programs in place before discharging patients from mental hospitals (Jansen 1986). The process of deinstitutionalization is inexorably advancing, however, and, particularly in the United Kingdom, is having a major effect upon the kinds of transitional work programs available for the mentally ill.

The United Kingdom

England was probably the first of the Western European countries to introduce industrial work units into its mental hospitals. With the encouragement of the Medical Research Council (somewhat analogous to our National Institutes of Health), industrial therapy programs were established in Banstead Hospital, Sutton, in 1955 and in Netherne Hospital, Surrey, in 1957 (Black 1970). These units were linked to transitional programs, including work on the wards and occupational therapy on the one hand, and sheltered industrial work, contracting with outside industry in the manner of what we have been calling sheltered workshops, and resettlement to outside sheltered or open employment on the other.

One of the earliest of these "Industrial Therapy Units" was established at Glenside Hospital, Bristol, by the consulting psychiatrist (medical director), Dr. Donal Early. He quickly saw the advantage of placing the workshops outside the hospital, to place the use of work as a therapeutic and socializing program in a more normal setting. His first factory was in a disused school building near the hospital, opened in 1960 with twenty-five patients. Dr. Early organized a not-for-profit company called the Industrial Therapy Organisation (ITO) (Bristol), Ltd., and employed as its manager John Turley, a skilled business manager with a graduate university degree in business administration. The ITO (Bristol) is noteworthy as the precursor of a number of ITOs, first at the Mapperly Day Hospital, Nottingham, which had become internationally famous for its experiments with aftercare services in the community, and at ITO (Thames), Ltd., in Southall, London. ITO (Bristol) also developed transitional and enclave placements in local industry that became the stimulators of the British sheltered industrial group program and the transitional employment program in the United States.

The British Ministry of Labour agreed to assist in the sheltered employment scheme, but only if those workers/patients accepted lived outside the hospital. The ministry met 75 percent of any deficiency incurred between costs and earnings, and the Bristol Corporation (local government) met the remainder. The ITO almost immediately faced a problem common to the deinstitutionalization movement in the United States: many patients had no homes or housing to go to on discharge from the hospital. Therefore, the ITO sponsored its own housing agency, and in 1963 the Bristol Industrial Therapy Housing Association, Ltd., came into being. The Transport and General Workers Union, one of the largest labor unions in the country, loaned money to purchase a hotel. Two years later the ITO took over tenancy of six houses built for it by the Bristol Corporation.

As the ITO (Bristol) grew, it moved in 1969 to a rebuilt factory. The equipment installed included cutting and creasing presses, guillotine, flexopress, gluers and conveyors, stitchers and heat sealers, all similar to what might be found in many sheltered workshops in the United States. This ITO, however, does direct manufacture of medical casenote folders supplied to medical authorities throughout southwest England. The relationship with Glenside Hospital has ended, and all of the clientele come from community sources. It seems to be a healthy program (Turley 1985).

During the 1960s there was a flurry of development of industrial therapy units in mental hospitals and in the establishment of ITOs. Their founding and continuation depended more upon the interest of a particular consulting psychiatrist at the hospital than for any other reason. Much of this interest began to evaporate during the 1970s, in part because of the move to community-based programs, the required cost of launching what is really a small business during a period of increasing economic stringency, and the difficulties in finding capable management and psychiatric interest. In addition, the United Kingdom has experienced deinstitutionalization, though not to the extent seen in the United States, and this has left an increasingly residual and low-functioning population in the mental hospitals.

As a number of ITOs were formed their directors joined in the National Association of Industrial Therapy Managers. In 1980 the association was reconstituted as the British Institute of Industrial Therapy. Among its leaders were the psychiatrists and industrial therapy managers who were instrumental in establishing the hospital units and the ITOs. The BIIT, as it has come to be known, serves both as a professional membership organization and as a "trade association." It offers technical assistance and guidance, courses in management, and legal advice; it also conducts training courses, publishes a magazine, and has an annual national conference. The BIIT plans to carry on research, particularly into mental health policy as it affects the use of work in therapy and rehabilitation. It acts as an advocate for the staff of the ITOs.

Under the Disabled Persons Act of 1944, the Ministry of Labour was empowered to organize a company called the Disabled Persons Employment Corporation, Ltd., which came to be known as Remploy, Ltd. Remploy now operates nearly ninety factories, employing nearly 9,000 disabled individuals, only about 17 percent of whom are psychiatrically disabled. The factories produce leather products, textile products, and furniture, and do packaging and assembling. Remploy enjoys preference in acquiring contracts for the manufacture or processing of goods for the government. It also bids for work in the open market. The wage rates are set by agreement with the trade unions, which participate in decisions as to a standard minimum.

In time, some of the ITOs were recognized as specialized (designated) Remploy industries (Black 1977). This has enabled the former mental patient employed in such sheltered workshops to participate in the full social insurance benefits afforded the employees of regular Remploy factories. Also, as is the case in the regular Remploy factories, governmental subsidies become available for operating deficits and capital outlays.

A very innovative approach to vocational rehabilitation for the mentally ill, which has been borrowed in the United States by certain of the psychosocial rehabilitation centers, was that of transitional employment and work enclaves in regular business and industry. As I have said, ITO (Bristol), Ltd., pioneered in the 1960s with placing individuals in selected jobs in local industry, entry-level positions in which the patient had an opportunity to test out capabilities and learn saleable employment skills. Then the ITO placed groups of patients in normal factory settings, under the supervision of a nurse and a regular foreman. Wage payments were made by the business to the ITO, which in turn paid the patient/employees. The British Manpower Services Commission has since developed the idea for all handicapped. This program now involves a three-way agreement between the commission, a sponsor (often REMPLOY or an ITO), and a host firm (Akabas 1984). As a service to the mentally ill, these sheltered industrial groups (SIGs) offer a great advantage. The patient is prepared for regular employment in a setting that is realistic, in which the working conditions approximate the real work-a-day world as closely as possible. For the schizophrenic patient, this is particularly significant in obviating one of his most serious difficulties, that of transposing experience from one setting to another.

The Manpower Services Commission (MSC) pays the sponsor the difference between the employer's payment to the sponsor and the minimum wage. The MSC can provide grants toward revenue costs, capital expenditure, training, and, in some circumstances, research. Revenue support is available to independent voluntary bodies to 100 percent of losses up to a ceiling of £2,380 per person, and up to 75 percent of approved capital expenditures. Through its Sheltered Employment Procurement and Consultancy Services, the MSC provides free advice to workshops (*Industrial Therapy,* Autumn 1983b). Akabas (1984, p. 14) issued some warnings about SIGs. She said: "A problem may occur if other workers regard subsidized disabled workers as a form of cheap labor. Availability of subsidies might be exploited, and disabled persons be pressured to agree to be registered under the quota system, as will be explained later." She agrees, however, that without a subsidy system, enclave employment at a regular worksite is all but unavailable.

Over the past twenty years the British have developed a number of resources for vocational rehabilitation of the disabled. A report of the Royal College of Psychiatrists listed the following (1980):

- Hospital rehabilitation units, including industrial therapy units, occupational therapy units, and hospital day units;
- Local-authority day centers;
- Local-authority rehabilitation and assessment centers;
- Industrial therapy organizations;
- Community-based industrial units;

- Sheltered workshops including Remploy factories;
- Sheltered industrial groups;
- Employment rehabilitation centers;
- Skillcentres;
- Residential training colleges;
- Colleges of further education.

The Department of Employment reported in 1970 that the largest group of short- or long-term unemployed among the disabled were the mentally ill. Verbal assurances confirm that the picture is the same today. However, the list above is no guarantee of the availability of resources for rehabilitation. The Royal College report points out that there are only two local-authority rehabilitation centers, only five industrial therapy organizations, and only some 200 places in sheltered industrial groups. In fact, the SIGs account for only 3 percent of the total United Kingdom provisions for sheltered work employment, and while it is expected that this proportion will rise to 10 percent in the next few years, SIGs are not a significant element in planning for the mentally ill.

In his report to the World Rehabilitation Fund, Dr. Lester John Nielson (1978, p. 5) indicates that "although between 2,500 and 3,500 people with mental and psychiatric disabilities enter Employment Rehabilitation Centres each year, some people derive greater benefit from a longer and less demanding course, but away from the environment of a hospital therapy unit." A personal visit to two of the centers a few years ago revealed that the psychiatrically disabled constituted but a small minority of those who utilize what are obviously excellent short-term training schools for upgrading or adding employable skills.

The key personnel from Great Britain's Department of Employment (successor to the Ministry of Labour) are the disablement resettlement officers (DRO), recently renamed employment advisors. The DROs, as they are still popularly called, are the links between the medical facilities and the array of training and work-testing facilities, both governmental and voluntary. The DRO has no real counterpart in the United States. The employment advisor has all of the responsibilities of what we call a job developer and some of those of a rehabilitation counselor, but without the postgraduate professional training we require of a vocational rehabilitation counselor.

Three problems are creating significant difficulties in the British system for rehabilitation of the disabled, and they are having a particular impact on schemes for the mentally ill. First of all, there have for years been questions about the lack of integration of services. The National Advisory Council on Employment of Disabled People concluded in its 1980 review that the existing arrangements for rehabilitation and resettlement of the mentally disordered into employment had produced a complex, disorganized, and inadequate system. A joint conference of the Mental Health Foundation and the British Institute of Industrial Therapy in 1983 found that "little progress has been achieved since then" (*Industrial Therapy,* Autumn 1983a, p. 16).

Secondly, deinstitutionalization has speeded up and resulted in policy changes affecting services to the mentally ill and mentally handicapped. The problems presented are very familiar (Williamson 1984/85):

- There is divided responsibility for discharged patients, split between the local health authorities and regional hospital boards (see Reagles 1980).
- The original locality where the patient might have lived fifteen or twenty years earlier, before hospitalization, does not consider that patient as a priority in allocating scarce resources.
- Local authorities have financial difficulties, and place mental health services low on the list for expenditures.
- Community services cost additional monies and appear to be more expensive than continuing hospital care.
- There is resistance from patients and families to moving patients out into the community.
- There is staff resistance, mainly from fear of loss of jobs if the hospitals wind down or close.

Added to this list is the fact that communities in Britain, like those in the United States, do not have the resources to absorb increasing numbers of the mentally ill who were formerly cared for in hospitals. Dr. Alan Whitehead (1984/85), director of the BIIT, reports that "employment considerations are often the last to be assessed when the overall care of the discharged patient is discussed. Consequently, circumstances exist on a widespread basis whereby individuals will have good housing, a good network of supported and social arrangements, but will have no prospect whatsoever of work or work therapy once discharged" (p. 10). He points out that the policy of the Manpower Services Commission is to discourage the formation of new sheltered workshops, opting for expansion of the sheltered industrial groups (SIGs). As I have already mentioned, the most optimistic forecast is that the SIGs will represent only 10 percent of total placements for all handicapped in sheltered employment by the end of the decade.

The third factor affecting work programs is the general worsening of economic conditions throughout the world and the increases in unemployment. Since this is a problem common to all of Western Europe, I will defer discussion until after describing the situation in other countries.

The Netherlands

The Dutch have developed a vocational rehabilitation program for all citizens of the Netherlands which is unique to the country's philosophy of social welfare and which recognizes the tripartite nature of its religious and political system. The philosophy embraces two concepts: *verzuiling,* meaning mutual cooperation and mutual independence, and *subsidiarity,* which holds that a function in society should be the responsibility of the lowest social unit capable of carrying out the task (Nash 1983). This has led to the development of social services and health services under the auspices of voluntary organizations, referred to as *particulier initiatief,* or "private initiative" (DeJong 1984) rather than under the control of government. These private-initiative agencies—PIs as they are known—have become the main providers of services for the disabled. Their organization is grouped into "confessional" divisions of the population—Catholic, Protestant, and nondenominational. Until recent years each such division was represented in the major political parties as well. In the 1970s, the government began to consolidate the PIs, and the strict "confessional" divisions began to blur. However, while the government does own and manage a number of social-service programs—including mental hospitals, a few vocational training facilities, and a number of the over 200 sheltered workshops—the majority of programs for the handicapped are owned by the PIs, over half of which still have religious connections (Nash 1983).

Holland has a means-tested general assistance program that applies also to all disabled persons, a general disability program, and a system of wage-related disability insurance as a third layer of protection. The General Assistance Act is financed wholly by the state; each of the other programs is financed by a combination of contributions from employers, employees, and the self-employed. There is also a Sickness Benefit Act that provides for a minimum benefit of 70 percent of regular earnings, starting on the third day of absence and continuing for one year. Employers supplement the sickness benefit to 100 percent of the last earned wage (Berkowitz 1985). All costs of illness and incapacity for disabled persons are paid for through the social and health insurance system (Reitsma 1984; for a brief though inclusive picture of these systems see DeJong 1984).

The Netherlands has been using sheltered workshops for the disabled longer than ony other Western European country. After the Social Employment Scheme for Manual Workers was enacted in 1949, the new sheltered workshops were utilized wherever possible for the mentally handicapped by the hospital aftercare services. Community-based sheltered workshops also began to be established. By 1966 there were

185 sheltered workshops located throughout the Netherlands, the majority of which were organized as nonprofit foundations or corporations, but very few had admitted discharged mental patients. The boards of managers or trustees for the workshops include municipal officials and representatives of industry. The national government certifies the shops, provides funds for capital and start-up, and to a large extent meets the deficits of operation. A training and oversight program for workshop directors was established under governmental control (Black 1970).

In an interesting reversal of the "Europe-to-America" transfer of the concept of transitional employment, a psychosocial club program patterned after Fountain House Foundation has recently opened in Amsterdam. It is called De Waterheuvel, and is a direct outgrowth of the dissemination education sessions and conferences conducted by Fountain House (communication from Fountain House Foundation, June 1986).

It is important to note that these "work-for-pay" facilities continue to draw clientele in a country that provides the most complete disability insurance and transfer payments coverage of any in the world. There is a built-in recognition of the importance of work in the Dutch character. However, the worsening economic situation across the world has had its effect here too, and funding for these programs has been decreasing over the years. The numbers of patients who can be served diminishes as government funds decrease. Placements in sheltered workshops have become long-stay, what economists refer to as "substitute permanent employment," and the wait for admittance to a program is now approximately one year (Jansen 1986; World Federation for Mental Health 1986a).

In Holland the move towards deinstitutionalization of the mentally ill and handicapped has been quite slow. The inpatient hospital system retains its prominence and has sufficiently modernized and improved services to retain control also of many daytime and outpatient services of discharged patients (Jansen 1986). A reorganization of outpatient mental health care has placed the authority in the hands of fifty-nine Regional Institutes for Outpatient Mental Health Care (RIAGGs) (World Federation for Mental Health 1986b).

Reubens (1970) has described a fundamental attitude of the Dutch toward the use of sheltered work as long-term or terminal employment, particularly for the mentally ill or retarded. She states that these become substitutes for, or supplements to, institutional or home care. Fewer personnel are needed in the work situation than in institutional or home care, thus freeing family members and caretakers for other work. "Furthermore," she says, "many who would otherwise be institutionalized are able to live in hostels, in boarding houses, in selected private homes, or with their families . . . But at the root of all Dutch calculations is the consideration that modern society tends to guarantee a minimum standard of living to all whether they work or not and that participation in the world of work is intrinsically valuable" (p. 18).

The Scandinavian Countries

Denmark, Norway, and Sweden have been characterized as "cradle-to-grave welfare states." Their national welfare schemes provide total unemployment and welfare insurances and complete health insurance coverage. Nationwide programs for all disabled were written into law in the late 1950s and 1960s, and complete services are indicated in vocational training and vocational rehabilitation. In each country there are examples of excellent integrated vocational rehabilitation services, but these are by no means distributed throughout the countries.

DENMARK

Denmark has a number of sheltered workshops for the disabled, primarily operated by voluntary agencies. Labor unions participate in setting minimum wages. There is also a very worthwhile program in many factories that allows groups of disabled workers to compose enclaves, although these workers are on the factory payrolls. The history of vocational rehabilitation in Denmark has moved through three stages (Gannik, Holst, and Wagner 1976). The first of these was characterized by the setting up of individualized programs to meet the needs of specific disabilities, much as we see in the United States today. During this phase there was the development of the disability pensions and of work settings for occupational rehabilitation.

In 1960 changes in the laws brought all of the rehabilitation services under one administration, the Department of Rehabilitation and Welfare of the Directorate of Social Services of the Ministry of Social Affairs. During this stage rehabilitation centers were set up in each county or administrative district, and rehabilitation advisors (mostly social workers) were attached to each center to coordinate grants to individual clients. Grants for support of facilities were made by a joint council in the center, although the rehabilitation actually took place in local nongovernmental organizations.

Despite what seems to have been a successful experience with the second stage—a state of integration of services greatly sought after by rehabilitation professionals in the United States—the Danes decided to abolish the separate rehabilitation system. The 1976 law defines rehabilitation broadly, making it an integral part of general human services.

Section 37 of the social reform law (see Gannik 1976) refers to "illness, pregnancy and child birth, failing possibilities of work, interruption of married life, military service or other changes in conditions for a limited period." The law says further that when a person is not covered by a pension or other maintenance allowance, "the public authorities will grant an aid of such size as to prevent the conditions of life of the person concerned and his family from being impaired to any considerable degree." The central-government-controlled rehabilitation centers were transferred to the counties. The Ministry of Social Affairs retains its National Board of Social Services (Socialyrelsen) and Disability Insurance Court, but local administration is under the county committee for hospital services and the county committee for social and primary health care services. The latter carries jurisdiction for disability pensions and rehabilitation services.

The number of rehabilitation clinics, training institutions, and sheltered workshops increased during the 1960s, but this growth came to a halt in the 1970s. There was an increasing tendency for rehabilitation to take place in hospitals and for training to take place in normal work settings. The demand for more places in sheltered workshops has continued, but this seems to have been met by increasing single sheltered work places in normal industry.

Redke reported (1975) that in spite of the all-encompassing welfare insurance coverage in Denmark, there seemed to be little disincentive in the desire of disabled persons to work in the sheltered shops or in the work enclaves. However, one Danish expert states that "in spite of good intentions . . . problems of sufficient staff, particularly of psychologists with clinical experience, training for staff, and high unemployment interfere with full realization of rehabilitation goals for all disabled persons" (C. G. Kongerslev, as reported in Schulman 1981, p. 33).

So far as the services to the mentally ill are concerned, Jansen (1986) reports that the system remains largely an institutional one. She says, "While the government policy is to utilize outpatient services as much as possible, these are generally associated with hospital facilities, and are frequently located on hospital grounds" (p. 9). Training for independent living, transitional work schemes, and sheltered employment are not usually found outside the confines of the hospital.

NORWAY

In Norway, vocational rehabilitation is the responsibility of a number of organizations. These include the State Labor Exchange, state rehabilitation institutes, sociomedical departments in hospitals, vocational schools, sheltered workshops, private industry, and public employment. Rehabilitation is conceived of as more than vocational, however, and a lot of emphasis is placed upon skills training, socialization, and residential care (Lereim, as reported in Schulman 1980).

SWEDEN

The Swedish National Labor Market Board administers all vocational rehabilitation and sheltered workshops. The corporation that coordinates an extensive network of sheltered workshops (approximately 345 workshops employing 25,400 persons in 1984) is known as the Swedish Communal Industries Group. Workshops are subsidized to 125 percent of the payroll of handicapped workers. The clients are paid about 90 percent of the competitive wage level in private industry; the rates are set by national agreements with the trade union organizations. Sweden has generous sick benefits; partial pensions are provided for the partially disabled (Berkowitz 1985). Regional Evaluation Centers undertake work evaluation and work adjustment.

The Swedish rehabilitation system is most noteworthy for an expansion of public-service job-training sites beginning in the 1960s. These are, for the most part, outdoor projects (Reubens 1970). They cater to three main groups: (1) those about to be discharged from institutions, including the mentally ill, alcoholics, criminals, and youthful offenders; (2) hard-to-place persons, who work for reduced wages, usually 15 percent below collective wage agreements; and (3) older workers, especially those living in isolated areas with few employment opportunities. Reubens (1970) explains that the Swedish view is that even if there is a high level of business activity, the need for sheltered employment for the disabled will remain high. The emphasis is on these "created jobs" serving as preparation for employment in the open market. No stigma, however, attaches to those who do not make this transition.

There are advantages and disadvantages to such outdoor employment projects. Among the advantages listed by Reubens are

1. Ease of providing labor-intensive work;
2. The rapidity with which projects can be started;
3. Low capital investment per worker;
4. Absence of conflict with the private economy;
5. Ability to establish separate work sites for different disability groups.

The disadvantages are

1. The low level of job tasks;
2. Poor preparation for transfer to the competitive labor market;
3. Unsuitability of the work for certain groups.

Outdoor work has a great attraction in services for the mentally ill, but the major sheltered employment in Sweden, as is true in Denmark and Norway, is centered in the mental hospitals or in day hospitals under institutional control. Outdoor work sponsored by the hospitals often takes the form of forestry work, nature work, and landscaping.

Dencker (1980) has described an integrated psychosocial rehabilitation program at Lillhagen Hospital, Göteburg. Here he uses work as therapy at the top step of a system in which the mental patient moves to less restricted living as functional abilities increase. The patient then moves out of hospital into supervised community living, with sheltered work available and leading, for those capable, to open employment. Description of this exemplary program has been widely disseminated in the United States. It is unique in that all facets of the rehabilitation services are integrated under one administration and in that patients are given continuity of care practically throughout their lives.

Another well-known Swedish program for the mentally ill is at the Regional Hospital at Örebro. Here, the Department of Psychiatric Rehabilitation conducts an integrated program from hospital to community, covering residential overview, physiotherapy, occupational therapy, industrial occupational therapy, psychotherapy, structured music, and art therapy (as reported in Örebro literature). The international Labor Organization (ILO) describes vocational training centers, particularly one at Skövde, that provide twenty weeks of training in social and work-coping skills (ILO 1979).

In recent years there has been a trend toward community-based care. Sweden has established a "sectorized psychiatry" for the chronically mentally ill in which each sector is responsible for developing its own system of comprehensive care (Jansen 1986). In a number of sectors there are now sheltered and transitional employment services. For some years now Stockholm has had a Fountain House, and since 1984 there have been such psychosocial club programs in Malmö, Göteborg, and the Kalmar District.

The Vocational Rehabilitation Division of the National Labor Market Board gives grants to private enterprises which employ both disabled and nondisabled people. Particularly interesting is the Swedish Archivist program, which puts disabled and other hard-to-place persons to work in public institutions such as museums. The government pays the full cost of many such white-collar projects; others are subsidized in part by municipalities. Sweden, like Denmark, has enclave work for the disabled in open-employment factories. Sweden has experimented with wage subsidies for hiring disabled workers, but reports of the experience have not been good.

France

As a treatment approach for the mentally ill *ergo therapy* (the French term for work therapy and sheltered work) appeared before World War II. However, French psychiatry tended to resist the introduction of group and milieu therapies, laying much stress on individual approaches, including shock treatments and psychochemical and behavioral types of retraining (Black 1970). The pioneering work in vocational rehabilitation was that of Dr. Paul Sivadon, who introduced work for pay at the hospital of the Ville Evrard, outside Paris. Shortly thereafter he was asked to direct psychiatric treatment for the Teachers Mutual of France (Mutuelle Générale de L'Education Nationale, or MGEN). In an unusual mental institution at the Château de la Verriere, near Versailles, Sivadon established workshops for occupational and work therapy. This program still continues, but the Teachers Mutual, no longer restricted to educators, operates programs elsewhere in the Paris region and in Trappes, Ruel, Rouen, Bordeaux, Toulouse, Grenoble, Lyon, and Lille. Some of these are day hospital programs (Chanoit 1983). Paul Sivadon's greatest contribution to rehabilitation of the mentally ill in France was linking his Atelier Thérapeutiques to the developing day hospital programs, first at L'Elan Retrouve in the Montmarte section of Paris, providing a large infusion of the activity therapies (thérapeutiques actives), including recreational and occupational therapy.

When sectorization of psychiatric services was mandated by the Ministry of Health in 1960, the way was open to build such ergo therapy services into each of France's departments (provinces). This step did not, however, result in the setting up of sheltered workshops. It has been suggested that resistance may have stemmed in part from the French people's experience with concentration camps during the German occupation of World War II, when banners were hung with the slogan *Arbeit Macht Frei* (Work Creates Freedom) (Gittelman 1975). It has only been in recent years that what we would recognize as sheltered workshops, manufacturing or processing goods in the real work-a-day world, have been established.

Today, each department has a commission called Cotorep (La Commission Technique d'Orientation et de Reclassment Professional) which registers any handicapped person. Cotorep has a team comprising physician, psychiatrist, psychologist, social worker, careers advisor, doctor from Social Security, and representatives from sheltered workshops and the Centres d'Aide par le Travail (CATs). This commission assesses the patient in terms of health, ability, and so on to determine the level at which he or she is capable of working, whether able to work part time in a normal environment, able to work only at simple jobs, able to work in a sheltered workshop, able only to work in a CAT, or able only to do home work. The CATs are similar to the Adult Training Centres and the Handicapped Centres in the United Kingdom. They include paid work, vocational training, medical supervision, and some socialization. The CATs were started by private organizations, and this origin may explain the old and reconditioned buildings in which many of them are located. The usual staff-to-client complement is nine professionals/paraprofessionals plus office staff and an accountant to each forty-eight clients. Those serving the mentally ill have a medical director along with the center director or manager.

There are combinations of sheltered workshops and CATs. The salaries paid the handicapped are determined by the director of the Department of Employment together with Cotorep. The amount paid is based on the average industrial wage (referred to as SNIC) for the task. Salaries in sheltered workshops can be from 90 to 130 percent of SNIC, depending on the profitability of the workshop. France expects the sheltered workshops to be as profitable as possible and allows them to employ up to 20 percent able-bodied workers. The CATs pay from 70 to 110 percent of SNIC based on productivity. Handicapped people in Paris travel free on Metro and buses. (For a fuller description of the CATs see Cole 1984.)

In the area near Grenoble the Centre pour la Readaptation Professionnelle et la Reinsertion Sociale operates a large sheltered work and training program for the mentally handicapped and the mentally ill, dedicated specifically to *readaptation* to agricultural trades. Workshops are organized as "teams" in four major areas: metalworking (iron works, mechanical work, plumbing); building (woodworking, masonry, painting); outside work (horticulture, gardening, lawn care, apprenticeship in agricultural implements, breeding rabbits and sheep); and cooking. Residences are maintained for the mentally retarded and developmentally disabled (literature from Domaine de Cotagon, 1984–85).

In Lyon and the vicinity, L'Association Industrie Service, affiliated with the Centre Hospitalier General "Lucien Hussel," now has a number of sheltered work sections. These include a shop to sew tablecloths and napkins, a packaging and assembly plant, a metalworking shop, and units that undertake painting and wallpapering, maintenance of lawns and gardens, clerical services, laundry, and the operation of two restaurants, in Lyon and Caluire. These enterprises all go under the trade name of Messidor (descriptions and literature supplied by Dr. J. Dubuis of the Centre Hospitalier General, "Lucien Hussel," March 1984). These workshops collaborate with the CATs for their areas. Residential services are available for both the mentally ill and the mentally retarded/developmentally disabled.

Other Western European Countries

Vocational rehabilitation programs are present in each of the other western European countries. In general, they have begun to follow the patterns described in the United Kingdom, the Netherlands, Scandinavia, and France. A few examples are of interest.

BELGIUM

Belgium's social welfare law of 1958 set up a council to undertake and support training, rehabilitation, and resettlement of the handicapped. In 1963, additions to the act made clear that it was applicable to the mentally as well as the physically disabled. Belgium has developed a number of sheltered workshops, under private support, although there has been increasing governmental subsidy. As the years have passed, a larger number of participants in the workshops are coming from among the mental handicapped and mentally ill.

SWITZERLAND

The Swiss Federal Disability Act of 1960 made clear that mental illness and disability are among the categories covered. The state provides subsidies to organizations serving the disabled, including costs of construction, establishment, and renovation of institutions and workshops, and some help with deficts in operation. The Assurance Invalide system (AI) provides social security disability insurance and vocational rehabilitation services. This system is very similar to the state-federal vocational rehabilitation system in the United States. In this respect it has an extensive evaulation and work-training component. However, unlike the American system, it offers disability insurance to any individual unable to work (Jansen 1986).

In most communities there has been little deinstitutionalization, and services are still primarily hospital-based. The cantons, like the states in the United States, have authority for determining health policy and practice. Much of the innovative work in community services for the mentally ill has been stimulated by Pro Mente Sana, a private organization which receives both public and private funding and which lobbies for effective services. Jansen relates, however, that unfortunately there is little emphasis on vocational rehabilitation.

FEDERAL REPUBLIC OF GERMANY

West Germany enacted rehabilitation legislation in 1974 and 1976. The pension age was lowered to 60 years in a 1978 law. However, rehabilitation of the disabled falls under the purview of five federal social insurance agencies, each of which contracts for services from public institutions and private nonprofit organizations. "In each system or agency, the responsibility for an individual's rehabilitation program is dependent on the cause of disability. Thus, a job-related disability is administered by the industrial accident program, whereas a disease-related disability is the obligation of the health insurance system" (Steinmeyer and Tracy 1985, p. 39).

The Federal Labor Office, by law, carries sole responsibility for job placement. There are a number of sheltered workshops in the Federal Republic of Germany, and these offer training for open employment as well as permanent employment for those whose disability is severe. Although sheltered workshops are required by law to accept disabled persons who are unable to function in competitive employment (Stude 1986), reports indicate that the workshops demand of the applicants so high a functional capability as to exclude the seriously disabled. Also, only a small number of disabled people make the transition from sheltered work to open employment.

West Germany began in 1979 to decentralize mental health care to a district plan. A few mental health centers have now begun to incorporate work programs into their therapeutic services. One example is the Haus an der Teutoburger, in Munich. This center, serving upper Bavaria, has a full complement of psychiatric services, including day and night clinics, halfway houses, and communal living homes. The center also operates a cafteria called the Schwalbenmel (Swallows' Nest). The cafeteria is used for evaluation, for job training, and as a medium to educate the public. The coffeehouse serves also as the focal point for crisis management; as a place for activities such as cooking, crafts, and singing; and as a center for counseling for average problems (oral report by Dr. Walter Winkelhofer, Center Director, June 1986).

The costs of the center are covered by public funds, but the Swallows' Nest is supported by earnings and the social service funding for the participants. The state Labor Bureau pays for a three-months' trial period in business for clients graduating from the program, and then subsidizes up to 70 percent for six months or more, depending on the amount of disability.

ITALY

In Italy a 1978 law authorized care of the mentally ill in general hospitals and health centers instead of in psychiatric hospitals (World Federation for Mental Health 1986c). In effect this called for the closing of the mental hospitals. It took a charismatic psychiatrist, Dr. Franco Basaglia, backed by a group of young psychiatrists of leftist ideology, to set a new program in motion in Trieste. The public mental hospital was closed, and a completely integrated set of community mental health services was established (Boffey 1984). According to Boffey, a World Health Organization study conducted by Dr. Douglas Bennett of the British Medical Research Council "found that the care was more 'supportive' than 'medical' in nature and that there was little evidence of psychiatric treatment. Even so, he concluded, those attending the centers or living in the group apartments appeared to be in 'much better' condition than those who remained in the hospital." (See also Jones and Poletti 1986; Lovell 1986; and Burti et al. 1986.)

One of the economic developments in Italy in 1973 was the organization of "workers' cooperatives," particularly in those provinces with strong leftist leanings. The idea of cooperative workers' management is characteristic of certain Eastern European countries, especially Poland and Yugoslavia. These were composed of twenty workers or more, chartered by the province for the purpose of making money. Each cooperative set its own policies about management, sharing profits, and the like. Italian unions set the wage rates for each type of job. There were mandatory deductions from wages for unemployment insurance, vacations, and separation pay. The Trieste Workers' Cooperative was the first in Italy to be organized by mental patients. Additional such cooperatives now exist in Venice, Genoa, Padua, and Arezzo (Crawford 1980). The Workers' Cooperative in Trieste has 120 members and is administered by two committees: the Assembly and the Administrative Council, chosen by the Assembly and including nonmembers from the town (e.g., a journalist, a businessman). The Administrative Council assists with getting contracts, negotiations with the union, and public relations and serves as an advisory group. All decisions affecting the cooperative are decided by the Assembly. Crawford (1980) states that the cooperative has proved to be economically viable. At the time of his visit there was a waiting list of thirty to join the Trieste Cooperative. Selection was dependent upon the applicant's ability to perform the job tasks.

A cooperative workshop, mainly for schizophrenics, was established in 1980 in Brescia (Gudmundsson 1985). Known as Cooperativa Fraternita Soc. Coop. a R.L. (Centro Fraternita), it is housed in two buildings with a capacity for a total of twenty people.

FINLAND

The Finnish programs do not follow the pattern of the other Scandinavian countries. In Finland private insurance plays an important role in the disability insurance program. There is basic protection by a means-tested welfare program, and then taxes paid by employers and employees provide for sickness insurance and a flat-rate disability pension with an earnings supplement. The sickness and disability benefits are administered by the Social Insurance Institution (SII), supervised by Parliament. There is universal coverage of all 16 years of age and over (Berkowitz 1985).

Pensions are granted on the basis of occupational disability: "The National Pensions Act defines a person as disabled if illness, defect, or injury makes him unable to maintain himself in his usual work or work suitable to his age, occupation, education, and place of residence. On these grounds he can be granted a pension for either a specified or an unspecified period. The pension is discontinued if the beneficiary regains his working capacity" (Jarvikoski and Lahelma 1980, p. 12). According to statistics for 1978, mental disorders accounted for 28 percent of the disability pensions in the working-age population of Finland.

Rehabilitation services have been available to the mentally ill in Finland since the 1960s (*International Conference* 1973). Most of these have been provided in connection with the mental hospitals, though in recent years there has been greater emphasis upon community care. The most interesting program from Finland has been an experiment between the Rehabilitation Foundation of Helsinki and the city government, carried on in the Port Authority, which has 900 employees, and the Water Works, which has 450 (Jarvikoski and Lahelma 1980). In this demonstration those persons already employed, with identified chronic physical, mental, or social symptoms which lowered or threatened to lower working capacity, were given service by a rehabilitation team.

Mental disorders were the primary diagnosis in 7 percent of the cases. The rehabilitation team was made up of a core group of part-time specialists, including an occupational health nurse, a rehabilitation physician, and a rehabilitation counselor. "Collaborative experts"—personnel chiefs, labor protection chiefs, delegates for safety and health—were added when job reassignment, changes in work tasks, or ergonomic changes were under consideration. The study found that mostly minor ergonomic improvements and job rearrangements were required. The study concluded that the work site is the most appropriate place to initiate early rehabilitation activity, since a person spends a third of his or her life there.

IRELAND

Ireland is a geographically small country, with a homogeneous population of 3.5 million and a strong heritage of the English dominance for hundreds of years, leaving a legacy of tradition and practice that has shaped its forms of institutional services (Smith 1982). Its major agencies having responsibility for various aspects of vocational rehabilitation are the Department of Health, The Department of Labor, and the Union of Voluntary Organizations of the Handicapped.

The Department of Health carries responsibility for Regional Health Boards and for the National Rehabilitation Board. This latter agency was established in 1967 as a quasi-governmental body with powers under the Minister of Health to supervise, operate, or arrange for the operation of services for the welfare of persons who are disabled as a result of a physical defect or injury, a mental handicap, or mental illness. The National Rehabilitation Board coordinates the work of voluntary agencies, gives medical treatment, assesses disability, gives vocational guidance, trains disabled persons for employment, makes arrangements for other agencies to train disabled people, and provides job placement services. It coordinates applications for financial assistance from the European Social Fund set up by the European Economic Community to supply investment resources to member countries. In Ireland the European Social Fund is supportive of programs to prepare handicapped persons for employment (Smith 1982).

The National Rehabilitation Board Industrial Service assists in advising on the establishment of sheltered workshops for the disabled. Somewhat like the National Industries for the Severely Handicapped (NISH) in the United States, it maintains contact with industry to identify revenue-generating work that can be undertaken in a sheltered workshop. The mental hospitals in Ireland have followed the English pattern of industrial therapy units and the establishment of industrial therapy organizations.

The Irish Department of Labor is responsible for manpower placement services. An industrial training authority, referred to as AnCo, an acronym from the Gaelic, was established by statute in 1967 and operates fourteen training sites throughout the country. These are not specifically set up for services to the disabled. Since 1974 AnCo has worked with the National Rehabilitation Board to provide training for instructors and/or supervisors in rehabilitation centers that train the handicapped. AnCo receives nearly three-fourths of its budget from the European Social Fund. Smith (1982) commented that the programs carried on by AnCo were not unlike those of the Comprehensive Employment and Training Act (CETA) in the United States.

GREECE

Formal vocational rehabilitation came late to Greece. The first attempts to deal with the handicapped provided only for disabled veterans and mandated the assignment of newsstands and kiosks as private businesses. It was not until 1979 that legislation broadened governmental support, and established the National Institute for the Rehabilitation of the Disabled (EIAA) and the Organization for Human Resources Development (OAED). The former certifies as to disability and the latter provides for training and employment opportunities (Coudroglou 1984).

For the disabled unable to enter the competitive labor market the OAED has set up Centers for Sheltered Work, which fabricate commercial products contracted by the state. The contracted employers pay the wages, at a competitive market wage, and the government supplies housing, health care, and other subsistence expenses. Rather liberal governmental subsidies are made to employers willing to employ the disabled. The state also provides all insurances and fringe benefits during the first year of employment, but nothing thereafter (Coudroglou 1984). This works well for the physically disabled (orthopedically handicapped) but poses problems for those with relapsing, exacerbating illnesses, including the mentally ill. (See also Stefanis, Madianos, and Gittelman 1986.)

Comments on the European Work and Employment Scene

In two major respects the use of work programs for the physically and mentally disabled in European countries differs from its use in the United States. In Europe, and increasingly elsewhere in the world, sheltered work is seen as long-term employment care for the most seriously disabled—"substitute permanent employment," as the economists refer to it. The idea that such programs can be used as transitional to open employment is not widely recognized. Culturally, the primary concern for handicapped people, in addition to medical concerns, has been with their economic viability. European social security networks are broad in coverage, yet there has been an underlying expectation that all those who can in any degree will contribute to the economy through their work. Sheltered work, then, is seen as the final contributing work setting, along with home work, in which the most severly disabled can make their contribution.

Along with this difference in the use of sheltered work has gone a fundamental difference in philosophy of vocational rehabilitation. The American attitude has been based on attention to the individual and his or her needs in a society in which anything in upward mobility seems possible. The problems of handicap are seen as those of the person, not necessarily those of the environment or the economic community. This has led to the development of professionals—vocational rehabilitation counselors and others—to assist the disabled person in overcoming the barriers to employment and advancement. In Europe, employment is seen as a right, and the efforts of the rehabilitation system are simply to assist the individual to that niche in the employment scheme into which he can best fit (see Stubbins 1982).

QUOTA SYSTEMS AND WAGE SUBSIDIES

Another part of the economic culture in Europe has been the requirement that public and private business provide employment to the handicapped. This concept originated after World War I, when great numbers of young men returned from the war with severe impairments and disabilities (Kulkarni 1982). Following World War II the countries with legislation covering disabled war veterans had it updated and broadened to persons other than war veterans; a number of other countries inaugurated mandatory employment of the disabled. By the end of the 1940s what has become known as the "quota system" was introduced in most European countries (Kulkarni 1982). For example, social welfare legislation in the United Kingdom in 1944, amended in 1958, set up a quota system requiring employers with twenty or more employees to employ registered disabled persons as at least 3 percent of their work force. In the Federal Republic of Germany the Severely Disabled Persons Act of 1974, based upon legislation that goes back to a first mandatory act in 1919, requires every employer with sixteen or more workers to employ from 4 to 10 percent disabled, the percentage depending on the industry and the region. Similar legislation exists in the Netherlands, Belgium, France, Sweden, and Greece.

Each of the acts contain "carrots and sticks." In Britain an employer who fails to satisfy the quota must offer every new vacancy to a registered disabled person unless a permit is obtained from the Manpower Services Commission. Without a permit the employer is liable to prosecution, although this has rarely been enforced. In West Germany each employer who fails to meet the quota must pay an "equalization levy" for each job in the quota remaining unfilled. Employers meeting the quota can claim a subsidy for each additional severely disabled person employed beyond the quota. There is also a provision that subcontracting work to a sheltered workshop for the disabled or providing homes or other forms of welfare to disabled people counts toward meeting the quota requirements. (See Kulkarni 1982 for a more complete account.)

In an attempt to increase the use of the quota system Britain has introduced a Job Introduction Scheme. This enables businesses to employ disabled persons on a trial basis for six weeks at a subsidy (£30 per week in 1976) (Kulkarni 1982; Stubbins 1982). This has similarities to the Targetted Job Tax Credit scheme in the United States (to be discussed later).

There is much difference of opinion as to the efficacy of quota or wage subsidy systems. The British Department of Employment (Manpower Services Commission) has been trying for some years to gain the system's repeal. It argues that the costs of administration are high in relation to the added job opportunities made available, that education of employers would be a better approach, and that other employees might regard subsidized or mandatorily employed disabled workers as a form of cheap labor (Piercy Committee 1973; Stubbins 1982). Such action is roundly opposed by unions, disabled people, voluntary societies serving the handicapped, and now the advocacy groups of disabled themselves. Their attitude is that the quota system does keep employers aware of the disabled and of their availability as workers. Stubbins (1982) quotes an experienced disablement resettlement officer as saying: "It doesn't work fully. But in the course of keeping records and seeking permits, employers are reminded of their moral obligation to retain and hire the disabled" (p. 27).

EFFECTS OF THE CURRENT ECONOMIC CLIMATE

Since the late 1970s inflation and rising unemployment have been facts of life in Western Europe. Referring to a 1982 study for the European Economic Community, Mary Croxen (1985, p. 46) points out that "joblessness has been the single greatest political and economic challenge to the Community. By the mid 1980s, unemployment will be in the order of 15 million in the ten Member States [which include Western Europe]. This number will not take account fully of the number of unregistered potential workers, the 'Silent Reserve', which will include a disproportionately high number of dispirited, disabled jobseekers. In Europe generally, this 'invisible' group is thought to be as high as a further 20 percent of the official figures for unemployed people." In terms of rehabilitation programs, over the past decade there has been widespread concern about the costs and effectiveness of rehabilitation, particularly as new client groups have evolved (those with mental illness, mental retardation, spinal injuries) and as medical advances and changes in health service policy have improved prospects of entering or reentering the labor market (Cornes and Hunter 1985, p. 53). Cornes (1984) has further emphasized that a technological revolution is changing the national economies, that the jobs which are disappearing most rapidly with the rise of automation are the ones in which the clients of vocational rehabilitation services were most readily placed.

There is no clear-cut response taking place to these changing conditions on either side of the Atlantic. However, there seem to me to be trends that are important to recognize. The move of Denmark, for instance, toward eliminating programs specially designated for the disabled in favor of a complete economic scheme that also includes them bears watching. A change in emphasis in vocational rehabilitation, particularly in Great Britain and perhaps in the Netherlands and Sweden, toward increasing professional counselling services and skill training for the disabled instead of focusing on job placement is of great interest, as is the reverse trend in the United States of developing more resources for "substitute permanent employment," such as the "supported work" movement. It is not always clear, however, to what extent the programs in Western Europe really meet the needs of the mentally ill. A comment made by Dr. Douglas Bennett more than a decade ago seems still largely true: "The great disadvantage in many European countries is that the psychiatrically disabled are still dependent on services designed for the physically disabled and therefore not particularly adapted for them" (Bennett 1973, p. 9).

7
Programs in Other Countries

During the past decade almost all countries of the world have been setting up or are elaborating on programs of services for their disabled citizens. The work of the World Health Organization and the designation of 1982–83 as the "International Year of the Disabled" by the United Nations have stimulated such developments. The focus in all instances has been upon the physically disabled and, to a lesser extent, on the mentally retarded/developmentally disabled. However, in a number of countries there has been a carry-over to vocationally oriented programs for the former mentally ill. Generally, such rehabilitation services for the psychiatrically disabled have been occasional isolated experiments or demonstrations, except in Eastern Europe and in the more economically developed countries elsewhere. I believe it is important to note these, as well as the major services for the physically handicapped upon which facilities for the mentally ill are most likely to develop.

Canada, Australia, and New Zealand

Canada, Australia, and New Zealand, considered part of the "developed" Western world, have forms of government and social security and health schemes that owe a great deal to the British model. Each, however, has developed a pattern of its own, though a little seems to have been borrowed from American experience. This is particularly true in Australia, for since World War II a number of its psychiatrists have received training in the United States.

CANADA

Canada has a comprehensive government-sponsored health insurance program. However, the system limits reimbursement for psychiatric services to direct patient care performed by physicians. There is a financial deterrent to collaboration and consultation, since these are not reimbursable (Nadelson 1986).

Unlike the United States, Canada has not moved precipitously into deinstitutionalization of its mental patients. While it is developing community psychiatric resources, most of the work therapy programs are, like those of the British, attached to mental hospitals. There are psychosocial clubs, particularly in Ontario, and a Fountain House model called Phoenix House in Regina, Saskatchewan (Propst 1984). Saskatchewan has a long history of experiments with community psychiatry. More recently a group of former psychiatric patients organized a work cooperative called the Crocus Cooperative in Saskatoon.

Two industrial demonstrations for the physically disabled in Toronto described by Akabas (1984) are worth mentioning because in time they are likely to be extended to the psychiatrically disabled as well. Molson's Brewery keeps light assignments for those with physical disabilities. However, these jobs offer lower pay, and workers are often unwilling to accept what they consider a demotion. Also, the Toronto Transit Authority reserves its tollbooth jobs for workers who become unable to perform their usual heavy or dangerous work. The tollbooth operators receive the same pay they had previously; bonus pay times and holiday work are used to make up the pay differentials. Regular medical checkups verify the continuance of the qualifying disability.

AUSTRALIA

Like Canada, Australia is a large country with concentrated population centers on its fringes and with vast agricultural and unsettled areas in its interior. Its large mental hospitals, therefore, have been situated in proximity to the largest cities, though some are a drive of an hour or so away. Australia, too, has followed the British pattern of cautiously moving towards decentralization. In the past few years deinstitutionalization has speeded up. The Richmond report for New South Wales, for instance, recommends rapid development of community resources and development of plans for scaling down or closing the large mental hospitals (Richmond 1983, 1985).

The large mental hospitals have invested greatly in "industrial therapy," somewhat after the British style. Gladesville Hospital in Sydney, for example, has a rehabilitation network including an assessment center, an industrial therapy unit, a molded products unit, a social skills unit, an offset printing and office practices unit, and a hobby shop (Black 1983). The procedures followed and the step system used are similar to what I have already described for sheltered work in American mental hospitals. What is unique to this hospital, and in fact to most of the Australian rehabilitation system for the mentally ill, is that these work-area programs are not operated by the hospital, but by outside community agencies. In the case of the Gladesville Hospital, the community agency is the Gladesville Auxiliary, Ltd., established in 1976. The auxiliary has a board of eleven members, of which three are appointed by the state health commission, with the others from the local community, and including the medical superintendent, the hospital manager, and the director of nursing. This auxiliary also runs a branch of a major bank on the hospital grounds, used also as a training site for patients, and provides a clothing shop and satellite housing in five home units and seven houses.

In Queensland, a psychiatric rehabilitation unit at Walston Park Hospital has a sheltered work program in converted ward rooms; the patients do simple contract work, some woodwork, and some sewing training. A larger and more sophisticated work program is carried on at the Baillie Henderson Hospital, in the town of Toowoomba, about 130 kilometers west of Brisbane. This industrial therapy facility is operated by a voluntary agency called Karakan (an Aboriginal word). The hospital supplies the facility with a building, at the edge of its large grounds, as well as a supervising male nurse and an occupational therapist. Income from sales provides salaries for the workshop manager and a skilled carpenter-cabinetmaker (Black 1983). In the state of Victoria industrial therapy is conducted in all of the mental hospitals by VATMI Industries, a unit of the Victorian Association for the Mentally Ill. In South Australia, that state's Aid to the Mentally Ill, Ltd., operates INVICTA, which runs five workshop centers. There are no such programs for the mentally ill in Western Australia, in the Northern Territories, or in Tasmania.

In Australia work programs for the physically disabled are more fully developed than are those for the mentally ill. Two excellent and large workshop programs that are much like "affirmative industries" of the United States are Centre Industries in Sydney, where the majority of clients have cerebral palsy, and Bedford Industries in Adelaide (Dickerson 1979; Bordieri 1986). To the best of my knowledge neither of these facilities accepts discharged mental patients. Centre Industries has developed a skills assessment procedure known as MODAPTS, a modification of which is used in the Commonwealth Rehabilitation Centres.

Australia has a national health system. The federal government pays about 85 percent of the cost of psychiatric services, and pensioners and social security recipients do not pay at all (Nadelson 1986). The Rehabilitation Service in the Department of Social Security was established in 1945, but it was not until 1977 that its services were extended to provide free social and vocational rehabilitation to virtually any disabled person in the broad working-age group who might benefit from the services. The Commonwealth Rehabilitation Service operates a number of general rehabilitation centers (Black 1983). Only one of these, Queen Elizabeth II, serves any volume of the mentally ill. Located in Sydney, this center serves the greater part of New South Wales. In addition to its assessment program, Queen Elizabeth II operates an arts and crafts center and a sheltered workshop, and offers clerical training and training in activities of daily living.

Under the Commonwealth government's Handicapped Persons Assistance Act financial help is made available to voluntary and other nonprofit organizations which provide employment training, activity therapy, and residential care. One important organization under not-for-profit nongovernmental auspices is the Psychiatric Rehabiliation Association (PRA) in Sydney. PRA manages a series of rehabilitation programs for the seriously mentally ill, including three sheltered workshops, psychosocial club programs in Sydney (Buckingham House) and Parramatta, an outreach program, and residential programs in Sydney, Newcastle, and Woolongong (Black 1983; PRA 1986).

There is one very recent discordant note, illustrative of the problems that rehabilitation programs for the mentally ill face across the world. A communication from PRA (letter of July 21, 1986) states that the Commonwealth Minister for Social Security has announced his intention of removing mental illness from the list of disabilities for which assistance can be provided to agencies serving them. His contention seems to be that mental illness is literally an illness, covered in the health services of the respective states, not resulting in the kind of disability covered under the Handicapped Person's Assistance Act.

NEW ZEALAND

Psychiatric services in New Zealand are similar to those in Australia. In fact, the two countries have a joint professional association of psychiatrists, the Australian and New Zealand Royal College of Psychiatry. New Zealand's Accident Compensation Act of 1972 served to bring together rather disparate elements of rehabilitation services for the physically disabled into a single system (Mitchell 1983). The emphasis, however, was upon injuries, non-work-related as well as work-related. The Accident Compensation Commission provides compensation at 80 percent of a person's loss of earnings. The New Zealand Rehabilitation League, Inc., a governmental agency, provides vocational training to disabled persons. There are five league centers, each staffed by a rehabilitation officer, a medical officer, a pychologist, a social worker, a vocational assessment officer, and a liaison officer. Each center operates a sheltered workshop (*International Rehabilitation Review* 1983c). Few of these services, including the activities of the Rehabilitation Liaison Officer Service of the Accident Compensation Commission, are available to those with mental disabilities.

The most significant program specifically for the mentally ill was the establishment of Framework House by the Framework Trust in Kingsland in 1985 (World Federation for Mental Health 1985b). This program provides employment assistance to people recovering from mental disorders. About thirty people attend the house each week; they perform light work, in similar fashion to the psychosocial clubs in the United States. Framework Trust also maintains a market garden where participants in Framework House can work. The trust is planning to establish similar houses in South and West Aukland. The Department of Social Welfare and the Mental Health Foundation of New Zealand both contribute to support of Framework House.

Eastern Europe

In no other countries of the world is work considered so integral a part of treatment and rehabilitation of mental illness as in the Soviet Union and other countries of Eastern Europe. This is in part an expression of central planning, which requires productive participation by all persons in the economic production of society, and in part an expression of the belief that occupation at work is a central philosophical theme in the treatment of mental illness. Two distinct patterns have evolved—the older use of "occupational therapy workshops" in the USSR itself and patterns of "cooperatives" and "collectives" in Poland and Yugoslavia.

THE USSR

The role of work carries a greater meaning in the culture of Soviet life than in Western society. Karl Marx wrote that "the mode of production of the material means of existence conditions the whole process of social, political and intellectual life. It is not the consciousness of men that determines their existence, but, on the contrary, it is their social existence that determines their consciousness" (Marx 1961, p. 217). The most authoritative recent review of Russian psychiatry (Babayan and Shashina 1985) states: "Work is one of the most important factors of mental health. It plays an exceptional role in the treatment of mental diseases . . . One can hardly imagine, therefore, properly organized rehabilitation of mental patients lacking such important elements as occupational therapy, job retraining, medical-labor expertise, and assistance in job placement. These are inseparable links of a single chain. Correct employment of mental patients is a factor which favorably affects the course of the disease, ensures rehabilitation and allows stable remissions" (pp. 313–14).

The great Russian psychologist Ivan Pavlov has been quoted as saying that "mechanical work and physical labor is a tremendous remedy in cases of disorders of higher nervous activity" (Field and Aronson 1965, p. 83; Babayan and Shashina 1985, p. 224). According to Wortis and Freundlich (1964, p. 123), the Pavlovian mechanisms involved in work therapy are (1) relief of inhibitory tendencies by the stimulus of work; (2) relief of excitatory tendencies by diverting energies into useful channels; (3) elevation of the functional tone of the cortex through the arousal of pleasant excitation; and (4) distraction of the patient's attention from distressing preoccupations (Pavlovian "sore points").

The use of work programs in treatment of mental illness has existed in Russia since prerevolutionary times. In the 1930s a program of linking "occupational therapy workshops" with the mental hospitals was systematized. World War II interrupted therapeutic work entirely, and it was not until the early 1950s that these programs were reestablished. By then great interest had arisen in the use of partial hospitalization, particularly in day hospitals (Volovik and Zachepitskii 1986). The USSR now has psychoneurological dispensaries in every large city and in every district of the larger cities. In rural areas the dispensaries function in association with district hospitals.

The tasks of the day hospitals have been described as follows:

(*a*) treatment aimed at the return to occupational activities of mental patients with temporary loss of ability to work;

(*b*) treatment of mental patients with a permanent reduction in work capacity in order to train them for alternate employment with partial utilization of former vocational skills;

(*c*) treatment and vocational training, while drawing them into the collective, of patients with symptoms of marked mental regression and withdrawal from social life . . . and their subsequent transfer (for continuing work therapy) to occupational therapy workshops preparing them for employment outside the system of neuropsychiatric institutions;

(*d*) complete treatment and gradual adaptation to normal life situations of patients after a course of treatment in closed wards of neuropsychiatric hospitals;

(*e*) diagnosis, determination of the degree of loss of ability to work, and evaluation of suitability for various occupations;

(*f*) sociological assistance to patients, settling labor and domestic problems, etc. (Babayan and Shashina 1985, p. 222)

It would be difficult indeed to conceive of day hospitals or of any aftercare service for the psychiatrically disabled in any Western country placing so much emphasis upon work as therapy or rehabilitation.

Occupational therapy workshops, resembling production workshops, are set up in connection with each day hospital as well as adjacent to the major psychiatric hospitals. These workshops are completely subsidized by the state; their aim is not profit. Wages are paid patients for work performed. There are privileges accorded by law to these workshops, including exemption from taxation and the setting aside of their income to improve cultural services for the patients, to improve their maintenance, and as a supplement to budget for equipment. The costs of spoiled materials and inadequate performance are not charged to the patient nor his relatives. There are occupational therapy workshops that utilize agricultural work, and some make use of home work.

The Ministry of Social Security runs specialized workshops at industrial enterprises for the occupational placement of mental patients. These are organized as integral parts of the businesses and perform either a complete production task or individual parts of a production cycle. Patients are selected for the workshops by a governmental Medical-Labor Expert Examination Board (VTEK), which is the body that determines invalidity status. As applied to disability generally the following rules are set for determining recommended occupation:

1. The character of the work must correspond to the functional capacities of the disabled person.
2. The job must conform to the education, training and vocational skills, and age of the disabled person.
3. The working conditions in the recommended job should facilitate maximum satisfaction of material and cultural needs.
4. The job should have advancement possibilities, particularly for young and middle-aged disabled persons. (Babayan and Shashina 1985)

The choice of jobs depends, of course, upon the nature of the business enterprise. Most usually it comprises small assembly or simple packaging. The working day is set at four to five hours, five days a week, with weekend, night, or overtime shifts prohibited. Say Babayan and Shashina: "A special law makes it incumbent on industrial enterprises to employ patients after the completion of a course of treatment and retraining . . . in accordance with the recommendations of the Medical-Labor Examination Boards. In view of the absence of unemployment and also because enterprises in the USSR belong to the state, rational vocational placement does not, as a rule, encounter great difficulties" (1985, p. 325).

Volovik and Zachepitskii (1986) describe a Moscow hospital setting for the mentally ill. The rehabilitation center comprises a day hospital, a therapeutic-occupational workshop, a socio-therapy club, and specialized dispensaries located at four industrial enterprises. From inpatient status the patient goes to the day hospital and begins to work in the sheltered workshop. After one and one-half months he or she may be transferred to one of the industrial enterprises, where working conditions, as referred to above, are less taxing than normal. In some places "night hospitals" are available. These reviewers conclude, "The experimental industrial rehabilitation of the mentally ill in large industrial enterprises has demonstrated that it meets the essential medical requirements and is truly effective only when a psychiatrist participates in the organization of the patients' work on a regular basis, observes them as they work, and ensures prompt delivery of the necessary therapeutic interventions" (p. 282).

While the differences in economic structure and social philosophy, not to mention the differences in psychological approach to mental illness, would make it extremely difficult to replicate much of the Soviet treatment structure in the United States or any other Western country, there seems to me to be a lesson to be learned in the training of psychiatrists. I have come across very few mental health professionals who are versed or experienced in the "world of work." The need for "occupational psychiatrists" should be as apparent as the growing recognition of the need for occupational physicians.

POLAND: INVALIDS' COOPERATIVE MOVEMENT

A form of work program that seems to have greater applicability across the world for disabled persons, though I doubt that it will be used extensively for the mentally ill, is that of "Cooperatives for the Disabled," developed most fully in Poland, where it is known as the Invalids' Cooperative Movement. Such cooperatives were founded after World War I by disabled war veterans who found it next to impossible to obtain employment in regular industry. The idea was revived in 1944–45 for the same reason but was broadened to include all disabled persons. State and local authorities supported cooperatives from the start. There is a law on cooperatives enacted in 1961, and revised in 1983. The Central Union of Invalids' Cooperatives sets standards, negotiates with the state, and relates to governmental central planning (Gudmundsson 1985; see also ILO 1978).

In Gudmundsson's review of cooperatives for the United Nations (1985) he reported that in 1980 the Invalids' Cooperative Movement in Poland provided employment and other services to over 238,800 disabled persons, about half of all disabled persons employed in the country. There were 435 primary invalids' cooperatives. About 70 percent of the members were in industrial employment, about one quarter of these in home-work schemes. Some 26 percent were in nonindustrial production, and the rest in trade. About 5 percent of the members were mentally ill and another 5 percent mentally retarded.

The state expects each cooperative "to be economically viable, to manufacture needed goods and provide socially useful services. It must also observe national prices, wages and norms." According to Gudmundsson (p. 83) the following services are included:

(*a*) Provision of suitable, remunerative work in line with the individual capacities and abilities of . . . disabled members.
(*b*) Vocational training (on the job and outside).
(*c*) Individualized rehab./vocational guidance.
(*d*) Basic vocational rehabilitation.
(*e*) Adaptation of working conditions and of tools, machinery and work places.
(*f*) Medical care and social benefits.
(*g*) Physical reconditioning.
(*h*) Leisure and other cultural activities.
(*i*) Scientific research and experimental facilities.

As is the case with the industrial workshops in the Soviet Union, I would expect that the actual kinds of work assigned to the disabled members depend more upon the patterns in the industrial facility than on the matching of capacities and capabilities.

Gudmundsson's U.N. report (1985) refers to concessions granted by the state to invalids' cooperatives to offset higher production costs and the costs of providing rehabilitation services. These include

- Reduction of taxes: up to 100 percent for cooperatives for the blind and for sheltered workshops run by the cooperatives.
- Partial reimbursement of premiums paid by cooperatives for social insurance of disabled workers. This subsidy is used for construction of sanatoria and holiday centers, sheltered workshops, and rehabilitation facilities.
- Preferential allocation of certain raw materials and machinery; establishment of long-term production subcontracts with public enterprises.
- Exclusive or priority rights to manufacture certain products or provide certain services.

The Polish state does not consider this assistance charity. As an earlier study of the International Labor Organization explains,

> All in all—in its balance sheet with the state treasury—the cooperative movement pays insurance premiums and taxes and receives a refund in the form of subsidies for the special fund with tax reductions earmarked mainly for the invalids' rehabilitation fund . . . From reductions alone cooperatives receive back some 50 percent of what they owe the State. It should also be added that the employment of disabled persons decreases State expenditure on invalids' pensions, because payment of a considerable part of the pension is suspended when a disabled person takes up work. Taking all this into account, it may be said that the Invalids' Cooperative Movement is not only fairly self-sufficient financially, but it can also earmark a part of its profits for national development purposes. (Szklarczyk 1978, p. 115)

In comparing invalids' cooperatives to sheltered workshops in the United States, Conte (1982) and Bordieri (1986) have identified several advantages and disadvantages of the Polish cooperative system. Among its advantages,

1. The cooperatives have succeeded in providing full-time, permanent employment for many disabled workers at competitive wages, with standard fringe benefits found in open industry.
2. They are semi-integrated, with about 30 percent of workers non-disabled.
3. The cooperatives provide home work for persons too severely disabled to come to the work place.

The disadvantages include the following:

1. Minimally disabled persons are segregated from competitive employment by working in cooperatives.
2. Most workers in the cooperatives are physically disabled; only 10 percent are mentally ill or mentally retarded.
3. There is a question as to whether separate cooperatives are really needed when there is evidence that there can be highly successful placement rates for the physically disabled in factories.

SOME NOTES ON COOPERATIVES

While I do not think there is much merit in comparing Polish cooperatives to American sheltered workshops, since the economic base of the two societies is so different, as is the underlying philosophy of sheltered work, it is important to note the similarities between Polish cooperatives and industrial workshops in Soviet industry. It is also important to keep in mind that for the most part these cooperatives do not to any marked degree serve the mentally ill, either those in hospitals or those in community care.

Nevertheless, both the International Labor Organization (ILO) and the Committee for the Promotion of Aid to Cooperatives (COPAC) of the United Nations do include the mentally ill in their urging that the undeveloped nations in particular use the cooperative system for their disabled citizens. COPAC points out that "in third-world countries, where massive unemployment and under-employment persist, a disabled person's prospects of obtaining work in the open labour market are minimal, if not nonexistent. In such conditions there is therefore an urgent need to create employment for disabled persons" (Gudmundsson 1985, p. 3). The ILO recommends small-scale industry, production workshops, and especially cooperatives for disabled persons.

Gudmundsson estimates that as many as half the trainees in vocational rehabilitation centers, even those of economically developed countries, remain unplaced on completion of training. He points out that "many, if not most cooperatives of disabled persons have been founded by such ex-trainees in search of a job" (p. 50).

The concepts underlying cooperatives for the disabled are outlined by Gudmundsson as

1. Self-help employment, with management objectives and use of assets controlled by the work force;
2. Membership of all workers;
3. A majority of the workers disabled;
4. Capital net surplus used as a reward for labor, *not* capital;
5. One person, one vote.

In Eastern Europe and in the developing countries, where financial support has to come from the state, the state in reality takes control of the cooperatives. Gudmundsson adds, "Because of traditional attitudes toward disabled persons, there will be an even greater tendency on the part of government officials to assume a paternalistic stance toward cooperatives of the disabled" (p. 38).

COPAC reports only a few hundred cooperatives for the disabled in Third-World countries, most of which are in India and serve the blind and the physically disabled. In the rest of the world there are scattered examples. I have mentioned cooperatives in Italy and in Saskatchewan, Canada, serving the mentally ill. Others, in the Pacific countries, in Latin America, and in Britain and the United States, seem mostly to be credit unions (often for the blind) or groupings organized for social and recreational services to the handicapped. Elsewhere in Eastern Europe, Hungary has a network of agricultural cooperatives, and Czechoslovakia and Bulgaria have industrial ones.

CZECHOSLOVAKIA

Czechoslovakia utilizes cooperatives for the disabled in much the same manner as Poland. Two of its programs seem to have particular relevance to the mentally ill.

Meta, a data-processing firm, has been operated since 1972 by the Union for the Disabled. Its Prague branch is a technology center, offering software services, analysis, and programming. It does management analysis for the chemical and food industries and offers courses in computer programming for the disabled. Salaries are based on the quantity and quality of work done. A great deal of the work is planned for home work. Supplemental allowances are provided for such living expenses as home utilities and use of apartments. There is a plan to enroll more young people, especially secondary-school graduates and college students (*International Rehabilitation Review* 1983a). When Czechoslovakia turns greater attention to services to the mentally ill, such a program as Meta will present opportunities for young schizophrenics.

The other facility of interest here is The Rehabilitation Center for Neurotics set up in Lobec in 1952. The main mode of treatment in this center is intensive group psychotherapy and use of the "therapeutic-community" methodology originated by Dr. Maxwell Jones (1953). About twenty-two to thirty patients are together for six to twelve weeks sharing in social activities and work. Patients work on a state farm from three to six hours a day and take care of the maintenace of the rehabilitation center building. A psychiatrist and a psychologist or social worker from the outpatient clinic in Prague visit one day a week. There is another therapeutic community for neurotics in the psychiatric hospital in Kromeriz, near Brno, founded in 1971 (Papiasvili and Papiasvili 1986).

YUGOSLAVIA: SELF-MANAGEMENT COLLECTIVES

After its break with the USSR in 1948, Yugoslavia reorganized its industrial system into self-management "collectives." Each industrial enterprise is managed by a workers' council elected by the employees (the collective). The workers' council elects its executive body, the managing board, and also chooses the manager or director for a four-year renewable term. The managing board supervises the director, makes up the annual plan, and directs its fulfillment (Vash 1984). Vash comments: "The role of the Communist League (party) is 'profoundly ambiguous.' In theory, it no longer exercises direct control; in practise, 'the more important decisions are made centrally by a small group of party leaders'" (p. 5).

The basic political unit in the country is the commune, for an average population of 30,000. It is the commune that carries the regionalized programs for medical care and rehabilitation centers. The rehabilitation centers have professional staff members—a social worker, a psychologist, and a psychiatrist—who keep in touch with the family and place of work, and who also train "factory mentors," workers who help disabled persons adjust to the job. Vocational rehabilitation, retraining, and creating jobs are responsibilities of the firms. By law, firms cannot dismiss workers who become disabled. Vash notes, however, that "in fact, few firms retrain or adapt jobs. There are no quotas for hiring disabled workers and no sanctions behind the legal responsibility to retrain workers and give them jobs. Usually when a person cannot resume a former job, s/he is moved to a lower skill position and the pension fund must pay any difference between the old and new incomes (occurs in about 75 percent of cases)" (1984, p. 23).

Associations of disabled people play important roles in providing community-based services, including transportation, sports and recreation, scholarships, and a number of sheltered workshops for the physically disabled and mentally retarded. The associations are active in sending delegates to political bodies and in representing the interests of disabled persons in social planning. There is no evidence as yet of an active advocacy for the mentally ill.

THE GERMAN DEMOCRATIC REPUBLIC

Vocational rehabilitation is administered in East Germany by the public health system. Locally, the rehabilitation commissions have representatives in the large factories throughout the country. The emphasis is on adaptation of the work place and the job to retain the disabled worker on a job (*Schonarbeit*). There is special attention now being paid to young disabled persons. By 1982 there were over 34,000 sheltered work places in industrial occuptions in East Germany, or about 2 places per 1,000 inhabitants (*International Rehabilitation Review* 1983b).

The World Health Organization (WHO)

Before looking at work programs in the less economically well-developed countries, we should note the efforts of the World Health Organization in promoting services for the mentally ill, including rehabilitation programs. According to Freeman, Fryers, and Henderson (1985), the most pertinent recommendations of WHO over the past decade have been the following:

- The size of large mental hospitals should be reduced.
- Alternative inpatient treatment should be provided in general hospitals alongside other medical specialties.

- Residential care should be as close to the population it serves as is possible.
- Outpatient facilities and day care should be available wherever patients' needs can be met without admission to a hospital.
- Nonmedical extramural care by social workers, nurses, and others should be developed.
- Mental health personnel should work as much as possible in multidisciplinary teams, serving defined populations.

To an increasing extent these recommendations are being followed. The emphasis across the world (for WHO is active in "developed" countries as well) is upon community care for the mentally ill. Mental illness and mental retardation account for almost half of the world's disabled. WHO estimates that severe mental illness affects one person in ten at some point in their lifetimes, and one person in every ten is so afflicted throughout his or her life.

In an earlier review of the WHO program for mental health, Harding (1976) described its main features as (*a*) an emphasis on prevention: controlling underlying disease conditions, early intervention, and influencing factors in the environment; (*b*) an intersectorial approach, involving social, educational, and vocational interventions; and (*c*) the use of simple technology as part of basic health services, rather than expensive, specialized services. He listed three "practical principles":

1. Management, as far as possible, should be within the community itself.
2. Throughout treatment the patient's family should remain in close contact both with the patient and with health workers. From the first contact onwards the family should be prepared for the patient's return to normal function, as far as possible.
3. The patient's activities during treatment should be maintained and should be relevant to his normal social activities. For example, in an agricultural society child care and farming would be more relevant than handicraft or industrial work.

"The poorer countries," said Harding, "are searching for low-cost strategies which will provide an increased coverage of mental health care at least for the priority mental disorders, while the richer countries recognize that resource allocation remains a critical aspect of programming, and that new concepts and models are no substitute for trained staff and facilities" (1976, p. 4). He notes:

> The traditional division between "treatment" and "rehabilitation" is no longer seen as relevant. The goal of maintaining the individual patient in society at the highest possible level of function requires a variety of tasks.

These can be carried out both by health workers and others in the community. The principles of rehabilitation form an integral part of such overall management and are taken into account in all task definitions. Rehabilitation is therefore *not* seen as a separate or even distinct entity in management of the mentally ill. (1976, p. 4)

Would that more governmental officials in the United States—local, state, and federal—were in agreement in practice with this principle.

Africa

In a review of mental health services in twenty-one African countries, Schulman (1981) concluded:

- Many disabled people do not receive rehabilitation services in Africa, and chief among this unserved population are the mentally ill. The primary emphasis in rehabilitation is on the physically and sensorially disabled.
- The trend is directed towards the development of self-reliance rather than just providing the disabled with financial and other support. In this regard there is serious consideration of work cooperatives.
- There is a tendency towards enacting legislation supporting rehabilitation and gaining governmental intervention in rehabilitative efforts.
- Innovative practices are concentrated on the physically and sensorially disabled, but those practices could be applied to the mentally ill.
- Agricultural pursuits and rural living arrangements predominate. The diversity of cultural orientations among the African nations must be kept in mind.
- The greatest barriers to services are insufficient finances and the lack of trained staff.
- Nevertheless, Schulman sensed a "positive outlook toward the establishment and management of rehabilitation procedures" (pp. 20–21).

NIGERIA

Nigeria, the largest black country in Africa, is a good example of the situation described by Schulman. Out of a population of 80 million it is estimated that there are 16 million with some form of mild mental illness, 8 million with serious mental disease, and 800,000 with incapacitating mental illness (Henry Williams 1983). There are critical shortages in trained personnel, including psychiatrists, social workers, occupational therapists, recreational therapists, medical technicians, and nurses, and no rehabilitation professionals. Williams believes that "while the imperative for developing work-oriented rehabilitation programs exists, it will be some years before professionals trained specifically in the field of rehabilitation join the cadre of care providers." He notes also that "Nigerians often regard mental illness as a cruel punishment that derives from unforseen and indescribable forces" (pp. 10, 32).

When Dr. Thomas Lambo, a native Nigerian trained in psychiatry in Europe, took over as director of Aro Neuropsychiatric Hospital in Abeokuta and as director of the Department of Psychiatry at University College Hospital at Ibadan, he developed a village treatment colony that gained international attention. The original Aro Village, usually referred to as the "Lambo Village," was opened in 1954 in the midst of four existing native villages. The discovery of oil, with its subsequent disruption in what was almost wholly an agrarian society, was still in the future at this time. Aro Village was not only a familiar cultural entity; it also met the needs of patients who had to travel long distances from their homes to the hospital as well as the needs of an institution that by no means had the capacity to take in the load of patient demand. Lambo began the village with a few shelters, into which a relative of the patient, and sometimes the entire nuclear family, moved in with the patient. He elicited cooperation from the traditional native healers. I remember Dr. Lambo's saying that the fact that he was of chieftain lineage aided him in this. The residents of the adjoining permanent villages were also cooperative, particularly with regard to social and group activities. The permanent villagers built additional houses to rent to patients. Piped water, sewage disposal, and the opening of additional jobs created a rise in general living standards.

The village set-up provided a positive environment for the patients. Asuni (1967) reported that "the need for standard occupational therapy is reduced as the patients are drawn into the normal activities of the village and are not left idle with time hanging on their hands" (p. 765). Patients were often able to secure work on local farms, and jobs were also available within the village complex in cleaning, maintenance, sanitation, and assisting tradespeople, a common activity in Nigeria and in many other African countries. These work activities provided an identification with normalcy and "speeded the day when patients could return to their native homes and villages" (Asuni 1967, p. 765).

When, in 1963, Dr. Lambo left, Aro Village continued as the Field Research Unit of the University College Hospital. In addition, two new villages, with a looser relationship to Aro Hospital, were started, but in the early 1970s budget restraints, transportation difficulties, and increased crime in the area closed them out. When Williams (1983) visited Nigeria he found three vestiges of the original village program. Aro Village continues as a unit of the University College Hospital. It is run by a smaller staff, four psychiatric nurses assisted by support staff. A psychiatrist from the hospital visits only once a week. In contrast to the original village, the availability of work for the patients is quite limited.

Although the hospital does supply some support services, such as drinking water, to a new and growing village outside of Aro Hospital, it refuses to accept any administrative responsibility for the program. Williams reported that while some patients are still able to find occasional work in the area, such as in roadside auto repair shops and assisting in selling cola and peanuts, in general "the formal activity or rehabilitative level of patients is low or nonexistent" (Henry Williams 1983, p. 29).

Village House, outside of Usulu Psychiatric Hospital, Benin City, offers eight rooms for patients and relatives. Patients are encouraged to participate in social and occupational activities at the hospital, but this is not a requirement for residence. Except that no work opportunities are available for patients or their relatives, the program follows the principles set by the Aro Village.

Even though these are but shadows of the Lambo Village program, Williams concludes: "The village system, by all measures, would have to be considered a major achievement. Mental illness was seen by many in Nigeria almost as a contagious disease to be shunned and avoided like the plague. That Lambo succeeded in establishing this system faced with that climate of reaction to mental illness, is both a personal and community triumph whose benefits should not go unnoticed in devising the future" (pp. 29–30).

ZIMBABWE

A program in primary health care is being developed in Zimbabwe, following the recommendations of the World Health Organization. Over two-thirds of Zimbabwe's population live in scattered rural villages, and at least half the population is under 15 years of age. In rural popular culture mental illness is associated with ideas of demons and angry spirits, prompting stigma and rejection. The Canadian Mental Health Association has developed a joint project with the government in Zimbabwe, a farm for mental health rehabilitation known as Tariro Halfway House (World Federation for Mental Health 1985a).

KENYA

The Kenya Mental Health Association reports that the government has begun decentralization of psychiatric services in the development of community support for patients discharged from the mental hospital

(World Federation for Mental Health 1984). This is a major step towards concern for rehabilitation services for the mentally ill.

ETHIOPIA

The United Abilities Company in Addis Ababa was established in 1964 by a group of eighteen physically disabled persons as an umbrella-manufacturing business. An initial grant was obtained from a charitable foundation. The company has now grown to a factory employing over 200 disabled persons of diverse disabilities, including the mentally ill. In addition to the umbrella-manufacturing division, there is now an auxiliary unit which makes metal components and parts for the umbrella frames. A factory making dry cell batteries was added in 1974 from the profits of the umbrella factory.

The company has no tax concessions, but it does have tariff protection against imported umbrellas. Its specialty is sturdy, simple, low-priced umbrellas in attractive colors. Sales are made across the country; sales and distribution are now managed by the Domestic Distribution Corporation, a branch of the Ethiopian government.

All employees, including salesmen, managers, and supervisors, are from among the disabled. Production is broken into units that can be undertaken by the disabled; the system used is one developed by the International Labor Organization in the general field of vocational training, called Modules of Employable Skill (MES). Training is on the job. There is now a long waiting list for employment in the factories, for turnover is negligible. (For the most complete description of United Abilities see Gudmundsson 1985.) While United Abilities Company is sometimes described as a "cooperative," it appears to me to be a valid example of an "affirmative industry."

Asia

The World Health Organization estimates that Asia has some 250 million disabled persons in forty-six countries, the majority of whom are dependent on family care. Mental illness is listed—along with blindness, deafness, physically crippling conditions, leprosy, poliomyelitis, and tuberculosis—as one of the main causes of disablement (ILO 1978). According to Schulman (1981), "Mental health care has been influenced by a legacy of Western influences—well intentioned—yet, in supporting a benevolent, custodial approach the mentally ill have been removed from their families and communities" (p. 21). In only a few places in Asia are there programs pertinent to the use of work in rehabilitation.

INDIA

The National Institute of Mental Health and Neuro Sciences (NIMHANS) was established in Bangalore in 1976 under orders from the president of India. It evolved from what had been a nineteenth-century lunatic asylum. A rehabilitation unit in the hospital had been operating since 1971, offering services to the chronically mentally ill. It was established with the cooperative backing of the Red Cross, the Canara Bank (a major bank in Karnataka State), and a number of small industries in the area. In 1973 the rehabilitation program expanded to include "day boarders," former patients who live at home. The program serves 100 inpatients and 100 "day boarders."

According to Bemak (1982) the program includes a rural unit, one part for men and one part for women, quite separated "visually and auditorially." The rural setting replicates an agricultural area in rural India. "The atmosphere resembles a village with sights, sounds, and smells to reproduce the feelings of home. Skills and crafts are taught, with the aim of preparing the patient towards economic independence" (p. 10). These include tailoring, weaving mats, baking bread and cakes, candle making, carpentry, pottery and leather making, bookbinding, printing, gathering fruits and vegetables, collecting bamboo and sandalwood, gathering silk, packaging incense sticks, making plastic joints and screws from molds, and production of a disinfectant. This work is put to use in meeting the needs of the hospital or in subcontract with local business and industry.

There is provision for placement in work settings, including the Canara Bank. Going rates are paid, and the ex-patients are treated as regular workers. A committee on rehabilitation, including prominent industrialists, philanthropists, and bankers, helps in procuring raw materials, obtaining subcontracts, selling of products, and placement of clients in jobs.

The rehabilitation unit is staffed by a psychiatrist, who also serves as administrator; a psychiatric social worker, who manages the day-to-day operations; and psychiatric nurses, who oversee medications. An organization of thirty-five to forty volunteers, Friends of NIMHANS, visit during recreation hours, teach sewing or knitting, visit families and raise money.

PAKISTAN

Pakistan is the only Asian country with a program on the Fountain House model (Lahore Mental Health Association 1985). The program is a project of the Lahore Mental Health Association, founded in 1962, which had developed a halfway house. The director of the mental health association, Dr. Muhammad Rashid Chaudhry, who was medical superintendent of the Lahore Mental Hospital, applied to his government and to the Social and Rehabilitation Services Administration, U.S. Department of Health, Education and Welfare, for the use of "counterpart dollars" remaining from transactions of World War II. He received a three-year research and demonstration grant to organize a rehabilitation program. John Beard, then director of Fountain House, New York, was sent as a consultant, and collaboration resulted in Fountain House, Lahore.

Fountain House, Lahore, follows the principles of the psychosocial club movement. There are daytime activities in clerical and kitchen work, running the snack bar, maintenance, and gardening. Courses are offered in flower-making, bookbinding, sewing, handicrafts, plaster of paris modelling, and so on. A "member leader" is appointed in each member unit, along with staff, a concept Dr. Chaudhry claims to have borrowed from China.

A transitional employment program (TEP) was funded with a grant from the National Institute of Handicapped Research, U.S. Department of Education. The TEP is mostly with the Rustan and Sohrab Bicycle Factory. Some TEP placements are available at local paint shops and in plant nurseries. However, outside jobs are scarce, and Fountain House, Lahore, has set about opening a small commercial business of its own, a canteen at the end of its grounds available to the general public. It is now arranging for what it calls a "sheltered" work site at the Rustan and Sohrab Bicycle Factory. From its description I would be inclined to describe it as "supported work." This is, of course, a variation in the basic Fountain House ideology, but not out of line with what is happening elsewhere among psychosocial facilities.

In 1982 the government of the Punjab allocated twenty-five acres of agricultural land, about forty kilometers from Lahore, to Fountain House. Fountain House has added a cottage industry to grow vegetables, operate a fish pond and a dairy, and raise poultry. Dr. Chaudhry states that research indicates agricultural work is particularly effective with schizophrenics.

Pakistan is a Moslem country. A mosque has been built at Fountain House and another at the agriculture site. Religious practices and music therapy are important elements in treatment. There are separate living and working facilities for men and for women. There is also a program for renting apartments off the site. The staff now comprises about sixty people, including psychiatrists as director and deputy directors, psychologists, social workers, vocational instructors, consulting psychiatrists, and physicians. While the Lahore Mental Health Association continues support with philanthropic gifts, the major financial support for

Fountain House is now from the federal government of Pakistan and the provincial government of the Punjab.

JAPAN

In communications and discussions during 1980 and 1981 with Dr. Yoko Kojima, Women's University, Tokyo, I was informed that there were no sheltered work programs for the mentally ill in Japan. Since that time I have heard of three (visits to Japan by Mrs. Mona Reeva, Executive Director, Rubicon Programs, Inc., Richmond, California, in 1983). Nishiyama Hospital, Kyoto, a private psychiatric hospital of 350 beds, has a limited sheltered workshop. Osakayama Hospital, Osaka, has a halfway house and a sheltered workshop. Hachi No Kai is a sheltered workshop operated by Takada-san in Kyoto. Hachi No Kai was founded over fifteen years ago by a parents' association; it now has support from the city and the prefecture. The workshop does some subcontracting, mainly packaging cookies. The client mix includes schizophrenics and mentally retardates.

In general, "Japan is still in the process of developing its vocational rehabilitation and vocational training facilities for handicapped persons" (Kulkarni 1982). State agencies, through the prefectures and provincial governments, provide services to one and a half million physically handicapped persons and one-third million mentally retarded. The National Ministry of Health and Welfare provides medical, social, and prevocational rehabilitation through governmental and private nonprofit organizations. The Ministry of Labor is responsible for vocational and industrial rehabilitation. Sheltered workshops are run by nonprofit agencies. There is an invalidity pension based on the Employees Pension Insurance Law, and an employment quota is fixed by cabinet order every five years. The quota varies between 1.5 and 2 percent, depending upon the occupation, but it applies only to physically handicapped persons.

Descriptions of sheltered work in Japan usually single out Japan Sun Industries, Beppu, started in 1965 for the physically disabled. Japan Sun Industries now employs 320 disabled and a small number of nondisabled workers, but there is no information that it accepts any mentally ill workers. It is primarily a profit-making business doing production work in the electronics industry (Bordieri 1986). Bordieri considers Japan Sun Industries a good example of an "affirmative industry," and so do I.

HONG KONG

Hong Kong provides a psychiatric day hospital for 40 to 60 patients in each of its districts with a population of about 500,000. There are supportive services in each day hospital, including, according to Schulman (1981), "sheltered employment if necessary, and job placement when feasible."

The Hong Kong Mental Health Association administers a halfway house and a hostel for male patients. The New Life Psychiatric Rehabilitation Association serves 170 persons at a time. Begun in 1959 as a mutual aid club for patients from the the Victoria Mental Hospital, New Life now includes a halfway house for men, a farm hostel and boarding house, a sheltered workshop, a halfway house for women, and a hostel (Schulman 1981).

PEOPLE'S REPUBLIC OF CHINA

Until quite recently little was known in the Western world about the structure and organization of services to the mentally ill in China. This was in part because the first visitors to China from the medical professions were interested in public health and in hospital-surgical programs and reported little, if anything, on what they saw of mental hospitals and community psychiatric care. In part, too, this was because mental disorders were not considered a special area of concern in traditional Chinese medicine. Dr. Tsung-yi Lin points out that "the basic concept of traditional Chinese medicine is that the proper functioning and reciprocal balance of the internal organs are central to physiological and psychological health; therefore, the origin of psychological dysfunction (mental illness) is thought to result from disorder or imbalance of the internal organs . . . Emotional problems, and a specific approach to them, simply did not exist as a separate self-contained area of inquiry until very recently" (Lin and Eisenberg 1985, p. 4).

Both Lin and others (see Schulman 1981) have referred to the great social stigma the Chinese attach to mental illness. The label is thought to attach to the family as well, particularly to its younger members. Chinese families typically avoid the stigma by denying or hiding mental illness. In addition, Lin indicates, the Chinese resist discussion of the negative aspect of emotional life, especially with outsiders. They focus instead on interpersonal situations, which has had the effect of retarding the development of psychiatry and psychotherapy in China.

The most authoritative information about mental health services, including work programs for the mentally ill, is in the report of Lin and Eisenberg covering a National Workshop on Psychosocial Aspects of Primary Health Care held in Beijing and in Shanghai in 1983. In this volume Lin and Eisenberg (1985) describe the historical development of psychiatric services, and published papers from the conference describe programs in various parts of China. I will summarize here only that information dealing directly with the subject of this text.

The public health system in China has evolved as an integral part of the overall social system. Grass-roots health activities are carried out by the same group of peasants or workers in the village or neighborhood who conduct the usual productive work. The group pressure of the work unit is paramount in almost every aspect of communal activities. It should be kept in mind that for a number of years there was a close rapprochement between the USSR and the People's Republic of China. A strong and lasting influence of Soviet psychiatry can be seen in Chinese psychiatry today. Pavlovian theory has affected every aspect of psychiatric thought. The open-door system in psychiatric hospitals and the development of work therapy, recreational therapy, and forms of group therapy came to China from the Soviet Union. Some of the key elements of the health care system show the Soviet influence, particularly the labor insurance system, total medical coverage for government employees, the mother and child health care system, the workers' sanatorium scheme, a senior party members' health care system, and the primary health care system, among others.

China is overwhelmingly an agricultural country, with more than 80 percent of the population living in rural villages. The public health system has had to develop a model that reaches into counties, communes, and brigades. Professor Liu Shi-Ji, of the Beijing Medical College, describes a tiered system of medical services, from Western-trained doctors to "middle-level" physicians with less training, to paramedical personnel, to "barefoot doctors" with high school education or less who receive a few months of training in primary and emergency medical care (Liu 1985).

Professor Xia Zhen-yi, director of the Shanghai Institute of Mental Health, describes the mental health system in a large metropolis (Xia 1985). Shanghai has a population of 12 million people in twelve districts and ten counties. There are twenty-five mental hospitals and sanatoria, one municipal psychiatric hospital with a branch hospital, twenty district and county hospitals, and three sanatoria. The current mental health program was organized in the early 1960s. Under the three levels of government—municipal, district (county), and neighborhood (commune)—there are coordinating committees for mental health. The corresponding committees in the districts and communes serve to communicate with their counterparts at higher and lower levels.

In each of the communes there is an occupational therapy group (station) which combines the services of a day center, halfway station, and sheltered workshop. Dr. Xia lists four factors that characterize the occupational therapy groups:

1. Occupational therapy stations are operated by neighborhood committees in the cities or by communes in the rural areas.

2. All the staff, administrative and support or technical, are volunteers and nonprofessional paramedics who have received a short course of psychiatric care. There is service from a psychiatric nurse and a psychiatrist from the district psychiatric hospital.
3. An occupational therapy station also serves as a unit of patient self-support through industrial production. Every occupational therapy group is expected to be self-supporting through its productive activities, providing entirely for the operation of the station, equipment, and supplies, as well as subsidies for patients.
4. The occupational therapy stations emphasize therapy through occupation, reeducation, job training, and recreational therapy, while they administer psychotropic medication.

The number of patients in each station varies from ten to ninety, most of whom are diagnosed as schizophrenic. The patients work six hours a day, six days a week. They are employed in processing semi-manufactured products (the usual assembling and packaging operations of sheltered workshops) and are paid according to the amount and quality of work they accomplish. Frequent recreational activities are planned between work sessions. The local government provides housing, the cost of upkeep of which is met from production income augmented by occasional small loans from welfare agencies and the community. As of 1981 there were 120 occupational therapy stations in Shanghai providing care for more than 2,700 patients. Some of the stations are now accepting physically handicapped and sensorially disabled people, a reversal of the usual trend.

"In recent years," writes Xia, "following the success of OT stations, some neighborhood committees have initiated a new program of welfare workshops. These are managed by the civil welfare agency, which is part of the system of collective ownership of the neighborhood. These workshops take care of fully recovered schizophrenics who cannot find jobs elsewhere. The welfare workshops provide them with work equivalent to employment. The patients in a welfare workshop work eight hours a day, six days a week. The nature of their work is more complicated than that in OT groups, and they accordingly receive a higher remuneration" (Xia 1985, p. 114). In two of the districts in Shanghai, neighborhood committees have transformed the occupational therapy groups into welfare workshops.

In addition to the occupational therapy groups and the welfare workshops, in each neighborhood committee there are a number of "psychiatric care units." Each such unit is composed of a family member, a neighbor, and a retired worker who assist in the care of a mental patient. They function like nonprofessional social workers to guide and advise the patient, help him or her solve social and psychological problems, and see to it that the patient takes prescribed medication. They also have the duty to observe the patient's mental condition and report to the health personnel concerned if there is disorderly or unusual conduct. In the suburbs of Shanghai thirty-six of the production brigades have set up such psychiatric care units, with 237 patients under their care. It is possible to see, from this description, how Dr. Chaudhry in Pakistan derived his system of having a club member serve as leader in his psychosocial units.

Latin America

BRAZIL

Brazil, the largest country in Latin America, emphasizes prevention of disabling conditions and primary health care rather than comprehensive rehabilitation. Vocational rehabilitation, focused on work-related accidents, is administered by the Social Security Institute (Instituto Nacional de Previdencia Social, or INPS), with centers throughout Brazil (Tate and Letsinger 1983). The program, however, is restricted to persons who are contributing towards social security and are thus in the active labor force. A person who has never worked, or who is born with a disability, is not eligible for benefits.

Priority is given to those who need less comprehensive rehabilitation care and can return to work in the shortest period of time. While rehabilitation programs have been developed for the mentally retarded, through Pestalozzi Societies formed in the 1930s (named after an eighteenth-century Swiss educator), there is at present nothing for the mentally ill. Harding (1976) referred to a plan to decentralize mental health care and promote psychiatric skills in general medical practitioners, but there is no indication that this has transpired.

CUBA

Cuba follows the Soviet pattern of emphasis upon work in rehabilitation. The chairman of the Cuban Social Work Association described six levels of rehabilitation of the mentally ill (Toyamil 1983). These are

1. Work on the grounds of the mental hospital;
2. Work on the wards of the mental hospital;
3. Sheltered group work in the hospital;
4. Residence in the hospital, with sheltered group work outside the hospital;
5. Residence in a group home, with work by groups in a work center, such as the Havana Botanical Gardens;

6. Residence in a group home or with the patient's family, and work in sheltered work or in previous (pretreatment) employment.

Bates and Whiteside (1985) described this program at Havana Psychiatric Hospital, a sprawling complex over 150 years old, housing between 4,000 and 5,000 patients. They reported that the hospital appeared "clean and busy." Patients were working in squads keeping the grounds clean and making boots, furniture, and other items needed to run the hospital. The hospital director explained that once the acute phase of illness has passed, a rehabilitation program is built around employment. Workers in sheltered factories are paid in cash, up to $60 per month. Patients move to community hostels and may work in jobs in the mainstream of industry. "Each employer knows that they must take their share of the disabled," explained the hospital director.

MEXICO

The major responsibility for providing rehabilitation services in Mexico rests with the Instituto Mexicano de Seguro Social (IMSS), the social security system (Kunce 1983). Outpatient rehabilitation centers provide major services in assisting disabled workers to resume employment after hospital treatment. In Mexico City there are two such facilities, one each in the northern and southern sections of the city. "Although inpatient services," says Kunce, "also provide services to persons with psychiatric problems and employment-related illnesses, such as toxic reactions, proportionally fewer of these persons seek outpatient services than those with physical limitations" (p. 5).

VENEZUELA

Venezuela, where the government covers 90 percent of the cost of psychiatric care, has developed psychiatric services in all provincial capitals, using a network of psychiatric hospitals, psychiatric units of general hospitals, and psychiatric clinics in the health units (WHO 1978). The World Health Organization has collaborated with the Venezuelan Division of Mental Hygiene to establish training programs in occupational therapy.

Two Countries of the Pacific

THE PHILIPPINES

Correspondence over the years has indicated that the Mental Health Association in the Philippines operates a traditional sheltered workshop. A more recent report (World Federation for Mental Health 1986) tells of the founding of small-scale businesses by the association to give jobs to those recovering from mental illness.

MALAYSIA

Hospital Bahagia, Ulu Kinta (HBUK), the largest of the two central mental hospitals in Malaysia (with 2,300 patients), operates a farm rehabilitation program. This was established in 1979 for long-stay patients, more than three-quarters of whom are diagnosed as schizophrenic (Krahl 1980). Krahl describes a setting of 260 acres of land with fifteen buildings for patients, accommodating up to twenty persons each. The program is staffed by a doctor, a clinical psychologist, a social worker, and six hospital assistants. The farm comprises an assessment farm, training farms, working farms, and hostels for men and women. Training is provided in fruit growing, flower gardening, vegetable growing, tapioca, maize and peanut cultivation, duck and fish rearing, basketry, tailoring, lawn mowing, and work in the canteen. The patients' progress is assessed "through discussions, interviews and an assessment rehabilitation scale" (Krahl 1980, p. 15).

When patients are placed on regular farms outside the program the hospital requires that employers provide food and lodgings. There is follow-up by the social worker, who, in addition to helping the patient over difficulties, "watches that the patient is not exploited or mistreated by the employer." Half of the patients are on psychotropic medication, mostly long-acting phenothiazines. Krahl comments: "The public prejudice towards former patients of mental hospitals is still very strong in Malaysia. Therefore, prospective employers are scared to employ ex-patients, commonly called 'orang gila' and considered to behave in a violent, disturbed or at least strange manner" (Krahl 1980, p. 15).

A Summation

I find great value in reviewing programs for the mentally ill in other countries, with different cultural settings, different economic situations, and different expectations. It brings into perspective our own value system and the paramount issues we have to deal with.

A common denominator in all parts of the world is the stigma and fear of mental illness. Those of us who treat or otherwise work with the mentally ill are inclined to forget how great is the underlying fear of mental illness in the general population. We Westerners may not think of demons or other extrasensory explanations, as is common in Asia or Africa, but the man on the street and the worker in the work place often perceive the mentally ill as "raving lunatics," at worst as highly dangerous people who need to be locked up, and at least as people to be avoided. Vocational rehabilitation counselors have long advised clients to explain periods of absence from work as due to "nervous breakdowns" or some other euphemism rather than admit to psychiatric hospitalization. The nomenclature in our federal-state vocational rehabilitation system is "emotionally disturbed," a much less frightening designation.

What may seem like differences in philosophical approach to dealing with disability may actually be artifacts of the practical conditions of different societies. There seems to be a dichotomy of belief, for example, between those who would treat the chronically mentally ill as permanently disabled, requiring services (including work) apart from the general populace, and those who believe in complete "normalization." Yet, as can be seen even in countries like Poland, the USSR, and Yugoslavia, where the emphasis is on as much return to or placement in the normal work environment as is possible, some special sheltered workshops still seem necessary for some of the psychiatrically disabled. Whether assignment to such a unit means final and permanent separation from "normalcy" or is just a lower rung on an open ladder we do not know. I suspect the former, and it would seem a shame not to allow for the remissions and an eventual stabilizing period so common in the mental illnesses.

Although governments, particularly in Eastern Europe, express noble desires about rehabilitation of the disabled leading to jobs commensurate with ability, offering maximum satisfactions and opportunity for advancement, it does appear that the opportunities available depend upon the actual economic and business situation in the country. We are prone to place great stock in evaluative and functional diagnostic assessments, much more so than other countries, in determining in advance the best rehabilitative procedures and job placement settings for our clients; and a lack of such "professional" methods is a recurring criticism of programs in other countries by rehabilitation visitors from the United States. Yet, in view of experience elsewhere, the increasingly difficult employment markets across the world, and the changing technology in production of goods and services, is this still the best approach in rehabilitation?

According to Dr. Norman Sartorius, director of the Division of Mental Health of the World Health Organization, "The field of mental health has never had a greater potential than in the present decade." He notes the advances in scientific knowledge, in etiology, and in treatment of mental illness. He believes that many governments, concerned with the increase in the number of persons who are disabled by mental disorders or by the psychological components of general disability, are coming to recognize that strengthening mental health services could significantly aid health care in general. He states that "the concepts of Western psychiatry seem to be becoming more appropriate for developing countries, East and West, than for the industrially-developed parts of the world. Perhaps this is because in many developing countries, mental health services have now reached the stage of development of the mental health services of nineteenth-century Europe, in which the concepts of Western psychiatry were created" (Sartorius 1983, p. 3).

3
Theoretical and Economic Considerations

8
Therapy and Rehabilitation

The World Health Organization (WHO 1980) categorizes medical conditions, according to limitations of the patient, as disease or disorder, impairment, disability, and handicap. It is possible, under this classification, for one to have an impairment that does not lead to a recognized physical disability, such as asthma or allergic disturbances that show up only under unusual conditions. It is also possible for one to have a disability which does not constitute a handicap. Such a situation would hold with a leg amputee who with a prosthesis could continue a relatively normal life in a sedentary occupation. A handicap would exist in this instance, however, if even with a prosthesis the individual could not return to work involving heavy labor, much standing, or walking. The terms *disability* and *handicap* are frequently used interchangeably, and have been so used in the preceding chapters. Nevertheless, the distinctions made by WHO are of value in understanding the differing approaches to illness, disability, and handicap of medical authorities (including the psychiatric and mental health establishments) and of those from the fields of employment, labor, and vocational rehabilitation.

The mental health services and the vocational rehabilitation services have each developed methods and techniques for dealing with the rehabilitation of the disabled mentally ill. Both sets of services have as their aims raising the levels of social and vocational functioning of their patients/clients, but, as I have intimated, their ultimate goals have been somewhat different. The psychiatric approaches evolve from therapies devised to minimize and stabilize the medical condition (impairment), the psychological symptoms, and any deviant behavior, thereby maximizing the possibilities of more normal living. The vocational rehabilitation approach has been directed toward increasing the likelihood of economic independence, and concomitantly addressing the social and psychological handicaps that present barriers or hurdles to its achievement. Economic independence, of course, implies income, usually from work, but where the greatest handicaps exist, this income derives from public or private benefits.

Each field has a set of methods which often draw from the same scientific concepts and some of which appear even to the initiated as the same processes. Mental health practitioners draw heavily upon a "medical model" that places first the "treatment" of illness, the alleviation of symptoms, with "rehabilitation" scheduled to follow, if at all. Vocational rehabilitation counselors follow methods learned in rehabilitation of the physically disabled which insist that rehabilitation be instituted as early in the course of illness or impairment as is possible. (For a more detailed exposition, see Anthony 1980.)

There is evidence that some rapprochement is occurring between the fields of services. In the previous chapter, for example, I quoted Dr. T. W. Harding of WHO as saying that "the traditional division between 'treatment' and 'rehabilitation' is no longer seen as relevant" (Harding 1976). More recently, Drs. Sands and Radin, of the Postgraduate Center for Mental Health, wrote: "Rehabilitation's philosophy, science, and art of practice are demonstrably transferable to the mentally handicapped, as are its concepts: physical restoration; focus on abilities; training in skills, abilities, and capacities to reach and maximize the individual's potential, habilitation, and adjustment to activities of daily living; and education of the community to accept the handicapped so that they can remain productive contributors to society. Thus society has accorded rehabilitation a central place in helping solve the problems of mental illness" (Sands and Radin 1979, pp. 30–31). On the other side, the program manager of a sheltered workshop writes: "My firm belief is that sheltered employment is an ideal way to 'maintain' the mentally ill person in the community. The sheltered shop can and should tolerate some degree of social deviancy. Environmental and production stress factors can be controlled by trained work adjustment supervisors who are able to take preventive action when individual approaches his threshold for stress tolerance" (Fortushniak 1983).

The major methodologies used by the psychiatric services that are applicable to preparing patients for return to or for initially entering the work-a-day world are (1) diagnosis: functional assessment; (2) milieu and/or group therapies; (3) occupational therapy: activities therapies; (4) dynamic intervention: behavior modification; (5) competency training; (6) social skills training; and (7) work therapy. The major methods in vocational rehabilitation are (1) vocational evaluation; (2) vocational counseling; (3) activities of daily living (ADL); (4) personal adjustment training (PAT); (5) work adjustment; and (6) job placement procedures.

The intent of this chapter is to present each of these processes briefly, referring the interested reader to much more detailed descriptions now available in the literature, and to comment upon their applicability to programs incorporating sheltered or transitional approaches to employment.

Psychiatric Methodologies

DIAGNOSIS: FUNCTIONAL ASSESSMENT

In institutional care the psychiatric diagnosis, which now most frequently follows the American Psychiatric Association's classifications in *DSM* III, has long been the commanding influence in the methods of treatment. To a limited extent, and generally dependent upon the interest and understanding of the physician, information from the social history of the patient or from observations of the patient by occupational therapists or the nursing staff has been used in planning future therapy. For the most part the emphasis has been upon the symptomatology and the behavioral deficits, these being the characteristics the treatment was designed to address. *Therapy,* according to a definition in use in one large mental hospital, "is the delivery of treatment utilizing specific modalities and clinical interventions for the attainment of stated goals and objectives in order to improve functional abilities" (Yood and Esposito 1986, p. 4).

The goals and objectives of most psychiatric therapy until recently were to deal with deficits. Very little attention was paid to the strengths and abilities of the patients. I recall, for example, conducting a survey in one large psychiatric institution to acertain which patients might be aided with an active rehabilitation program, including activity therapies. Almost every schedule was returned with the section on strengths and abilities blank, though much information was provided on behavioral deficits. It was not until the deinstitutionalization push was on to discharge patients from the institutions that assessments of functional abilities began to appear as part of the diagnostic and discharge planning records. New York, and other states, began to develop measures of "levels of care" to indicate which patients might be moved into what levels of less restrictive institutional or community care. In a few places these schedules have been utilized for, or converted to, assessment methods designed to help in planning rehabilitation services, including assignment to sheltered workshops or work activity centers.

A good example of such a use is the conversion of the New York "level of care" survey schedule to a "level of functioning" assessment by

Central Islip Psychiatric Center (Yood and Esposito 1986). The Level of Functioning Survey is based on a four-point scale in four treatment areas and on a measure of "activities of daily living." In brief, it is as follows:

Medical Treatment Area

Level 1. Incapacitated.
Level 2. Impaired. Needs assistance with or without assistance device.
Level 3. Impairment, with minimal limitation.
Level 4. No limitation.

Social Treatment

Level 1. Uncommunicative, isolated, and nonparticipatory most of the time.
Level 2. Responds minimally when approached. Will participate with urging.
Level 3. Responds to others. Participates in activities with minimal encouragement.
Level 4. Initiates conversations and social interaction. Spontaneity with involvement in activities.

Emotional Treatment

Level 1. Extremely hostile or withdrawn most of the time.
Level 2. Passive or aggressive most of the time.
Level 3. Exhibits passive or aggressive behavior some of the time and appropriate emotional responses some of the time.
Level 4. Exhibits appropriate emotional responses most of the time.

Cognitive Treatment

Level 1. Actively delusional, hallucinatory, confused, or disoriented most of the time. Severely impaired attention span.
Level 2. Actively delusional, hallucinatory, confused, or disoriented some of the time. Moderately impaired attention span.
Level 3. Delusions or hallucinations do not interfere with functioning. Fair to good attention span.
Level 4. Rarely delusional or hallucinatory. Good attention span.

Activities of Daily Living

Level 1. Completely unable or unwilling to independently care for personal hygiene and maintain living quarters.
Level 2. Requires close supervision in personal hygiene and maintenance of living quarters.
Level 3. Requires minimal supervision by staff in personal hygiene and maintenance of living quarters.
Level 4. Completely willing and able to care for personal hygiene and maintain living quarters.

While these characterizations are very helpful in determining into which of the programs available the patients may be placed, and can even be used in designing programs to meet the needs of groups of patients with similar characteristics, they do not supply sufficient information for planning community rehabilitation efforts.

MILIEU AND GROUP THERAPIES

So much has been written about the uses of group and milieu therapies in the treatment of mental illnesses that it is not necessary to repeat it here. (See, for example, Jones 1953; Black 1971.) Suffice it to say that when the group approaches and the "therapeutic community" are properly used, they do aid patients in reality testing and in taking hold of some decision-making in their lives, thus raising these areas of functioning capabilities. In addition, patients' regular association with other persons at their own level of social communication has the effect of setting the stage for increasing social networks, so necessary a component for successfully living in the community.

OCCUPATIONAL THERAPY: ACTIVITIES THERAPIES

Probably the oldest of the mental health disciplines having an interest in and concern with positive functional behavior is occupational therapy. Occupational therapists were employed in the mental hospitals during World War I, when crafts and skills that had been found valuable in restoring physically disabled soldiers were adapted to the "shell shocked" and other mentally disabled. The methods employed were within the medical model of using specific tasks on prescription of the physician to obviate specific symptoms, such as social withdrawal, aggressive tendencies, or incontinence of bladder or bowel. Later, as social and recreational activity programs were introduced, many occupational therapists accepted responsibilities for conducting them. This led to a dichotomy of interests, with many occupational therapists holding to the medical-prescription nature of their duties and others enjoying the larger management functions of the activities. In time, occupational therapists were joined by other specialists, including therapists in education, art, music, drama, and poetry. In more recent years these specialities have been combined in many hospitals and community mental health facilities into a category called activity therapy.

After World War II many occupational therapists became leaders in the development of sheltered workshops and industrial therapy in the mental hospitals. This was particularly true in the psychiatric hospitals of the Veterans Administration in this country and in the industrial therapy organizations in Britain. Rackow (1959) listed the duties of occupational therapists in mental hospitals as including teaching skills in the activities of daily living, including community care and adjustment; directing arts and crafts and hobby clubs; testing and evaluation (of vocational aptitude and skills, work tolerance, work habits, and interests); and providing prevocational exploration, training, and work experience. Therapists' duties are very much the same today.

There is no hard and fast rule as to the use of occupational therapy as a modality of treatment. The Joint Commission for the Accreditation of Hospitals requires that a patient's medical record specify the prescribed nature of occupational and other activity therapies in relation to symptoms or behavior, but I have found little indication that assignments to activity therapies or to rehabilitation procedures actually result from such prescriptions. An interesting comparison between occupational therapy, in its pristine form, and work therapies is given by Landy and Raulet (1959): "Occupational therapy involves the patient in a creative task of some kind, in which something is produced which is primarily of value to himself. Work therapy, or industrial therapy, involves the patient in a task of some kind, in which he may or may not actually create or produce something, but in which his energies are expended toward accomplishment of something of use to others" (p. 74). While occupational therapy continues to be of value as a treatment modality, both in hospitals and in community mental health services, it is more in terms of the definition just given. Occupational therapists have been particularly valuable in directing activity and rehabilitative services for the mentally ill (see Allen 1982; Palmer 1985).

DYNAMIC INTERVENTION: BEHAVIOR MODIFICATION

Direct, dynamic intervention to effect changes in the behavior of patients has been tried in many mental hospitals over the years. Usually, the techniques of operant conditioning or behavior modification have been used with an individual, under the direction of a psychologist trained in the methods. The aim has been to correct some deportment that is interfering with the application of more standard therapies, such as chemotherapy or group or individual psychotherapy. In some instances the methods of behavior modification have been applied to groups of patients, usually a ward in the mental hospital, for the most part using the process of "token economy." This process involves payment of some kind to award proper behavior, thus reinforcing its repetition, and a penalty for unacceptable behavior or performance, thus reinforcing its abolition. In my experience the token economy methods always work—so long as the tokens are available (either money or chits exchangeable for food or small personal grooming items or meals or cigarets). But such a program is difficult to maintain for long, because of the extra expense of the tokens, or the special training required by staff, or interruptions by the turnover of patients and staff that is common in the public bureaucracy. As soon as the token economy ends, the patients return to their previous behavior.

This is not a fault of the behavior modification procedure, however, but more the fault of the short or truncated length of time it is carried on. Changing habits of behavior takes time, measured in months, not weeks or days. Another complication of the token economy is illustrated in the experience of a Veterans Administration hospital (Moriarty 1970). Applied to a ward of patients, the program resulted in the majority of them being able to leave the hospital, live in the community, and return each day to work in the sheltered workshop. Participants in the program materially reduced aberrant behavior, increased their performance at work activity, declined in overt physical and verbal hostility, and reduced their need for medication. The difficulty is that since no control or comparison group was available, it is not possible to ascribe all of the changes to the behavior modification techniques themselves.

One six-year experiment, however, which did use scientific comparison, was the work of Gordon L. Paul in Illinois between 1968 and 1974 (Paul and Lentz 1977). Paul devised a treatment technique to assist minimally functioning schizophrenic patients to achieve greater self-sufficiency. He designed two psychosocial programs—milieu therapy and social-learning therapy—for two experimental groups and compared their progress with the progress of a control group of patients in usual hospital programming. In the psychosocial programs "85 percent of each resident's waking hours was devoted to acquiring skills to overcome specific deficits in behavior . . . The remaining time was allocated to unstructured activities (12 percent) and to drug administration (3 percent)" (Rhoades 1981, p. 13–14). In the regular hospital regimen 63.8 percent of patients' waking hours was unstructured time; classes, meetings, and focused activities accounted for 4.9 percent; morning and evening routines, 6.3 percent; drug administration, 6.3 percent; and meals, 18.8 percent. In the psychosocial programs, meals and regular routines were programmed as focused activities.

Paul based his conceptual framework upon what he called an "interaction/educative model." He "assumed for the study that the problems of these schizophrenic patients were the results of inappropriate maladaptive learning that occurred in bizarre environments (including the traditional mental hospital) and in the absence of appropriate skills for dealing with a complex world" (Rhoades 1981, p. 28). He adopted ten basic rules for all residents included in the study: each resident was expected to

1. Care for himself or herself and present a desirable appearance.
2. Perform his or her own housekeeping chores and share in those of the unit.

3. Think, talk, and act straight, in ways that made sense to others.
4. Show gentlemanly or ladylike behavior.
5. Show respect for the rights of others, for himself or herself, and for property.
6. Participate cooperatively and actively with other residents, staff, and others.
7. Attend and participate in all scheduled activities.
8. Acquire work habits and skills that would provide for an income after discharge from hospital.
9. Move through the program and return permanently to the outside community.
10. "NOT act 'crazy'!"

This listing brings to mind the rules developed by a schizophrenic patient who never stopped working through four bouts of acute disease:

> I started slowly to learn the five basic rules of how not to appear insane. These I called my "sanity rules" . . .
> 1) Never mention any hallucinations you are having to anyone, not even your own friends and relatives.
> 2) Never transmit telepathically on any account.
> 3) Never talk about telepathy or psychic power to anyone.
> 4) Avoid fights and physical violence of any sort.
> 5) Most important rule of all—I had to secretly learn all I possibly could about defense against telepathy and psychic force in whatever form this might take. (Wing 1975, pp. 30–31)

Thus, the motivating force of work to *not* act crazy.

In Paul's experiment the milieu therapy unit operated as a therapeutic community. The staff members were instructed to follow these precepts: "Change agents [the staff] were to encourage desirable thoughts, feelings, and actions by making positive statements, providing positive feedback, and giving residents [the patients] opportunities to behave well . . . Change agents were to decrease inappropriate behavior by providing negative feedback, removing the opportunity for the behavior to occur . . . and avoiding negative statements. Negative feedback was to follow undesirable behavior and inform residents that behavior is inappropriate and should not occur again" (Rhoades 1981, p. 31).

The social learning therapy was predicated upon the "law of effect" and the "law of association by contiguity" (Paul and Lentz 1977; Rhoades 1981). The law of effect promulgates that frequency of behavior depends on the effects or consequences it produces. The repetition of consequences reinforces the behavior. The law of association by contiguity promulgates that objects, actions, and so on that occur simultaneously come to be associated or to mean the same thing. Therefore, tokens can be used to mean acceptable behavior. They become forms of secondary reinforcers (in place of food, cigarets, or other desirable acquisitions) of major importance to learning. Residents earned tokens for appropriate behavior and lost them through fines ("response costs") for inappropriate behavior.

Paul found that social learning therapy was superior to milieu therapy on every measure. Milieu therapy was superior to the ordinary hospital regimen. Rhoades (1981) reports that "Paul's 'social learning' approach is painstaking and time-consuming, spanning years to prepare patients for community living." I have found very little attention paid to or knowledge of Paul's studies or writings among vocational rehabilitation or mental health personnel in the United States, but a great deal of interest among psychiatrists interested in rehabilitation in West Germany and in England.

I observed an interesting form of reverse token economy in a hospital near Melbourne, Australia. There, since all patients receive a Social Security pension from the Commonwealth, they are required to put $1.00 per week into a "kitty" for ward services and special activities. On a point system this fee can be reduced to nothing for acceptable behavior. Behavior in the sheltered workshop, a very popular activity, is included in the point system.

Dynamic intervention can also be conceived of as the method of modifying the environment to allow for better behavior or performance on the part of the patient. While environmental modification is little used in the hospital or clinic setting, it is frequently used in the workplace. There are tales galore of particular environments found to be better or easier for persons of a given personality to function in. For example, it has been long considered that the "graveyard" shift in the post office and radar observing on a ship are ideal for the withdrawn personalities of those with schizophrenia of schizophrenoform disabilities. Sheltered and transitional work can often be altered to meet the specific problems of the worker. "At first glance it would seem that a repetitive bench assembly task or maintenance service offers much less opportunity for matching the activity to the patient's need. More careful consideration reveals, however, that the real work situation has a diversity of elements in it, no matter how mundane the work task, that far exceeds the complexity of the arts and crafts situation. There are opportunities for using the group situation dynamically; the skills are often more complicated than they initially appear; the procedures of production, quality control and supervisory relationships can be modified to meet a range of patient needs, as can motivations and working conditions" (Black 1970, pp. 5–6).

COMPETENCY TRAINING

Competency training is a term that was originally used to designate forms of vocational or occupational education. It relates to the teaching of "tasks," and calls for task analysis, the preparation of curricula, and lesson plans. Educational goals and objectives are set for learning the procedures of accomplishing the task. For a full explication of competency training of this sort see Pruitt 1983. In previous chapters I have referred to training programs offered by sheltered workshops in particular skills, expected to be transmissible to outside employment. The training process is essentially on the job or by short apprenticeship. (See also Nelson 1971.)

Another form of competency training has come to be recognized in connection with the growing interest in "preventive mental health" (Buckner 1985). This is competency building to teach self-growth, self-awareness, and self-control, as well as ways of coping with stress, coping with failure, and enhancing social relationships. Two references are of interest, one of which describes categories of problem-solving programs, whether cognitive, developmental, or task-specific (Durlak 1983), the other of which discusses skill training for personal competence building (Danish 1983).

SOCIAL SKILLS TRAINING

The most popular mental health approach to competency building has come to be known as social skills training. In the United Kingdom this therapeutic approach developed from the work of theoretical social psychologists (see Argyle 1969), and in the United States it is based upon assertiveness training as developed by Wolpe (1958; see also Eisler et al. 1973 and 1975). Its basic idea is that some of the evidences of mental disorder can be cured or alleviated by training in social skills (Spence and Shepherd 1983). Social skills training is described by Spence and Shepherd as "an active performance-based treatment. The core methods are modeling, verbal instructions, practice (role playing) and homework assignments. It can be done individually or in groups . . . SST begins with an assessment and this tends to take the form of a short role-play test . . . Once the assessment has been completed, then the treatment targets may be set. The conventional approach tends to focus on behaviour, but if cognitive processes seem to be important then some kind of cognitive therapy might be initiated. Similarly, if the deficit is a simple performance one, then graded task assignment might be used" (pp. 11–13). The book edited by Spence and Shepherd (1983) includes a number of descriptions of the use of social skills training, including training with psychiatric inpatients, with long-term clients in the community, and with adolescents in institutions and as psychiatric outpatients.

A careful review of the use of social skills training was done by Wallace and associates. In this review they clearly outline the steps in the training procedure.

> In a prototypical training session the patient is first asked to act out an interpersonal situation either with the trainer or a fellow patient. The trainer then reviews the patient's performance, reinforces the correct behaviors, and provides instructions to use certain other behaviors that will presumably result in a more socially skilled performance. This cycle is repeated until the performance meets a criterion specified by the trainer. Video taping may be used to aid in the reviewing process; modeling and coaching may also be used to demonstrate and prompt the more effective behaviors, although instructions alone are frequently effective . . . Homework assignments are frequently used to extend the effects of training beyond the immediate session. These are assigned tasks that require patients to practice outside of the sessions the socially skilled behaviors that they have been taught. (Wallace et al. 1980, pp. 44–45)

"Social skills training has proven to be an effective way of increasing the social competence of chronic mental patients," says Dr. Robert P. Liberman. "The learning disabilities experienced by many chronic psychiatric patients require the use of highly directive behavioral techniques for training social skills . . . It is important to tailor social skills training procedures to the needs of the individual patient, as patients present different constellations of social abilities and deficiencies" (Liberman and Phipps 1984, p. 22).

A number of commercially developed modules for social skills training are on the market. For example, one set provides audio tapes covering practice sessions for a number of skills (Goldstein, Sprafkin, and Gershaw 1976). These include starting, carrying on, ending, and listening to a conversation; conversations expressing oneself (e.g., giving a compliment, asking for help, etc.); conversations responding to others (e.g., praising, apologizing, persuading, responding to failure, expressing anger, complaining, etc.); planned skills; alternatives to aggression; and a series of "application skills," including finding a place to live, managing money, job seeking, job keeping, eating in a restaurant, using leisure time, and so on. The program recommends groups of patients, six to twelve trainees, with two trainers. Each session is to last two hours or less, with meetings two to three times a week. The developers recommend three to fifteen sessions depending on the needs of the patients.

Liberman and his associates at the University of California at Los Angeles have been developing videotape modules of instruction in many of these areas (Liberman and Fry 1983). Whether these will be of value in preparing mental patients for entry or reentry to the work-a-day world it is too early to predict. Spence and Shepherd concluded (1983, p. 14) that "in general . . . [social skills training] has not been very successful in generalizing improvements outside the treatment setting and in maintaining them over time." Wallace and colleagues (1980) offered as explanations for "the less than satisfactory generalization of social skills training to 'real life' situations" that "the total duration of training is often less than 10 or 12 hours; this is rather brief and may offer too little practice to firmly establish the skills in the patient's behavioral repetoires . . . generalizations may be less than adequate because the focus of topographical features [e.g., eye contact, hand gestures, body posture, speech diffluencies, voice volume, latency of verbal response] ignores other elements that are critical in the process of producing social skill behaviors" (p. 58).

WORK THERAPY

As I explained in Chapter 2, the use of work tasks as part of the prescribed therapy in mental hospitals came to an end with the *Souder vs. Brennan* federal court decision in 1973. Slowly in recent years there has been a revitalization in the use of work programs for patients in the hospitals and to some extent in the outpatient services as well. This has for the most part taken the form of using work activity centers, already described, as part of activity therapy programs. There has also been an increasing use of the old-time hospital tasks (cleaning and maintenance, laundry work, clerical work, etc.) as extensions of a sheltered workshop, with payment made at sheltered workshop wages and with central supervision by a workshop manager, an occupational therapist, or a vocational rehabilitation counselor.

Whether these work activities should be considered "therapy" is open to question. The director of Woodley House, one of the earliest halfway houses for the mentally ill in this country, quotes a consulting psychiatrist: "You have probably noticed I have carefully avoided any reference to work therapy. Unfortunately, therapy has become something that is done to patients, something that is free from social demand, something not quite real. Work should be active, demanding, reality oriented. To be most therapeutic it should just be work" (Doniger 1970, p. 69). I would that more psychiatrists and other mental health professionals shared that view.

In a review of accounts in the literature on work therapy Anthony (1980, p. 9) reports, "The evidence to date indicates that work therapy alone does not increase the patients' probability of remaining in the community or obtaining employment." In writing about the use of work therapy for long-term chronic psychiatric patients Mackota (1976, p. 97) concludes that "the alternative, which is much more appropriate and does not foster regression and undue dependency, is one which combines work therapy and social therapy in a mix that is tailored to the needs of each patient." She points to another difficulty which I have referred to in the use of work in psychiatric rehabilitation: "Emphasis on work is considered bourgeois. To a large extent, lower-level, entry jobs or sheltered workshop activities are looked down upon and not considered worthwhile. There is much preoccupation with the 'dehumanizing' aspects of the assembly line, the monotony of routine work, and the nonintellectual nature of nonprofessional work. The result is that the benefits that derive from working—the feeling of being productive, the sense of being needed, the social outlet in terms of one's relationships with coworkers—are all largely neglected." She goes on to point out: "If work therapy is to be used to its fullest advantage, more middle-class professionals need to guard against the tendency to view nonprofessional work in terms of their own, subjective reaction to it. . . . Doing any job well is generally highly regarded in circles other than those of mental health professionals" (Mackota 1976, p. 97). My experience has been, as has been Mackota's, that many patients see work as desirable and less demanding of social skills than a number of other activities.

Methods Used in Vocational Rehabilitation

VOCATIONAL (WORK) EVALUATION

The cornerstone of vocational rehabilitation is referred to as work evaluation or, more frequently, as vocational evaluation. There have been many definitions of vocational evaluation, but I like the inclusive definition of Hoffman (1970, p. 9):

> Work evaluation is a technique of assessment that utilizes work or aspects of work to assess vocational strengths and weaknesses. Techniques of work evaluation include, but are not limited to, work samples, situational work settings and job tryouts. Work samples are either actual samples of work from a job, a mockup of an actual industrial operation or a test resembling work which assesses a specific trait. Situational assessment usually refers to the placement on a production job in a sheltered workshop for assessment. Job tryout refers to the placement within a job either in an institutional setting, a rehabilitation facility, or in business or industry in a community.

Pruitt (1977, p. 3) adds that "vocational (work) evaluation incorporates medical, psychological, social, vocational, educational, cultural, and economic data to assist in the attainment of the goals of the evaluative process."

Vocational evaluation as a formal process relies heavily upon psychological testing, following the concept that tests or instruments can be used to understand present behavior and predict future adjustment. In the 1968 amendments to the Vocational Rehabilitation Act, Congress added vocational evaluation and work adjustment services to vocational counseling as eligible for funding through the federal-state system. Today, almost every rehabilitative service for the physically disabled includes a formal vocational evaluation process in its program, and most services include vocational or work adjustment as well. Special training courses have become available in a number of universities, in addition to those for vocational rehabilitation counseling, that prepare specialists in vocational evaluation.

In those rehabilitation facilities that have turned their attention to also serving the mentally ill, vocational evaluation has continued to be a primary service, generally using the work-sampling approach. In the psychosocial club movement and in rehabilitation programs developed under the auspices of such psychiatric facilities as community mental health centers and community support services, there is much more reliance upon the use of situational assessment and job tryouts. I do not believe there is any fundamental difference of philosophy involved here. It is much more likely that the availability of funding for vocational evaluation to the rehabilitation facilities stimulates the use of psychological and other testing and of the work samples that lend themselves to instrumentation. The psychiatric facilities are more likely to be funded from mental health sources that do not prescribe specific vocational evaluation procedures.

The use of work samples has been a major characteristic of vocational evaluation in recent years. As Pruitt has pointed out, "A paper and pencil vocational interest or aptitute test has little construct relationship to the world of work. A performance test has some (but not much) relationship to actual work. On the other hand, a work sample is either an actual sample of real work or a simulated sample of real work, and only an expert can tell the difference. Work sample evaluation lacks only the physical and psychological conditions of real work" (1977, p. 65). There are limitations, of course, to work samples. One cannot include samples of all the kinds of jobs in which clients may be placed, and technological changes may make actual job samples obsolete. The field, therefore, has come to rely upon the *Dictionary of Occupational Titles* put out periodically by the U.S. Department of Labor. These volumes define jobs now used in the American labor market and classify them by industries, by required worker traits, physical demands of the job, and working conditions.

Pruitt lists five approaches to devising work samples:

1. Doing a job analysis of potential jobs;
2. Using the *Dictionary of Occupational Titles* (*DOT*);
3. Using an "occupational group arrangement" from *DOT;*
4. Using "worker trait groups" from *DOT*, which categorizes jobs according to a common worker function;
5. Using "isolated-trait work samples"; factor analysis of a variety of work samples from the *DOT.* (Pruitt 1977, pp. 70–71)

The first standardized and normed work-sample battery was the TOWER System (the Testing Orientation and Work Evaluation in Rehabilitation System), produced by the Institute for the Crippled and Disabled in New York (1967). This system, developed with a grant from the federal Vocational Rehabilitation Administration, combined ninety-three work samples in fourteen areas of the *DOT*. It was hailed as a breakthrough in assessing the capabilities and future rehabilitation developments for the physically disabled, but it proved clumsy and expensive in dealing with the mentally ill. Tower was followed by the JEVS (Jewish Employment and Vocational Services) Work Samples, developed with a grant from the U.S. Department of Labor Manpower Administration. This battery was designed to evaluate the work potential of disadvantaged persons with limited reading ability and is still used for the mentally retarded and the mentally ill (JEVS 1968). Other work samples followed, many now commercially available, and some of which are used more broadly than for vocational evaluation of the handicapped—for instance, to assist in career choice for high school and vocational school students and for those about to be discharged from correctional institutions, and to an increasing extent in large industry for job placement.

The more generally used of these work samples are described in detail by Pruitt (1977). Those I have seen more widely used with mental patients are

- JEVS, already mentioned, based upon twenty-eight work samples and ten worker trait groups from the *DOT;*
- TAP (Talent Assessment Program), based upon eleven independent work samples in occupational clusters;
- VALPAR, based on a trait and factor approach to twelve independent work samples;
- McCarron-Dial, based on five neuropsychological factors for seven-

teen work samples in five occupational groups, a battery devised specifically for the mentally retarded and mentally ill;
- Singer Corporation, using twenty independent work samples and set up with modules for testing, with instrumentation computer-controlled;
- WREST (Wide-Range Employment Sample Test), using ten independent work samples.

Whether work samples are used as part of the vocational evaluation process or not, all programs I am familiar with use situational assessment in determining work capabilities and forecasting future rehabilitation plans. "Situational assessment," writes Pruitt (1977, p. 128), "may be defined as a systematic procedure for observing, recording, and interpreting work behavior. The effectiveness of this approach depends almost entirely upon the sensitivity and skill of the observer." The concern in situational assessment is with performance at the work station; the focus is upon the work personality of the client. As I mentioned earlier, the term work personality was coined by Gellman (1967) at the Jewish Vocational Services in Chicago. He defines work personality as "the characteristic pattern of work activity displayed by a person in a work situation. The work personality incorporates work attitudes, behavioral work patterns, value systems, incentives and abilities. It is the behavioral configuration regarded as necessary to function effectively in a work setting. It is a constellation distinguishing work roles from other societal roles" (p. 20).

The major problem with situational assessment in vocational evaluation in psychiatric settings is that frequently the evaluator is a mental health professional with little or no experience in the business or industrial work world. Judgment as to the meaning of behavior and performance in sheltered or transitional work settings for placement in competitive work can be biased by negative attitudes toward chronicity of illness on the one hand or, on the other, by invalidly high expectations for the patient being assessed.

A number of rehabilitation programs dealing with the mentally ill and other disabled clientele have developed handbooks or service manuals describing their vocational evaluation procedures in some detail. An indication of the range of factors considered is included in the Service Manual of the Arnold Center, Midland, Michigan:

1. Physical and psychomotor capacities
2. Intellectual capacities
3. Emotional stability
4. Interests, attitudes, occupational information
5. Personal, social, and work history

6. Aptitudes
7. Achievements (e.g., educational, vocational)
8. Work skills and work tolerances
9. Work habits (e.g., punctuality, attendance, concentration, organization, interpersonal skills)
10. Work-related capabilities (e.g., mobility, communication, hygiene, money management, homemaking)
11. Job-seeking skills
12. Potential to benefit from further services
13. Possible job objectives
14. The individual's ability

Two points are significant. One is that this evaluation process—like most programs using formal evaluation procedures—involves the patient/client as a participant in the process. (Indeed, patient involvement is a requirement for all programs depending on funding via the federal-state vocational rehabilitation system.) This means sharing findings, eliciting suggestions and interpretation from the client and the family, and arriving at subsequent steps acceptable to the participant. The other point is that the comprehensiveness of such an evaluation process offers opportunities for including the therapeutic modalities of behavior modification, competency training, and skills learning in the assessment as well as in work adjustment.

Examples of some other rehabilitation programs having handbooks or service manuals describing vocational evaluation are

- Southeastern Kentucky Rehabilitation Industries, Corbin, Kentucky. This program uses a battery of psychometric tests, the Pennsylvania Bi-Manual Work Sample, and six of the work samples in VALPAR.
- Goodwill-LARC Rehabilitation Center, Adrian, Michigan. This agency uses the JEVS and the McCarron-Dial systems as well as the Michigan Occupational Information System (MOIS).
- RCS (Rehabilitation Center of Sheboygan, Inc.), Sheboygan, Wisconsin. This program has a vocational assessment center and uses the Singer Graflex Evaluation System and situational assessments on subcontract jobs.
- Portland Habilitation Center, Inc., Portland, Oregon. This agency uses batteries of psychometric and aptitude tests, the Pennsylvania Bi-Manual and the TOWER Collating work sample, and a Lamp assembly work sample.
- Community Services of Lane County, Inc., Eugene, Oregon. This program uses work samples developed at in-house work stations.

In the use of vocational evaluation, and particularly of work samples, two warnings from the literature are worthy of note. Nadolsky (1985) points out that vocational evaluation really involves two kinds of measures, those designed to *assess* and those designed to *predict*. These call for different technologies, and the separation has not yet been developed. As regards the use of work sampling, Coker and Blakemore state: "There are a large number of studies demonstrating that performance on work tasks involving motor skills shows marked improvement with practice . . . These findings cast doubt upon the validity of competitive norms and industrial standards with simulated work tasks" (1985, p. 148). They describe a way of meeting this problem by repeating work sampling some small number of times and fitting the findings to a learning curve or equation. The use of a microcomputer affords rapid extrapolation to a more valid conclusion. I must point out, however, that studies in England years ago determined that the learning curve for schizophrenics follows a different pattern from that of normal persons. My own experience has been that much more time is required for the severely mentally ill to reach the same plateau of learning as those not mentally ill.

VOCATIONAL COUNSELING

The person responsible for coordinating and directing the services to the individual in the federal-state vocational rehabilitation system, and to the greatest extent in the community-based rehabilitation facilities, is the vocational rehabilitation counselor. The counselor may be a psychologist, a social worker, a vocational counselor, or, increasingly, someone from the newer profession of vocational rehabilitation counseling. Educational programs leading to master's degrees in vocational rehabilitation counseling are offered at a number of universities across the country. The national professional organization, the National Rehabilitation Association, has established an accreditation for those engaged in rehabilitation counseling, the certified rehabilitation counselor, or CRC. I believe, however, that at this time the greater number of rehabilitation counselors serving the mentally ill come from the field of social work.

A study some years ago of the tasks engaged in by rehabilitation counselors (Muthard and Salomone 1969) listed them in the following order of importance:

1. Vocational guidance activities and services;
2. Therapeutic counseling;
3. Job placement;
4. Rehabilitation planning;

5. Group procedures;
6. Vocational and psychological appraisal;
7. Supplying medical and occupational information.

These would generally be the current array of tasks of the rehabilitation counselor serving the mentally ill. However, the development of a "case-manager" approach to serving the chronically mentally ill has had a carry-over to rehabilitation counseling. In the case-manager model, Kemp (1981) lists the tasks of the vocational rehabilitation counselor as

1. Diagnosis (including evaluation);
2. Counseling (therapeutic relationship with client);
3. Planning and organizing services;
4. Procuring and expediting services;
5. Keeping records of services given and costs incurred;
6. Advocacy and salesmanship (to represent the client);
7. Organizing and managing of a caseload.

TRAINING IN ACTIVITIES OF DAILY LIVING AND PERSONAL ADJUSTMENT

Many seriously deteriorated or seriously ill handicapped persons require training in common elements of daily living. Such daily tasks as personal grooming, handling money or transportation, cooking meals, and shopping have been forgotten or never learned. For the mentally ill, this was especially so for the long-term institutionalized. Programs in teaching activities of daily living (ADL) were devised, borrowing from those developed for the physically disabled and particularly those for the mentally retarded. Many of these programs are under the direction of occupational therapists. While not usually thought of as adult education, some of the best ADL teaching I have seen was by special education and adult education teachers of the Rochester, New York, Board of Education, serving adult patients referred from the community mental health agencies.

WORK ADJUSTMENT

The logical outcome of vocational (work) evaluation is to place the client in a program that will lead to employment. The process of using work settings under professional counseling and supervision to modify behavior is known as work adjustment. According to Leshner (1970) the purpose of work adjustment training is "to produce an individual with a sound self-image of a particular kind of worker with identifiable capabilities, vocational goals, and motivation for continued vocational self-development. When he is finished, he is ready for entering into training or in competitive employment" (p. 33). Anthony (1980) points out that "it is essentially an *in vivo* training setting which imposes gradually increasing demands and tasks on the client as the client learns new skills" (p. 133).

All sheltered and transitional work programs for the mentally ill I have seen or read about employ some form of work adjustment training. Pruitt (1983), in a very comprehensive analysis and description of work adjustment, classifies the different models as follows:

1. The medical model. In this approach, work is looked upon as therapy. However, the judgments made are very subjective and gross (e.g., "poor work habits," "can't work an eight-hour day," "unmotivated").

2. Counseling models. In this approach, work, together with counseling, constitutes the therapy. There are several such models.

(*a*) The Chicago Jewish Vocational Services' "vocational adjustment shop." The goal here was to develop a "work personality." The shop program reproduces a normal development with exposure to the work milieu. "Success, praise and reassuring supervisory attitudes foster motivation. Competition is minimal . . . Work tasks are selected which are meaningful to the client and which engender a sense of satisfaction. Wages induce a feeling of independence. The client works in an atmosphere which maximizes the image of himself as a worker" (Pruitt 1983, p. 14).

(*b*) The critical role transition model, pioneered by the Vocational Guidance and Rehabilitation Services (VGRS) of Cleveland, Ohio. "*Critical role transition* is a sociological term which describes the transition or passage from one behavioral role to another during a crisis period" (p. 16). The model requires the mastering of tasks in each of four transitional phases: "settling in," learning, growth, and job readiness. There are psychological and environmental tasks for each phase.

(*c*) The STEP (Selective Training and Evaluation Programming) Model, developed at the Milwaukee Jewish Vocational Service. Clients move from one step to the next in seven phases until ready for job placement. The agency uses subcontract work, counselors, and work supervisors to train clients to work. The steps include

1) Vocational assessment;
2) Function shop, with individualized training in a limited number of areas;
3) Behavior shop, with training to relate to work supervisors and co-workers;

4) Basic integrated training (BIT), with focus on total job readiness;
5) Training-oriented production (TOP), with emphasis on self-worth in relation to good work habits and productivity;
6) High integrated training (HIT), using group techniques to explore vocational fields and the current job market;
7) Placement employment pool (PEP).

3. Work-habit and skill-training models.
4. Behavior-modification models.
5. The individualized work-adjustment model. This model's emphasis is upon individualized planning and implementation, including the voluntary involvement of the client. Pruitt (1983) believes that this "represents the best of our knowledge within the current state-of-the art" (p. 30). He describes the process in detail in his book.

JOB-PLACEMENT PROCEDURES

In the United States great emphasis is placed upon job placement in competitive occupations as the ultimate goal of rehabilitation services to disabled persons. In almost no other country is this so: elsewhere, the emphasis is upon placement in substitute employment in sheltered work or in special cooperatives or other enclaves for the handicapped, although there is greater concern with maintaining workers who become handicapped while already in employment. The basic tenet of our federal-state vocational rehabilitation system, however, is eventual placement in a job; therefore, employment counseling and assistance with job seeking are considered major services to the clientele.

The person about to embark upon a job search "is confronted with the problem of obtaining as much information as possible regarding vacancies within a labor market characterized by constraints on employment opportunity. The solution to this problem lies in the development of a search strategy that minimizes to the maximum extent possible the negative impacts of labor market constraints" (Dunn 1981, p. 117). Over the years, but to a lesser extent with decreasing governmental budgets, special employment and job-placement personnel have served the disabled through state labor department employment or manpower services. In addition, vocational rehabilitation counselors are expected to provide job-seeking counsel as part of their duties.

One of the more highly effective approaches for the mentally ill has been a variation of the Job-Finding Club first described by Azrin and colleagues (1975). This group approach required the client "to be occupied full-time in such activities as phoning, being interviewed, writing letters, and contacting friends and relatives. Counseling sessions were arranged daily to provide a structured setting for these activities and to review the job search activities he performed outside of the session" (Azrin, Flores, and Kaplan 1975, p. 20). Liberman and his staff (1984) have used the Job Club to great advantage with psychiatric patients. That program, as well as a number of others I am aware of, now use videotape playbacks of practice job interviews and access to computer-assisted job-opportunity listings as aids to club members. A CETA work program with chronic psychiatric patients in an institutional setting has used a group approach patterned after the Job-Finding Club quite effectively in helping clients to find entry-level jobs in the open labor market (Black, Carpenter, and Robinson 1986, pp. 24–29).

It is important to emphasize that persons with psychiatric disabilities have much greater difficulty in finding a job in the first place than in keeping the job after they are placed in it. The extensive analysis of the experience in Britain over a number of years by Wansbrough and Cooper (1980) makes this quite clear. In bad economic times, when work is scarce altogether, and with the severe stigma applied to mental illness, the mentally ill person requires all the help possible. Dunn points out that for the disabled in general, "about 50% . . . are able to get a job either on their own or with minimal assistance from a rehabilitation counselor. Almost all of the remaining 50% can be assisted in getting a job by using intervention strategies based on applied behavior analysis and behavior-change techniques. Only about 5% of disabled persons cannot be adequately assisted using available technologies" (1981, p. 141). I would like to believe that this is true also for the psychiatrically disabled, but it will hold only if "substitute" types of employment, such as Fairweather groups or supported work, are included.

One interesting concept, not widely used, is that of considering "psychological prostheses" in seeking the kind of job best suited to an individual client. There has long been recognition that certain kinds of jobs seem best for certain personalities and even obviate certain symptom behavior. Thus, work alone or on a night shift seems to suit withdrawn persons, and outdoor work with a lot of movement is calming to one likely to be agitated. I have found that placement in a familiar work field, even though the new work might be mundane in comparison to former employment, serves to bolster acceptable work behavior. I have in mind a former advertising professional who, after a psychotic episode, was placed in a clerical capacity with another firm. He was able to announce he was still "on Madison Avenue."

9
Business and Economic Aspects

A number of years ago I described sheltered workshops as presenting three faces to the world: a welfare and social services face; a public health face (in that the approaches to stabilize a handicapping condition or to prevent its recurrence constitute *tertiary prevention* in the public health nomenclature); and a business and industrial face (Black 1965). Practitioners of vocational rehabilitation and those in the mental health services have had no difficulty in recognizing the first two faces, but until quite recently the third face rarely evinced a nod of recognition. Just two years ago the Advisory Committee on Sheltered Workshops to the Wage and Hours Division of the U.S. Department of Labor pronounced in its statement of principles (*NARF Rehabilitation Review,* June 4, 1984) that the purpose of a sheltered workshop is "to serve its handicapped workers rather than to achieve productivity. While productivity is essential to the successful operation of a workshop and provides a service for handicapped workers, this should be kept subordinate to the needs of the individual" (p. 3). The Advisory Committee is composed of sheltered workshop directors. However, even an economist, in reporting to the U.S. Department of Labor (Reubens 1970), had described the primary purpose of a sheltered workshop as "not to produce goods and services or to seek profitable operations, but to provide a steady flow of work with a suitable variety of jobs at good pay for the maximum number of handicapped workers at the minimum annual subsidy per worker" (p. 34). It is not possible to meet these conditions for operating the sheltered workshop, or for operating any other transitional work program for the disabled, without meeting the standards of a profitable business enterprise.

More recently, an economist who is familiar with rehabilitation enterprises stated unquivocally: "We have come to the conclusion that the way to understand sheltered workshops is to view them as organizations that provide services to workers through the medium of work. We do not view them as having twin objectives. We do not view the operators of sheltered workshops as being persons who maximize income through contract work on one hand and who maximize services on the other. We view them as people who seek to maximize services subject to certain constraints, and these services are provided through the modality of work" (Berkowitz 1980, p. 28). There is an old adage in the rehabilitation field, to which I subscribe, that rehabilitation for the world of work is best carried on in a setting that teaches real work habits and methods; that the closer the rehabilitation setting approximates the elements of a business enterprise the more useful it becomes for therapy. As Berkowitz puts it, "The people in the workshops are not playing games. They are living in a real-world atmosphere and this enforces a discipline, not only upon the worker at the bench, but also upon his foreman, his supervisor, and workshop manager. It is a discipline that one cannot simulate, one cannot play at it. Its only virtue is that it applies to the real world where we all live" (Berkowitz 1980, p. 29). It is this "real world" of business and economics that this chapter will discuss.

Types of Work and Procurement

Many types of work have been mentioned in the descriptions of programs in the preceding chapters. In general, three types of work have been predominant: subcontract assembly and packaging, direct manufacture or assembly for sale by the program, and contracts for service trades activities. By far the most prominent type of work in sheltered workshops has been subcontract—doing a piece of an assembly operation in which the larger or more complicated pieces are performed by the firm that let the subcontract and/or packaging items provided by the firm that manufactures or assembles them. In the transitional work programs, service trade contracts such as cleaning, yard work, gardening, and sometimes clerical tasks and storeroom work have been most popular. In only a few instances have workshops developed a product which they manufacture "from scratch" and sell on the open market.

The kind of subcontract work undertaken is greatly dependent upon the kinds of manufacture that exist in the neighborhood of the workshop. Some programs are fortunate enough to exist in an area with many small to middle-sized industries, which can be induced to subcontract some of their processes to the workshop. Often these are salvage procedures, as when a telephone company or an electrical parts manufacturer desires to save for reuse parts of equipment which have been damaged in manufacture, delivery, or use, or whose style or design has changed so that the original item is no longer saleable. Sometimes an assembly or packaging procedure would require an additional work force that the prime contractor does not desire to set up for a single operation. Often the work is seasonal: packaging in preparation for Easter or Christmas sales or for the opening of a school year or for the summer season.

The difficulties with these types of work are that they are frequently of short duration, or that the parts for assembly or packaging do not come in a regular flow, or that the source of work dries up at inappropriate times. A workshop must have a variety of such tasks, arranged if possible in overlapping sequence to cover the entire year. One workshop I know of, for example, packages filters for air conditioners all spring for the summer sales, in the summer starts packaging school supplies for the fall, then is engaged in assembling and packing items for the Christmas trade. It fills in gaps with salvage work for an electric company until the filters arrive again. Delays in delivery of supplies, changes in the contractor's delivery schedules, modification in design, not to mention a slowdown in sales, and even the failure and demise of the contracting firm can each cause consternation for a workshop.

Many a manager of such a subcontract workshop—in the business world referred to as a "job shop"—thinks longingly of the workshop's manfacturing its own product. The case for doing so was put most clearly a quarter-century ago by a British hospital superintendent who operated a large workshop manufacturing paper party hats and favors for sale throughout the United Kingdom:

> In the unit producing its own product, one is probably taking on more difficulties because of the problems of finding the right product both from the point of view of the range of the patients' working abilities, and the hospital's ability to find suitable markets. On the other hand, there are opportunities for designing tasks which are particularly suitable for patients . . . While more staff are required in a self-contained sheltered workshop than in a subcontract workshop for such extra functions as toolmaking, work preparation, inspection, dispatch, office work, etc., the resulting profit margin from the sale of one's own products nevertheless more than pays for such staff and may also pay or contribute to overhead costs as well as permit extra payments for patients . . . When one is involved from beginning to end in the manufacture of the product, it does mean that one can create a variety of jobs, and, of course, the bigger one's factory becomes, the better chance there is of finding the right job for the right person. Inevitably, in subcontract work, there is a tendency for reduced choice of tasks for patients to perform, and one is much more exposed to a fluctuating market with consequently less control over supply and demand. (Wadsworth, Wells, and Scott 1962, p. 780)

For the community-based workshop in the United States, however, it is well to keep in mind that the possibilities for a "profit margin" such as Dr. Wadsworth mentioned are reduced by wage and hour regulations applicable to patients, which the British psychiatrist did not have to deal with, and are further reduced by the cost of space for the workshop, which Dr. Wadsworth also did not have to include in his calculations.

The facts of business life, as the manpower economist Reubens (1970) has pointed out, are that sheltered workshops must of necessity favor labor-intensive methods. Profitable direct manufacture often entails the use of expensive machinery. Moreover, the workshop cannot usually provide more than one working shift a day, and this results in inefficiencies that affect sales and profits. Reubens concluded that there are financial and organizational advantages in subcontracting over those of production for direct sale. The latter, as Dr. Wadsworth intimated and as I can attest to from personal experience with the management of a workshop, requires a large staff of nonhandicapped employees to advertise, sell, and conduct the business side. Also, storage of parts and of finished goods requires much more floor space than is needed for most subcontract work, and this can become a sizeable expense to the business operation. Nevertheless, direct manufacture remains the dream of many sheltered workshop managers, and particularly of the directors of the newer supported-work programs and affirmative industries.

Set-Asides: The Role of NISH

A great assist in achieving direct production work was the passage by Congress of the Javits-Wagner-O'Day Act in 1971. This act extended the Wagner-O'Day Act of 1938—which had been established to make the workshops for the blind eligible to contract work from federal agencies—to make federal contract work available to any program serving the disabled. A statutory committee (the Committee for the Purchase from the Blind and Other Severely Handicapped) was established to decide what products and services could be "set aside" for the workshops. The statutory committee felt that it could best serve this diverse field if there were but one organization to represent it, and so the National Industries for the Severely Handicapped, or NISH, was established. NISH is a nonprofit corporation set up by six national volunteer agencies: the Association of Rehabilitation Facilities (now, through merger with the National Association of Sheltered Workshops and Homebound Programs, known as the National Association of Rehabilitation Facilities), Goodwill Industries of America, the National Association of Jewish Vocational Services, the National Association for Retarded Citizens, the

National Easter Seal Society for Crippled Children and Adults, and the United Cerebral Palsey Association. NISH acts as the go-between for the interested local agency and the statutory committee.

The procedure to be followed by a program interested in contracting for work with a federal purchasing source is briefly this (Clements 1977, pp. 16–20):

1. The workshop or other agency (e.g., a mental health agency or psychosocial club desiring to contract for cleaning or other service work) must meet standards set by NISH, including a nonprofit tax status, must serve severely handicapped persons to the extent of at least 75 percent of direct labor employees, must have an adequate financial base, and must have capacity for production.
2. NISH researches the commodities and services available from federal government purchasing sources, and if it believes a participating workshop or program can match the program's resources to the requirements of the government, it asks the statutory committee to have the item assigned to (set aside for) that workshop.
3. The statutory committee then asks clearance from the National Industries for the Blind and the Federal Prison Industries, which have prior legislative claim. It also consults with the federal Small Business Administration and obtains information as to whether removing the item from general competitive bidding will have a serious financial impact upon any business or industrial firm that has been a constant supplier to the government.
4. When these hurdles have been cleared, NISH is asked to prepare a detailed plan with the applicant for acquiring materials and equipment. Costs are compared to fair market prices derived from most recent competitive bids. The statutory committee is then requested to place the item on the official federal procurement list.
5. After proper notices in the *Federal Register,* the federal procuring agency buying the commodity or service must obtain it only from the designated workshop for as long as the item remains on the list. Pricing is reviewed from time to time.

Most of the major federal agencies are involved in the Javits-Wagner-O'Day (JWOD) program, including the General Services Administration, the Department of Labor, various branches of the Defense Department, the Veterans Administration, the Department of Health and Human Services, the Department of the Interior, and the Federal Aviation Administration. The work available has included the manufacture of office furniture, desk lamps, paper clips, wiring harnesses, circuit boards, hospital gowns, and pallets, and such services as grounds maintenance and janitorial work. In 1984, NISH identified 110 items for possible addition to the procurement list.

NISH charges a modest fee, added to the cost determination for each commodity or service obtained for a workshop. From this income NISH operates a small office, holds an annual conference for participant agencies and procurement offices, and makes loans to be used for equipment inventory or other start-up costs for entering a JWOD program. In 1984 NISH made interest-free loans to eight workshops; maximum amount of $10,000 per workshop, to be repaid in two years. NISH was responsible for adding $25 million value of work to the procurement list in 1985. This added 900 job stations, bringing the total of job places performing contract work under JWOD to over 5,000. Although over 1,000 sheltered workshops have been verified to participate in the program, only 241 were actually producing work in 1985. It is estimated that 3,800 of the 4,500 workshops that carry certificates from the U.S. Department of Labor are eligible to participate in the JWOD program (*NARF Rehabilitation Review,* May 21 and Nov. 12, 1984; December 16, 1985).

Claiming that the National Industries for the Blind was delaying inordinately its decisions in the statutory committee procedures, thereby losing contracts for other agencies even though the NIB finally did not desire them, NISH filed suit in U.S. District Court. The judge's ruling (August 30, 1985) was that the statutory committee has the right to set a limit to the amount of time the NIB can take in clearing items for the procurement list (*NARF Rehabilitation Review,* September 9 and 16, October 21, 1985).

Not all agencies and workshops have the resources to abide by the rigid standards of quality and production required in federal contracts. An example of one that does is Elwyn Industries, Elwyn, Pennsylvania, which has contracts with the Defense Personnel Support Center, Philadelphia, for "Food Packet, Long Range Patrol," "Food Packet, Survival, Aircraft, Life Raft," and "Bandage, Muslin, Compressed, Camouflaged":

> The Contract involves the assembly and packaging of government furnished food components into individual packets, according to rigid specifications. As many as 150 workers are engaged in a variety of sequential production tasks resulting in the finished product. Sound industrial engineering principles are utilized in establishing assembly line production groups. Special gravity feed bins, material handling containers, conveyor belts, high speed package sealing machines, adhesive applicators and pallet handling equipment are used to make the operation efficient. Production lines receive close supervision by experienced staff personnel and are under stringent inspection by both Elwyn and Defense Department quality assurance inspectors. (Elwyn Industries 1983, p. 2)

Elwyn Industries is a unit of Elwyn Institutes, with programs in Delaware, Pennsylvania, and California, serving close to 300 persons, mostly mentally ill or mentally handicapped, in its sheltered workshops.

Other examples of qualified programs are Allied Services, Scranton, Pennsylvania, and Altro Workshops, which was described more fully in Chapter 2. Allied Services was enabled to take on through JWOD a variety of nonwoven hospital items, such as nurses' and surgeons' caps, T-binders, vaginal sponges, isolation gowns, and mortuary packs (Gallagher 1977). Altro Workshops manufactures such items for the Veterans Administration and the Department of Defense as men's and women's operating-room clothing, convalescent suits and bathrobes made of high-temperature-resistant and flame-retardent fabrics, electronic data processing items, and metal tent pegs (Kase and Gerber 1977). Abilities, Inc., of Florida Rehabilitation Center produces printed circuit board assemblies under a JWOD contract (Nunn 1977).

The great significance of these contracts is that they are long-time and offer all of the advantages for training and work adjustment. While the problems of delivery of goods, changes in design, and so on remain, these are inherent in any business contract. The JWOD contracts relieve the workshop of the marketing and sales requirements they would have to face if they manufactured products of their own design and making. Nevertheless, there are restrictions to accepting the federal contracts, especially the stringency of quality demanded and the time constraints on delivery of finished products. Workshops, therefore, would like to be able to obtain contracts from other sources as well. Also, the vast majority of governmental work of the sort that workshops believe they could do well is now set aside for general small business competition. The federal Office of Management and Budget would like to restrict all federal contracts to general competition by small business. The National Association of Rehabilitation Facilities (NARF) has obtained the assistance of a U.S. senator who is a friend of services to the handicapped, to introduce a bill in Congress to include rehabilitation facilities in the small business "set-asides." There is opposition from the law firms representing several small businesses, as well as from the National Federation of the Blind (*NARF Rehabilitation Review,* March 17 and 24, 1986). A similar bill was introduced in the House (ibid., January 20, 1986).

Types of work are changing rapidly in the business and industrial world, and sheltered and transitional work for the disabled are also affected. While there will be subcontract work of the "goesinter" kind (this goes into that) for years to come, as well as some salvage work and small assembly and packaging with runs that are too small to warrant automation, the nature of direct contracts has already shifted. Technology has displaced labor in an increasing number of manufacturing processes. Products are made with replaceable modules rather than with repairable parts, or they have "built-in obsolescence." Workshops like Goodwill Industries and the Salvation Army find fewer and fewer household items like toasters and clocks that can be repaired or refurbished and resold. A recent report of the New York State Education Department illustrates another aspect of this changing scene. It says:

> Clearly, New York is changing from an economy based primarily on the manufacture of goods to one based primarily on the creation and sale of services . . . The fastest growing segment of services are "producer services," or those services which support the work of businesses and industries. These services include activities such as planning, product control, marketing, automated recordkeeping, data analysis, finance, and several others . . . Another significant change occurring in business and industry is the adoption and use of computer-related technologies. (*The Benchmark* 1985).

Most significantly for agencies serving the chronically mentally ill is the necessity that clients have the educational capacity to undertake these new types of work. Remedial education will become as important a rehabilitation service as vocational evaluation and work adjustment are now.

Wages

In the United States the wages paid to disabled employees of sheltered and transitional work programs are subject to the regulations of the Fair Labor Standards Act of 1938 (as amended; see P.L. 99–150). The U.S. Department of Labor has the legal responsibility of ensuring that work programs are in compliance with Section 14(c) of this act, which sets up special provisions for sheltered workshops and work activity centers. In general, the wages for disabled workers in such programs must be related to the prevailing wage rates paid for similar work in industry. In no instance may the wage rate paid be below the federal minimum wage rate, though the actual dollars paid the worker may be less than the minimum if his or her productivity is less than that of a normal worker. Even then, the Department of Labor sets an absolute minimum for most workshops, usually at 50 percent of the hourly minimum wage. This is generally set lower in work activity centers. Detailed explanations are available in reference guides to the Federal Wage and Hour Law issued by the U.S. Department of Labor and in an excellent publication of the National Association of Rehabilitation Facilities (NARF 1984a).

Prevailing wage rates are those paid for the same or similar work by business or industry in the same area in which the workshop is located.

Most frequently, either the rate paid by the contracting business is used, or a time study is conducted using nonhandicapped workers to determine the normal productivity rate upon which an hourly wage can be determined. Time studies must include allowances for personal time and fatigue. Workshops frequently use staff members in time studies. Often the processes of assembly or packaging lend themselves to determining piece rates, and the clients can then be paid directly on the basis of their productivity. Invalid or poorly constructed wage rates are all too frequent among the work programs for the disabled. Managers of such programs, in their anxiety to obtain work, sometimes fail to include in their time studies the time spent in all the preliminary, clean-up, and other irregular operations.

In nearly 500 investigations of charges of violations by sheltered workshops in 1983, the U.S. Department of Labor found the most common violations to be failure to pay commensurate wages and improper determination of piece rates (*NARF Tech Brief* 1984). More recently, the General Accounting Office (an arm of Congress) reported that noncompliance with the Fair Labor Standards Act's minimum-wage and record-keeping provisions is a serious and continuing problem and that employers who violated these provisions were often not penalized (*NARF Rehabilitation Review,* January 27, 1986). Earnings in sheltered workshops are often very low, and low wages constitute one reason that programs prefer transitional employment and enclaves in industry. The average earnings per week in the sheltered workshops in Virginia in 1982, for example, was $33 ("A Discussion" 1982), with the range from $7 to $110. Wages did not increase significantly even for those who remained longer in the programs. An analysis of the reasons for this revealed the following, all business issues:

1. There was inadequate supply of work, most of it being overly simple, poorly priced, and low-paying subcontract work;
2. There was inadequate technology, lack of automated equipment, and lack of industrially trained staff;
3. There was inadequate training of the clientele on the job; and
4. The budget and financing of the workshops was inadequate.

The ability to accomplish the therapeutic and rehabilitative aims of sheltered workshops is obviously undermined by poor business practices.

Cost Accounting, Pricing, and Bidding

While there is always professional concern with management of the patients in work programs for the mentally ill, there is often too little attention paid to financial management. The program that focuses its fiscal eye only on the wage rates paid the patients is headed for business failure in the long run. Concern must be paid to such matters as cost accounting, the pricing of work, accurate bookkeeping, provisions for capital costs, and the funding of operating deficits.

A business firm includes a number of items besides the cost of labor in calculating the cost of manufacturing or assembling a product. It would add to the labor costs such items as the cost of direct supervision of the workers on the job; a proportion of the costs of administrative salaries; applicable costs of light, heat, rent, and depreciation of building (if owned by the firm); insurance; costs of raw materials if the firm supplies them; costs of transporting materials and supplies and of delivering finished goods; depreciation of tools and equipment; costs of the storage of raw materials and finished goods; and costs of borrowing money to pay for wages, supplies, and equipment in advance of receiving payment for work done. A profit-making firm would also include a proportion for profit, out of which stock or share owners would be paid and a reserve established for future expansion.

Where, in a subcontract, the contractor bears directly certain of the costs, such as the raw materials, or the loan of machines or equipment, or the cost of transportation of supplies and finished items, they can be eliminated from the pricing calculations. However, the practice of some programs in not including costs that are covered by the hospital or mental health center, such as professional supervision, use of agency trucks or vans, and converted therapeutic space, is very questionable and opens the program to charges of unfair labor competition. At the same time, costs that derive from built-in inefficiencies because of longer production time, increased supervision, and the like cannot be seen as valid charges to a business customer.

An understanding of proper accounting practice is a *sine qua non* of work-program management. Since many of the programs are under an umbrella that includes rehabilitative and therapeutic elements along with the business ones, a combination of business and nonprofit accounting is necessary. In recent years a number of aids to accounting have been made available. The Advisory Committee on Sheltered Workshops to the U.S. Wage and Hour Division has produced booklets on cost-estimating procedures, the National Rehabilitation Association has literature on the subject, and the Stout Vocational Rehabilitation Institute of University of Wisconsin—Stout has monographs on the subject. These and others are listed in the appendix at the end of this chapter.

A most important use of proper accounting is in the determining of prices to charge for work done and in bidding for additional work. An illustration of the accounting issues to be considered in arriving at a bid is afforded by the recommendations from the business faculty of a state university called upon to advise a sheltered workshop that found itself in financial trouble (SUNY 1978). The faculty pointed out the need for time studies to assess the direct labor input per unit. This calls for understanding fixed costs:

- Costs allocable to a specific job (e.g., job set-up, material procurement, storage for the job, transportation for the job, specialized jigs and unique machinery);
- Indirect overhead;
- Physical plant costs (e.g., rent, heat, light and power, telephone, general supplies and equipment, vehicles operation, depreciation of building and equipment, insurances);
- Personnel costs (e.g., supervisors' salaries and benefits, marketing salaries, payroll taxes, administration salaries).

Each job should be costed to determine bidding. The faculty recommended a "generalized bidding formula," as follows:

$MB = VC + SFC + Y(IFC) + X(PFC)$,
where
MB = minimum bid on a specific job,
VC = variable costs allocable to the specific job,
SFC = specific costs indigenous to the job,
Y = client days needed for specific job as a percentage of total client days in the year,
IFC = annual indirect personnel costs,
X = work space needed for job as a percentage of total usable work space multiplied by number of days specific job is in workshop as a percentage of total number of work days workshop is open, and
PFC = annual fixed costs for physical plant.

The business consultants added, "Bidders should realize that if a workshop is to maintain a long-term existence, operating at a breakeven level is a basic requirement. However, some provision for growth should be added to the 'rock bottom bid' to insure a healthy growth for the workshop. Although the exact bid is left to the discretion of the bidder and the workshop's philosophy, a suggested bid is 120 percent of the minimum bid." I would add that while this recommendation is analogous to the profit margin of ordinary business, workshops are unlikely to have sufficient surplus margin to provide for additional capital construction. Like most nonprofit enterprises, they must obtain separate funding for any substantial physical growth. The "surplus," should there be one, is more likely to be needed to offset the inefficiencies in production methods resulting from low productivity; at best, it will be used to better the amenities in the shop for the clientele.

Capitalization and Funding

A major financial problem of the nonprofit workshop is the availability of funding for capital expenditures of normal business. By this I mean the money available for investment in equipment, overhead, purchasing power, credit, and bettering methods of production. For example, if there is a gap between completion of a job and payment from the customer, the workshop must still have funds to pay the wages of patients/clients and staff. It is not infrequent in assembly work that a job can be only partially completed when one element has been delayed. Nevertheless, labor has been expended and must be paid for. Other costs that require capital on hand are

- Jobs in which the shop must acquire the raw material itself and include the cost in its price;
- Opportunities to buy materials or supplies more economically in larger quantities;
- The costs of redesigning jigs or fixtures during the early phases of production or where there is greater complexity in initial learning, when the potential return will come later with increased productivity;
- Investment in new equipment to increase work potential.

I have referred to aid with capital expenditures provided by governments in the Netherlands and other countries. In the United States there is no such general assistance available. From time to time, aid with costs of expansion to serve greater numbers of the disabled or to serve an additional handicapped group has come from federal grants or contracts through the Rehabilitation Services Administration or, more usually, through the state divisions of vocational rehabilitation. Occasionally a state mental health, mental retardation, or welfare authority will make grants for capital costs to sheltered workshops. The New York State Office of Mental Health, for example, recently granted start-up costs for opening new sheltered work programs for the mentally ill. But such funding is unusual, and agencies must turn to raising funds from the public or from private foundations for help with long-term capital funding.

In the short term, however, work programs for the disabled must do what business does—borrow from banks. The repayment cost plus interest charge is then included in the pricing structure. In recent years, for instance, Altro Workshops has used bank loans for the purchase of the sizeable amounts of piece goods it needs for the manufacture of garments under its JWOD contracts. When Altro decided to remodel its plant to provide better working space, make room for a new work program, and replace obsolete equipment, it obtained financing through a combination of public fund-raising, foundation grants, and mortgages on its existing buildings. The costs of amortizing the mortgage and the interest thereon became a charge first against business income and then against future fund-raising.

It should be remembered that, with rare exceptions, health and welfare nonprofit funding makes no provision for capitalization. An amount for depreciation of equipment, for example, a perfectly normal business expenditure, is not considered a charge against operating budgets. When the machine wears out, application is made for a grant to replace it. If the roof leaks, the section under the leak may be closed off until funds are granted for repairs. No business can function for long under such conditions. A broken machine must be repaired without delay, an obsolete one must be replaced forthwith, or contracts will be lost and business will fail. For sheltered workshops, as with any business, good faith and good will depend upon being able to satisfy customers with quality and timeliness of delivery.

Marketing and Sales

Marketing is a key and necessary function of any business. Selling the products is an obvious responsibility if the workshop manufactures for sale on the open market. The marketing function does not seem so obvious with subcontracting or with JWOD or other set-aside contracts. Yet the need for selling and marketing is just as important in the latter situations. There, it becomes a matter of selling the workshop operation rather than just a product; it becomes the task of opening markets of jobs to be done. The business advisors to the workshop I mentioned pointed out: "The individual sheltered workshop can survive if it can seek out new profitable contract sources. This can be done primarily through 'leg work' and constant visitation to customer plants. The average customer will 'throw' some work to the workshop when asked, but the old adage 'Out of sight, out of mind' is unfortunately true. Since the traditional market for subcontracts is shrinking, new markets must be sought. . . . This implies a skilled salesman with some production knowledge and a lot of persistence" (SUNY 1978, p. 3).

Workshop programs frequently complain that they cannot afford the services of a professional marketer or sales engineer, and that their staff members lack the necessary business expertise. Without such help the program is likely to stagnate and fail. In a number of cases, work programs in the same community have joined forces in employing the kind of salesperson who can keep them all supplied with work. In my own experience I have found it wise to consider expert marketing as a valid charge against start-up capital expenses.

Engineering and Quality Control

Business consultants believe that a sheltered workshop needs much more industrial engineering skill than a shop in the industrial sector of similar size and product mix (SUNY 1978). Even though there is desire to employ as many clients in the workshop as possible, it does not pay, either in the business or in the rehabilitative sense, to promote inefficiency. The aim should be to develop work processes engineered to provide the simplest and quickest way of performing each task. Modern work programs recognize two adages from industrial engineering. One is that "the best way to handle materials is not to." This simply calls attention to the costs involved in moving materials about. New work programs that inherit space, as in hospital wards that have closed, or that split up assembly operations in different locations to bring the work closer to the patients often do not realize the extent to which they are increasing the costs of production.

The second adage is that whenever equipment is available to do a job more efficiently, it should be substituted for hand labor. It may seem at times that to follow this adage will eliminate work that has some therapeutic value for some patients, but in the long view that is costly both for patients and for the workshop. In the business consultation I have referred to, for example, the business experts pointed out that

> approximately 30 workers were unnecessarily employed on the GE contract (from an efficiency point of view). Although beneficial in the sense that it keeps people busy, such a policy of "featherbedding" has many unfavorable results:
>
> (1) The client does not get rehabilitated in a realistic environment and becomes more out of touch with the way business operates.
> (2) It hides the availability of surplus labor and leads to bidding for subcontracts based upon the faulty premise that the workforce is totally employed. The real operating advantage of taking on low mark-up work as a contribution to fixed expense is entirely camouflaged.
> (3) It encourages poor supervisory habits which lead to losing sales through too high bidding based upon inefficient work standards.
> (4) It lulls supervisory employees into a false sense of security about the need for competitive efficiency and effectively stifles initiative in engineering systems to meet client needs. (SUNY 1978, p. 5)

Quality control is a very necessary component in all business operations. As I have intimated, stringent quality-control methods are included in all JWOD contracts. When work is subcontracted, the quality standard required by the contractor is the determining one. In the past I have stated that the cost of quality control is almost always higher in a workshop dealing with the mentally ill than in one dealing only with the physically handicapped. I said, and I believe this still to be true, that "this is in part because consistency in behavior is not one of the attributes of the patient-employee. Too often inexperienced supervisors watch a patient at a task for some time and then assume that because all is going well, it will continue to do so and then discover sometime later, to their consternation, that without his necessarily being consciously aware of a problem, the patient's quality of performance has declined and work is ruined or not done" (Black 1970, p. 153). Either spot-checking on an ongoing basis or a final quality check on every item, which could be done by another patient-employee, will ensure that work done does not leave the shop at below acceptable quality standards.

Personnel

Two groups of personnel are employed in sheltered and transitional work programs for the disabled: the patients/clients served by the program and the group of supervisors, instructors, and nonpatients on the production line who ensure that the necessary management, supervision, and training are attended to.

In the United States, and indeed in most other countries, the patients/clients who work in the programs must be treated the same as workers in business and industry. They are eligible for protection under the Fair Labor Standards Act and, except for inpatients of hospitals, must be covered under liability and workers' compensation laws. It has become standard for sheltered work programs that the working conditions for all workers, including client-employees, be spelled out in writing, usually in a manual for workers. The field now recognizes the rehabilitative value of having clients eligible for all of the "fringe benefits" and working conditions accruing to regular employees of business and industry.

The one exception to this attitude I have come across is in Canada, where as recently as October 1985 a judge ruled that employees of a workshop accused of running an unsafe establishment do not qualify as workers under the Ontario Occupational Health and Safety Act (*Canadian Human Rights Advocate* 1985). In this case a client had damaged his hand on an electric saw not equipped with a blade guard. The Ontario act exempts inmates "of a prison, a psychiatric institution or mental health or retardation centre or rehabilitation facility," thereby denying them compensation or liability against the workshop. The Canadian Advocacy Resource Centre for the Handicapped is trying to have the Ontario act offset with the broader, more inclusive provisions of the new Canadian Charter of Rights and Freedoms in the Canadian Constitution.

Supervisors and instructors, as well as managers, of sheltered and transitional work programs for the mentally ill come from a wide variety of backgrounds. For the most part they are from such disciplines as vocational rehabilitation counseling, social work, occupational therapy, and psychology, but there are also a smattering of nurses and educators and a small number of persons trained in college programs specializing in sheltered workshop management. By contrast, in most of the programs elsewhere in the world, and increasingly in the larger programs in this country, there is a turning to personnel skilled in the business world, especially in the fields in which the shop is producing. Although I understand the values in having professional staff who can handle vocational evaluation and work adjustment measurement, and although I do appreciate that tradesmen may not be necessary to supervise very simple bench assembly and packaging, I believe I have made clear my preference for experienced business folk in the clearly business tasks and management. As Vash has written, "Grass roots service providers, like professional service providers, are SERVICE PROVIDERS, not entrepreneurs or businesspeople. The temperament, attitudes, knowledge, and skills needed to imagine, establish, and run a successful business are either absent or dormant" (Vash 1984, p. 30).

Public Relations

In all of its facets, a work program serving the disabled requires good public relations. In fact, because of the stigma attached to mental illness, being able to present a positive and successful image to the public is very important. To customers and to those providing grants and other funding support it is a way of ensuring continuing good will. The business advisors to the workshop I mentioned earlier listed the following business reasons for good public relations:

1. It increases the exposure of various levels of government to the Workshop's programs and successes.
2. It increases the exposure of the community at large to the Workshop's civic contribution.
3. It serves to constantly remind industry of the Workshop's capability and availability. "It serves to keep a foot in your customer's door. It is, in fact, a low pressure sales call." (SUNY 1978, Exhibit I).

All programs now provide at least brochures or printed releases of some sort describing their services to clients and the work they can perform. Many work programs have special booklets or advertising monographs for distribution to prospective sources of clientele or of work. Annual reports, special reports, publication of news, and magazine articles about the programs are used by many agencies. Some have turned to radio and television spots or special segments to advertise and explain their services. A few of the larger programs have a regular newsletter or a journal made available to those who subscribe to fund-raising as well as to other interested parties.

A most important component of a work program for the disabled, is the board of directors or advisory board. This board should consist of influential business, governmental, and professional people in the local community, as well as labor leaders, if possible. Such a committee can be looked upon as a primary public relations responsibility of the program, but it is also a valuable component of the business operation. The right kind of support from community leaders, and the best available business advice from successful leaders of business, law, government, and labor can make the difference between a faltering service or one soundly organized as a small business venture.

Standards and Accreditation

Beginning in the mid-1950s the National Association of Sheltered Workshops and Homebound Programs worked on developing a set of standards to raise the general quality of these workshop programs both as rehabilitation services and as business enterprises. After the merger of the National Association with the Association of Rehabilitation Facilities to form the National Association of Rehabilitation Facilities (NARF),the federal Rehabilitation Services Administration assisted in the establishment of the Commission on the Accreditation of Rehabilitation Facilities (CARF). In 1966, CARF was set up within the framework of the Joint Commission on Accreditation of Hospitals (JCAH), at the offices of the American Hospital Association in Chicago. Later, CARF separated from JCAH and is now located in Tucson, Arizona. An increasing number of work programs for the disabled, including the larger services for the mentally ill, have sought CARF accreditation.

At the present time, thirty-four states require CARF accreditation for an agency to be eligible for vocational rehabilitation funding; fifteen state mental health and mental retardation agencies require certification or accreditation (CARF being one of the acceptable accrediting bodies), and eleven states accept CARF accreditation to qualify for insurance payments. However, few of the psychosocial agencies are CARF-accredited, even though in 1983 the Board of Directors of the International Association of Psychosocial Rehabilitation Services recommended that its member agencies consider obtaining such accreditation (Nessel 1985). The major barrier for the psychosocial centers—in addition to the costs of accreditation review, which many of the smaller agencies consider to be too great for them to afford—is that the standards call for formal programs in vocational evaluation and work adjustment. Few of the psychosocial rehabilitation programs subscribe to such formal approaches.

The basic standards that CARF requires for accreditation are as follows:

1. The purposes of a rehabilitation facility shall be established and stated so as to govern the direction and character of its programs. Its operations shall be directed to the primary objective of fulfillment of these purposes.
2. The rehabilitation facility shall be organized and administered so as to effectively implement its programs.
3. The rehabilitation facility shall provide services essential to implement its programs. These services must be of high quality and effectively applied through its programs.
4. The rehabilitation facility staff shall be competent, ethical, and qualified to provide the services essential to the conduct of its programs. It shall establish and maintain personnel policies which contribute to the effective functioning of its staff.
5. The rehabilitation facility shall maintain accurate and complete records necessary to the conduct of its programs. It shall prepare and distribute reports that demonstrate and interpret the level of fulfillment of its purpose.
6. The rehabilitation facility shall manage its fiscal affairs consistent with the purposes of the organization and in accordance with sound practices and legal requirements.
7. The rehabilitation facility shall be designed, located, constructed, and equipped so as to promote effective conduct of its programs and to protect the health and safety of its clientele, staff, and equipment.
8. The rehabilitation facility shall actively participate in community planning, organizations, and programs, as they relate to rehabilitation. (CARF 1985).

CARF has developed detailed standards based upon these larger standards for facilities in a number of areas, including, in addition to sheltered work, facilities for alcoholism and drug abuse treatment, comprehensive inpatient and comprehensive outpatient rehabilitation, developmental disabilities, and residential and respite programs. In some areas it is not clear which accrediting body best qualifies the agency. A few of the larger programs serving the mentally ill are accredited both by CARF and by JCAH. The accreditation by a national standard-setting body has value beyond the requirements of funding and governmental agencies. Programs with such accreditation proudly announce the qualification in their publicity.

Competition with Normal Business and Industry

Every so often there are questions raised as to the practices of sheltered work programs, whether they are exploitative of their handicapped work forces and whether they constitute unfair competition with business and industry. During the 1960s such criticism arose in Washington State and in New York City, where striking labor unions demanded cessation of subcontract work in sheltered workshops affiliated with the struck industries. In 1970, social workers criticized what they called the suborning of rehabilitation needs to those of industrial production (Kase 1970).

Also in 1970 a series of newspaper and magazine articles erupted, first in the *Wall Street Journal,* then in *U.S. News and World Report* and in various local newspapers, such as the *San Francisco Examiner.* These started with the work of two investigative reporters (Kwitny and Landauer 1979a, 1979b) following up complaints about workshops for the blind made to the U.S. Department of Labor and the National Labor Relations Board. The articles were most critical about the wage structure, and the claim was made that blind workers received so little (as low as 10 cents an hour in one case) as to be exploited; the reporters also criticized the high salaries paid some administrative staff and the opposition of the service agencies to unionization of their blind employees. Some months later, the reporters made similar charges about workshops for the mentally retarded, adding that physical working conditions were often below standard (Kwitny and Landauer 1979c; *U.S. News & World Report* 1979; *San Francisco Examiner* 1979).

Though harshly critical, the reporters did fairly present the answering arguments of those from the rehabilitation fields, essentially that a few bad apples should not be used to damn important fields of service to the disabled. I believe that the airing of faults in the press had salutory effects. A review of inspection findings by the U.S. Department of Labor was made public; the Advisory Committee on Sheltered Workshops, which had been dormant, was resuscitated; and ammunition was provided for further development of standards by CARF.

More recently, the federal Small Business Administration published a report entitled *Unfair Competition by Non-Profit Organizations: An Issue for the 1980s* (*NARF Management Review,* July 1985). The SBA ascribed the unfair competition as due to tax exemptions and public funding of the rehabilitation agencies. Even though the SBA claimed its criticism was not directed at sheltered workshops, a group calling itself the Business Coalition for Fair Competition did attack nonprofit business ventures in a publication it called *Unfair Competition in the States.*

As I indicated in the chapters on transitional and supported types of work (Chapters 2 and 3), criticism of sheltered workshops for the mentally retarded stimulated at least some of this attack. The federal commissioner of Administration on Developmental Disabilities, in the Department of Health and Human Services, has been quite critical of sheltered workshops. He claimed that only 10 percent of the retarded in such shops hold jobs that pay a minimum wage or more. He said that too often people who are ready for competitive jobs are "stuck in low-paying sheltered workshops because employers underestimate what the retarded can do or because workshop officials don't want to lose their best workers" (*NARF Rehabilitation Review,* June 25, 1985, p. 3). Dr. Lou Brown, an expert on mental retardation of the University of Wisconsin, agreed, adding, "I don't think people with severe intellectual disabilities should go to activity centers or workshops" (ibid., August 12, 1985, p. 3). To which the National Association of Rehabilitation Facilities replied, "In advocating this position, Brown has continually criticized activity centers and sheltered workshops as inappropriate segregated environments and as exemplifying the worst models one can find, while ignoring the fact that community-based, sheltered rehabilitation facilities at this time in our industry's development represent what if not always the best, is frequently the only service available to the individuals with which Brown is concerned" (ibid., p. 3).

Some of the criticisms of sheltered workshops have come about because of the recent business recession and the greater competition for work and jobs. Dr. Beatrice Reubens was prescient when she wrote in 1970:

> How do trade unions and employers view the expansion of workshop employment and the competition with ordinary industry? As long as full employment prevails, price and wage levels are respected, and the workshops have only a small share of the market, the sale of workshop products occasions little adverse reaction. Even less conflict arises when subcontracts from industry are accepted . . . [However] if there should be a severe recession in these countries, the favorable situation might be altered because private firms and unemployed workers would compete for a smaller volume of subcontract business. (Reubens 1970, p. 34)

Reubens points out that the practice of including union and employer representatives in the administration of sheltered workshops contributes to good relationships. It is not unusual in European countries, in contrast to the United States, for labor unions to be represented on the boards of directors or advisory councils of sheltered workshops. Akabas noted, also, that in the United Kingdom, "unions are potentially valuable partners for disabled persons seeking protection of their employment after onset of disability . . . There are many examples . . . of maintaining employees at the worksite after they become disabled" (Akabas 1984, pp. 7 and 12).

Some Other Economic Issues

The majority of the work programs for the mentally ill are very small—so small, in fact, as to be uneconomic. They are dependent upon only one or a few sources of work and rely heavily upon subsidies through payments for the rehabilitation counseling, evaluation, and work adjustment tasks of the program. As I have repeatedly pointed out, there is a real question as to whether such programs can be considered truly rehabilitative. In some countries, as Reubens (1970) has stated, small units are combined under one roof, to effect economies in joint management, securing contracts, purchasing, and marketing. She reported: "In Holland, federations of workshops are organized on a provincial or interprovincial basis to avoid competition among workshops, coordinate price policies, regulate sales, canvass for contracts, and advise on general policy issues. Some Swedish county councils achieve the same ends by taking responsibility for all the workshops in their region" (p. 35). In a sense, the Remploy Industries in the United Kingdom are a series of sheltered workshops working together under one administration. In the United States there is very little of such coordination, except for the few instances in which work programs join forces to employ a salesperson to solicit subcontracts.

BUSINESS COMPETITION

Changes in the international business picture have, over the past twenty years, brought changes in the mix of work available to programs for the disabled. Many items formerly assembled and packaged in the United States are now handled abroad. For example, the assembling of inexpensive watches, formerly a sizeable job for Altro Workshops, was shifted to Hong Kong and Taiwan, because labor was even cheaper there than in the workshop here. Many articles of clothing formerly sewn in small shops in this country are now cut and assembled in Taiwan, Korea, Malaysia, and elsewhere. Items in the toy trades and in small electronics once popular in sheltered workshops are wholly made overseas and shipped ready for sale. The threat of movement of such jobs to less economically developed countries is constant for workshops wholly dependent upon subcontract work.

Competition among workshops serving the disabled is a matter of concern in urban areas, particularly where workshops serving discrete handicapped groups have been organized. The shop for the mentally retarded, for example, might underbid a shop for the blind or the mentally ill, or vice versa. This can become a thorny issue when a state mental hospital opens a sheltered workshop or work activity center in the midst of a number of community workshops. It was for this reason that Dr. Harold Kase and I some years ago recommended "partnerships in industrial therapy" (Black and Kase 1973).

TARGETED JOB TAX CREDITS

In the United States, one of the incentives for the employment of the disabled has been the targeted job tax credit. Until its expiration at the end of 1985 this act provided that job seekers who were welfare recipients, poor youth, poor Vietnam War veterans, disabled persons, ex-convicts, or poor teenagers seeking summer jobs could present vouchers from their state employment agencies to employers. Upon hiring, the employers could deduct from federal taxes half the wages for the first year of employment and one-fourth of the wages for the second year, up to a total of $4,500. The targeted jobs tax credits program has just received a three-year extension in the Tax Reform Act of 1986. Under its new provisions the employer may credit 40 percent of the first $6,000 in wages after an employment period of 90 days or 120 hours. There is no credit for the second year (*NARF Rehabilitation Review,* October 6, 1986). In the Congressional hearings that led up to the tax reform passage, a spokesman for the Committee for Economic Opportunity stated that the program had saved the taxpayers $418 million in 1985 through reduced welfare costs (*New York Times* 1986).

Not everyone is satisfied with the targeted job tax credit. A recent report of the U.S. Department of Labor states that the two major problems of the program are low employer participation and uncertain cost effectiveness (*NARF Rehabilitation Review,* September 1, 1986a). Only 5 percent of employers participate at any one time. A small number of firms—mostly eating and drinking establishments, hotels, and motels— account for a large share of certifications. The effect on the handicapped is not clear; the focus is mainly on disadvantaged youth, though the handicapped represent the third largest percentage of the certifications. In a letter to the *New York Times,* a Fellow of the Brookings Institution expressed the belief that "the targeted tax credit provides a two-edged sword for a disadvantaged job seeker. On the one hand, it makes him more attractive to a prospective employer because the employer can collect subsidies if the applicant is hired. On the other hand, if his eligibility for the tax credit is made known, he may be stigmatized by it . . . many employers seem to interpret this discount as evidence that the workers are 'damaged goods' " (Burtless 1986).

This problem seems similar to that of registering under the quota system laws in Great Britain and other countries (see Chapter 6 above). Only if the incentives are great enough—such as the provision of other benefits in Japan (loans, special aids, preparatory allowances, training allowances) or in the Federal Republic of Germany (medical and vocational rehabilitation allowances, additional leaves, protection against dismissal)—do they offset the danger of stigma (Kulkarni 1982).

WORK AND WELFARE PAYMENTS

In Chapter 1 I discussed the disincentives presented by the availability of Social Security Disability and Supplemental Social Security Insurance for persons with disabilities. There is great danger that a person who elects to enter a work program for the mentally ill will lose rights to disability payments or at least have great difficulty in reestablishing such payments at the end of the training period. The greatest concern is that even if income payments through a work program are sufficient for normal needs, they will not cover medical expenses met through the federal-state Medicaid program. Bills have been entered in Congress to eliminate these barriers or at least to lessen their disincentives to enter rehabilitation programs. The major provision in law is section 1619 of the Social Security laws. At present it requires that recipients of SSDI and SSI who earn over $85 per month receive a reduction in benefits. The first $85 in earnings is exempt; then 50 percent of wages earned are deducted from monthly benefits. If a person earns $300 a month, benefits are terminated. Most SSDI and SSI payments are over $500 a month, so that it is easily possible for a person in a rehabilitation program to find himself or herself without benefits and without sufficient income long before the training period has been completed. While there are rules that are supposed to allow a nine months' period of "trial work" before earnings are considered substantial gainful activity and come under the provisions just described, they seem to be more "honored in the breach" (*Federal Register* 1984).

With the passage of the Employment Opportunities for Disabled Americans Act (P.L. 99-643), Congress has made section 1619 permanent. As of August 1985, there were 2,611,900 disabled persons on the SSI rolls. Only 5 percent had some earnings. About 55,000 had been covered by section 1619 for some period since 1981. The participants under section 1619 were reported to be much younger than the SSI disabled population as a whole. Over 40 percent of them are mentally retarded; the second greatest disability is psychiatric (*NARF Rehabilitation Review,* September 1, 1986b). It is interesting that the federal report that produced these findings comments that the results "suggest that the majority of section 1619 participants would not lessen work efforts in order to retain Medicaid eligibility."

In a conservative-minded world and with a conservative-minded government there is a substantial amount of push for work programs as an offset to welfare (transfer) payments of any kind. In a proposal from the president to Congress entitled "Community Work Experience Program," all able-bodied recipients of public assistance would be required to "work off" their benefits in unpaid community service jobs. The merits of such mandatory programs—now being tried in a number of states and localities and popularly referred to as "Workfare"—are controversial, and their possible effect upon programs for the disabled, particularly the mentally ill who show no physical limitations, is unknown (Carter 1982; Dickinson 1986).

ECONOMICS OF DISABILITY

While the focus of this book has been somewhat narrowly directed towards those programs that seek to provide roads to the work-a-day world for persons with mental illness, it is important to keep in mind the larger perspective of what the prospects for services are for all disabled persons. The magnitude of disability across the world is vast. Rehabilitation International estimates that there are at least 500 million disabled people in the world and that 350 million of them live out of reach of rehabilitative services of any kind (Hammerman and Maikowski 1983). The World Health Organization (WHO) predicts that by the year 2000 there will be another 200 million people in the disabled population.

In reporting on a study by Rehabilitation International in cooperation with the U.N. Department of Social and Economic Affairs, Hammerman and Maikowski (1983) state:

> Few, if any, nations fully recognize the complex matrix of interactions that take place among the varying provisions offered for social benefit transfer payments, rehabilitation assistance, and labor market placement of disabled people. More often than not, the interaction is neither understood nor planned. Labor market problems are "medicalized." Social benefits may become "disincentives" to both rehabilitation and/or work. Efficient outcomes of spending in one aspect of the rehabilitation process, such as a successful medical or educational intervention, may be virtually eliminated as a result of some failure further along the line; for example, the medically or educationally rehabilitated person may be unable to leave home or to take transportation to work because of architectural or service system barriers. Varying entitlements and eligibility criteria, as well as funds originating from

different sources, administered by different agencies or government services, and delivered through a multiplicity of channels, may mean a maze of confusion for the disabled person and his/her family members, a maze to progress though without any assurance of achieving the rehabilitation objective glittering at the end. (P. 178)

By this time the scenario for the mentally ill should be a familiar one to the reader.

The report of Rehabilitation International comments:

> The industrialized world is experiencing a paradox: workers living without jobs at the same moment as there are jobs in want of workers. Increasing specialization of work tasks, changing definitions of productivity and attitudes toward work, new patterns of demand for labor—all are combining to force less able workers from the work place. Disabled workers, in whom more time and training may be invested in order to achieve marketable skills, are typically among the first groups to be laid off and discharged when economic indicators turn down. They may have less flexibility in adapting to the demands of new job requirements and consequently are at greater risk of being unable to return to the work force once dropped from it. These factors can sharply reduce any gains achieved by rehabilitation investments in disabled people. Even more significant may be the loss in self-esteem for the out-of-work person within societies that place a high value on productivity and that structure a great deal of social interaction around the workplace. (Hammerman and Maikowski, p. 183)

Even where authorizing legislation and resources are available for rehabilitation of newly disabled workers, "the world-view of counselors is one in which this has a low priority. In frustration, companies turned to private rehabilitation firms or to in-house return-to-work efforts" (Bowe 1986).

The significance for the future of rehabilitation of mentally ill persons, as I see it, lies in the changing patterns of treatment. As more and more of the therapeutic and rehabilitative efforts are centered in the community without lengthy hospitalization except for the very few, there becomes greater need to provide rehabilitative support so as not to disrupt a worker's employment; and unless apathy and lack of understanding of mental health and rehabilitation professionals hold sway, it is in the workplace that the major rehabilitation efforts of the future are called for. A new term for this is coming to the fore: "disability management." Demography is aiding this point of view, for it is the increasing proportion of persons in the middle working years (ages 40 to 60) who make up the bulk of the adult disabled population, and these are the experienced and productive workers that business and industry can least afford to lose (*Journal of Applied Rehabilitation Counseling* 1986).

The National Alliance of Business has produced an analysis of the demographic changes that will affect our economy over the next decade or so. In brief it shows:

- "The number of youth entering the workforce will decrease as the number of minorities, as a percentage of the youth workforce, increases."
- "Youth unemployment is expected to increase, even though the absolute numbers of young people are on the decline."
- "The incidence of female headed households will continue to increase, contributing significantly to rapid increases in the population on welfare, particularly among minorities."
- "Prime age workers (25 to 54 years of age) will account for about 75 percent of the 1995 workforce, up from 64 percent in 1982."
- "The prospects for permanent dislocation of workers are expected to increase. An estimated 1.5 million workers are already permanently displaced, their skills obsolete due to a continuing shift from manufacturing to high technology and service industries and to international competition. These conditions will continue."
- "The population 55 and over will increase. At the same time, the current trend of early retirement is expected to continue."
- "The nature of work will change. It is not so much that jobs will become 'high tech' but that technology will alter how they are performed." (*NARF Management Review,* September 1986, pp. 1–2)

The report states: "Our ability to improve education, training and retraining will affect all segments of the workforce and all sectors of the economy. No sector can afford a growing underclass that cannot get or keep jobs. While government at all levels has a significant role to play, government must be joined by the business community to address these problems" (ibid. p. 2).

Appendix: Some Sources of Business Advice

The following are some suggestions of sources of information dealing with the business problems of sheltered and transitional work. They are not at all inclusive but are intended to supplement standard texts on general business management.

SHORT MONOGRAPHS, BRIEFS, SEMINARS, AND WORKSHOPS

1. The National Association of Rehabilitation Facilities (NARF) has, in recent years, provided a great deal of training materials and programs for workshop managers. NARF publishes a monthly periodical called *Voc/Dev Management Review,* which carries short explanations and ad-

vice on a wide variety of subjects. For example, the January 1986 issue contained the following articles:

"Develop a Blueprint for Tomorrow"
"Managers Must Now be Strategists"
"Internal Risk Management Programs Can Prevent Liability Expenses"
"Do You Know When Not to Delegate?"
"Build a Strong Board for Leadership"
"Noise in the Office: How to Deal With It"
"Computerizing Your Facility: How, What, When?"

In other months, some of the titles were

"Control Absenteeism through Seven Guidelines"
"Ten Reasons Why Marketing Plans Fail"
"The Used Equipment Marketplace"
"Effective Time Management Leads to Greater Productivity."

NARF also publishes an occasional release entitled *Tech Brief* that deals with management issues in somewhat greater detail than the *Management Review.* One issue, for example, was entitled "Fixing Production Mistakes."

In addition to its publications NARF offers seminars and workshops from time to time and now maintains a "hot line" for its members, offering advice on business as well as vocational rehabilitation matters. As of this writing the hot-line number is 800-368-3513.

2. New York University's Employment Research and Training Center offers two-day workshops on such subjects as developing marketing and sales techniques.

3. The Center for Enterprise Development, Washington, D.C., in association with the federal Small Business Administration, offers workshops on such subjects as quality control, reliance time and motion study, marketing ideas and how to use them, new product development, and practical business training for nonbusiness managers.

TEXT REFERENCES

Cost Estimating Procedures for Sheltered Workshops. 1978. Washington, D.C.: Advisory Committee on Sheltered Workshops, Wage and Hour Division, U.S. Department of Labor.

Lorenz, Jerry, et al. 1981. *Selected Aspects of Financial Management in Rehabilitation Facilities: A Resource Manual.* Menomonie, Wis.: Materials Development Center, University of Wisconsin—Stout.

Smith, Christopher A. 1985. *Effective Determination of Overhead Rates for Pric-*

ing Goods and Services. Menomonie, Wis.: Stout Vocational Rehabilitation Institute, University of Wisconsin—Stout.

———. 1986. *Inventory Control for Rehabilitation Workshops*. Menomonie, Wis.: Materials Development Center, University of Wisconsin—Stout.

Wolinsky, Daniel, and Breakstone, Arthur L. 1975. "Reporting for the Rehabilitation and Sheltered Workshop." *Journal of Accountancy* (July).

The RPM Press, Verndale, Minnesota, publishes a series of management and training materials, including the following:

Work Measurement Handbook
Selling to Industry and Government
Basic Production Management for Work Supervisors
The Industrial Engineering Handbook for Sheltered Workshops
Engineered Performance Data
The Sheltered Workshop Board of Directors
Safety Handbook for Work Supervisors

10
The "Eternal Balance": Conclusions

In facing the problems of running the dual enterprise of a rehabilitation service and a sheltered workshop for disabled people twenty years ago, I wrote: "The sheltered workshop is a socioeconomic institution that, in business parlance, deals with two products—the items it makes, packages or distributes, and the ill or handicapped people it serves. For each of these products, there are problems of demand and supply, of productivity, of quality control, of management, of personnel, of marketing and sales, of public relations. There is an eternal balance required, but in this sheltered workshop 'business,' the service to client comes first. However, we have learned from long and sometimes sad experience, that the adequacy of service to customer and to community often determines the preservation of service to client" (Black 1965, p. 235).

Balance between Customer and Client

The key is the "eternal balance." There is seldom a match between what are the perceived or evaluated therapeutic needs of a disabled person and the type of work in which he or she can be placed. Occasionally, a very meticulous client might be assigned to small electronics assembly requiring unusual attention to detail; a withdrawn but artistic person might find a niche in a photographic darkroom; or an overactive but brawny young man might be placed in a truck-loading crew. The reverse is also rare, that the demands of a job might find just the right attitude, interest, and skills in a client waiting for assignment. Most usually compromises are required with the disabled, as they are for most of us.

The result is an enterprise that always has the potential of swinging in one direction or another, either towards stressing therapeutic needs to the exclusion of good business management of the work program or towards such concern for productivity and sales as to discount the needs of the client except as a worker on the specific job to be done. Thus, it is not unusual to hear the kinds of complaints I noted in the previous chapters—for example, that overconcern with therapeutic or rehabilitative maneuvers, including therapeutic community meetings, evaluation, and work adjustment is making it impossible to meet production schedules or marketing needs, and that overconcern with meeting business demands is keeping clients in the shop who should be ready to move to less restrictive, "normal" work settings. Work activity centers are good examples of programs in which the pendulum has swung sharply in the direction of therapy over work; the affirmative industries in this country, the occupational therapy workshops of Russia, and the cooperatives of the disabled in Poland may, for reasons of philosophy, have swung in the other direction. However, the Eastern European programs do provide for rehabilitation services; and it is interesting to note that the U.S. Congress has just passed a revision to the Fair Labor Standards Act that will eliminate the separation of work activity centers from sheltered workshops (*NARF Rehabilitation Review*, October 6, 1986).

Resolving Conflicts

There is no optimum formula for balance between therapy and business/industry that will fit all occasions. The ultimate goals of rehabilitation cannot be compromised, but in individual instances choices have to be made between what appear to be conflicting principles. In small organizations the very working side by side of work supervisor and therapist or counselor can lead to collaboration on solving problems that would otherwise wreck the program: "For example, the bringing in of additional patients to complete a task when the patient-worker assigned becomes ill may mean that the therapist has registered understanding of the importance of quality and delivery while the work manager has learned something about the nature of the illness of his workers. Together they may plan a backup system for the next time such an episode occurs" (Black 1970, p. 171). I recall an instance when a work manager "fired" a client worker who appeared intoxicated on his first working day. After the therapist's explanation that the client had reverted to a habit he had not indulged in for over a year, out of anxiety that he might fail, the work manager allowed the client to have another chance. In order for such a process to be successful, both work supervisor and therapist or counselor must be thoroughly competent in their fields.

When the program is larger, such informal channels of resolving differences become unavailable. Then there have to be more formal procedures. One of these is to provide formal training of staff, both the rehabilitation specialists and the work supervisors. Care must be taken that such training include explanations for understanding the roles and responsibilities of the other. It is not helpful to try to teach work managers to be therapists or counselors to be business supervisors. There is some special training available for work managers in Holland through state-supported training schools, in England through the British Institute of Industrial Therapy, and in a few university locations in the United States. Short-term training of this sort is also becoming available through NARF and in the form of workshops and seminars by some of the larger rehabilitation programs.

Much more widely used for the advance resolution of problems is teamwork. Including work supervisors and managers in work evaluation, in the determining or rehabilitation plans, and in plans for discharge helps to forge understanding and the ability to effect the necessary compromises. In a study of Altro Workshops twenty years ago, Etzioni and Lehman (1968) suggested that a theory from the sociology of organizations explained the roles of staff in effecting the "eternal balance" required. They referred to the needs of the organization as including both "instrumental" and "expressive" leadership. The instrumental needs are to supply the resources required by the unit's activities and to allocate these resources among the components. The expressive needs they described as "the commitment of [the unit's] members to one another as members of the group (i.e., their loyalty or solidarity) and their commitment to the shared values and norms the group supports" (p. 51). They decided that workshop managers were "instrumental" and social workers (who exercised the roles of counselors and therapists) were "expressive." Together, these constituted a dyadic relationship that assured that both customers and clients would be served.

Personnel Relations and Treatment Relationships

One peculiarity of work programs for the mentally ill is that often the patient/client enjoys two entirely different roles in the organization. In the one, he or she is a patient or "client," depending on whether the program is closer to the psychiatric treatment milieu or that of vocational rehabilitation. In the other, he or she is a worker, an employee. We have already explored the value of having the work environment as real as possible and requiring the client/patient to perform as much like a real worker in the real working world as is feasible. The combination of roles, and the different statuses they import, can present problems to management. In the work setting the client/patient, along with having the privileges and responsibilities of being a worker, can be expected to want to exercise concern for working conditions through the usual processes of personnel practices, even including labor unions.

It is recommended practice in industrial relations that a work program have a manual of personnel procedures. In this the requirements of work are clearly described, as well as hours of work, holidays and vacation rules, expected deportment on the job, general methods of computing wages, fringe benefits, and so on. Such a manual is expected also to state how and to whom complaints and grievances are to be reported. CARF accreditation imposes the same requirements on work programs. A most serious issue arises, however, when the work force desires to participate directly in the setting or changing of personnel policy. Some workshops have faced unionization and have yielded insofar as staff and nonhandicapped employees were concerned. Some have resisted unionization of any kind. The argument that two of the main tenets of labor unions cannot be yielded on behalf of client/workers—that neither job security nor seniority of employment can hold for persons in a rehabilitation process—weakens in the face of extended employment in sheltered workshops of the growing development of supported work. For the most part, labor unions have thus far backed away from organizing rehabilitation clientele, but whether this will continue I do not know.

Although movement of a client/worker to higher levels of work and higher pay will continue to be in great part a therapeutic and rehabilitative determination, it is very likely that in the future the work force will be participating in setting the rules. Some form of worker representation has become expected in sheltered workshops; enclaves in industry and supported work programs are likely to follow whatever forms of worker representation exist in the firms in which they are located.

This still leaves the dilemma of the role of the client as a patient or as a worker, the one denoting dependency, the other independence. While the increasing practice of having the patient/client participate more fully in the therapeutic decisions that affect him or her will help resolve many problems, only the most careful and skilled handling of the triad of counselor, work supervisor, and client/worker will ensure complete satisfaction.

The problem, of course, is how much representation and how much self-determination there should be. The program manager fairly quickly will discover that a representative committee of the patient/workers is not the same as a patient-management committee. As I have said before (if the reader substitutes "workshop" for "industrial therapy"),

The industrial therapy committee . . . even with seemingly minor demands, can effect major changes in productivity, costs of production, delivery schedules and other matters that affect business operation. Suddenly even the most sympathetic industrial therapist finds himself reacting to employee organization as the average employer reacts to labor organizing. Again the problem of balance between the objectives of business and therapy is joined. The answer, easier to enunciate than to practice, is that the apparent requirements of therapy for patients are not always pre-eminent over the rights of workers. People cannot really always be treated as both by industrial therapy. (Black 1970, p. 170)

The Family and Advocacy

Possibly the greatest change of significance to the development of work-related programs for the mentally ill, and perhaps for the mental health delivery system as a whole, has been the recent concern for the family as a focus of treatment and the growth of an advocacy system for the mentally ill. The first has taken off from the long-standing treatment modality of family therapy, but has developed new connotations as greater understanding of the nature of mental illness has come about. Now that there is recognition of an organic base for psychotic and depressive conditions, and there no longer seems to be any necessity for therapists to blame the family as a repository of ills that stimulate or aggravate the symptomatology, there has come to be an interest in inviting the family to participate in the therapy. This has called for developing new psychoeducational methods to help other family members understand the illness, the medications used, and its behavioral and social management. Since the vast majority of mental patients, certainly those in the working-age ranges, return to live with or at least stay close to their families, this makes pragmatic sense in an era in which there are more patients out of than in mental hospitals. (For descriptions of the newer family therapies see McFarlane 1983 and Falloon 1985.) Among the questions that family members inevitably raise is whether and when their ill member can return to work or get a job.

Although organizations made up of the formerly mentally ill and members of their families have existed for years (e.g., Schizophrenia Fellowship, Grow), only in the past few years has there been a concerted effort to forge associations among patients and their family members that can really act as advocates for better care and understanding of mental illness. In the United States, the National Alliance for the Mentally Ill (NAMI) was formally launched in 1979 and has grown by leaps and bounds. The national president of the alliance announced recently there were some 50,000 families already organized into hundreds of chapters in every state, and the numbers seem to be increasing geometrically. Already, in New York State and elsewhere the alliance has had a positive effect upon the course of legislation for mental health. In its membership brochure NAMI describes itself as "the leading self-help advocacy organization for families of persons with severe mental illness." It calls itself a self-help consumer/advocacy movement whose goals are:

- to provide support to families learning to cope with problems presented by mental illness
- to advocate for a system of care in every community adequate to the needs of those who suffer severe and disabling mental illnesses
- to secure increased support for research from the federal government and from private sources
- to eradicate that stigma associated with mental disorders
- to help mental health professionals understand mental illness from the perspective of the family.

Leading members of the NAMI, both nationally and in a few states, have assured me privately that high on the agenda of the National Alliance is the provision of work programs for their disabled family members.

Some Clinical Issues, Demonstrations, and Research

This newer interest in considering the family constellation as a locus of therapy and a participant in rehabilitation has raised for me an old question. In thinking of vocational rehabilitation in its "social welfare" face and in terms of the effect of the economy on successful outcome to the world of work, why must it be only the disabled family member who is eligible for services? Among a very large proportion of the seriously mentally ill, family economics play an important part in the outcome for the disabled family member. Might it not aid the rehabilitation process for the patient/client if an unemployed or underemployed nonhandicapped family member were "rehabilitated" to a paying job? I know of one experiment along these lines, at what was the Lincoln Community Mental Health Center in the Bronx, New York, during the 1960s (Bauman and Grunes 1974). Developed during a period when "the Great Society" was in vogue and the federal vocational rehabilitation agency was for a time merged with the welfare services into the Social and Rehabilitative Services Administration, this demonstration workshop did address that question. The Lincoln CMHC accepted into its sheltered workshop any member of the family ready and able to work and unable to find a job, while at the same time it guaranteed mental health services to the psychiatrically disabled person. The results, at least from an anecdotal viewpoint, were highly successful, but when federal funding ended, there was no disposition by the mental health center or its funding bodies (state and local mental health and vocational rehabilitation agencies) to continue the experiment. It seems to me that it would be worth replicating.

Recently, a rehabilitation counselor working with the chronically mentally ill asked me, "If lack of motivation is a characteristic of these patients, how do I get them involved at all in work tasks or in any social activities? They insist they are quite satisfied to do nothing." In an era of "patients' rights" this is a troublesome issue. The answer, it seems to me—and this is based on practice, for there has been no research, to my knowledge—is to find the "hook" that arouses the patient to participation. The psychosocial rehabilitation field does more of this than any other I know. The director of Thresholds, the large psychosocial center in Chicago, states:

> Staff members in the rehabilitative centers believe that motivation can be created by several characteristics:
> - A strong professional desire to influence the member
> - An ability to develop a feeling of "dynamic hopefulness" in the member
> - Creativity that enables the worker to use the center for the members' involvement
> - Professional tenacity in the face of symptoms, regression, hostility, and resistance
> - Genuine ability not to be fearful of the member's illness
> - Frequent interpersonal contact
> - A deep-seated investment in all areas of the member's current life situation. (Dincin 1985, p. 19)

Another issue from the clinical world is that we do not really know a great deal about the longitudinal history of severe mental illness. In the first chapter I referred to a twenty-year follow-up study of patients rehabilitated from Vermont State Hospital. This seemed to indicate that the length of time before stability in symptoms is reached may be as short as ten years for many, if not most, patients, thus giving hope that rehabilitative efforts and their costs are not facing a "bottomless barrel." Strauss and his colleagues (1985) have been conducting a "prospective" study of a cohort of seriously psychiatrically ill patients and are able to prove with scientific rigor that the course of illness does not follow a straight line or an even curve. The ups and downs of the course, though, have meaning, and these researchers believe that a proper therapeutic interpretation of these fluctuations can help keep these disabled individuals functioning in their social lives, including work, in spite of their symptoms. Though there seems to be a reluctance on the part of funding agencies to give support, more such longitudinal studies need to be undertaken, for they hold the promise of yielding the information needed to keep ill individuals in "productive participation" in society. We also know too little about the effects of psychotropic medication upon functioning capabilities at work, and this, too, might be explored in longitudinal studies.

Another interesting finding, from the research of Wansbrough and Cooper in England (1980), is that the discharged mental patients who seemed to make the easiest transition to the workaday world were those who had been out in the community for a time, even without working. This may, of course, be a manifestation of the problem I have already referred to, that of the difficulty of making numerous changes in one's living arrangements all at once. It might also be an artifact of the normal gyrations in the course of illness, as revealed by Strauss and his colleagues. Nevertheless, it is an interesting enough question that one sheltered workshop director announced at a meeting last year that he will no longer accept referrals unless the patient has been in the community at least six months. I am not sure that there is any magic in the six months' period, but it does seem to me to be worthwhile exploring what the explanation for the British finding may be and whether it warrants inclusion in rehabilitation planning for the patient.

After reviewing the literature of research in work as therapy and as rehabilitation, Carpenter and I concluded: "In general, the studies reported on in the published literature have not been very good . . . Few of the studies included identify or delineate clearly the diagnostic categories of the clientele. The general finding that psychotic patients are less successful than the non-psychotic does not add much to prior knowledge. Findings showing that patients with good premorbid histories of work and education do better than those lacking this background help but little in attending to the problems of the chronic schizophrenic" (Carpenter and Black 1986, p. 75). We do not need to prove, as was necessary when I started in psychiatric rehabilitation a generation ago, that a person who comes out of a mental hospital can work or be trained to work. "What is needed now are more and better studies and evaluations of therapeutic work programs as well as work training programs with careful attention to describing the clients served as well as their structure and the techniques employed" (ibid., p. 77). For example, at the least we need careful comparisons as to whether the various types of work programs I have described actually serve the same or different mentally ill population groups.

Serving Multiple Handicaps

From time to time I am asked whether it is better to set up rehabilitation programs, particularly those involving work activities, to serve more than one handicapped group of people. One can make equally good arguments for restricting the program to persons of similar disabilities as for opening the program to a mixture of handicapping conditions. This is really an old controversy, stemming in good part from the differences of opinion as to whether categorical or general assistance should be provided for the disadvantaged. In my opinion the answer has little to do with an assessment of patient/client needs. It has to do with the available funding and the attitudes of those who supply the funding or the clientele.

There was great validity in setting up services specifically for the blind, the deaf, and the mentally retarded when no other program was willing to accept these handicapped persons. While the argument can be made that specialized services tailored to the needs of one disability can better be provided in a specialized workshop, the fact is that many programs open to a variety of disabilities have been able to give equally good service. As we have seen, there are programs of both kinds serving the mentally ill. I do not believe that it is this distinction that determines the quality of the service.

One complication that does affect the operation of programs for the mentally ill is the attitude of professional personnel, and now of parents in the advocate groups, about the kinds of work offered in sheltered and transitional work programs. Complaints are made that the work is too mundane and unstimulating, particularly for younger and better-educated patients. The complaints are more likely to come from parents than from the patients themselves. Even though professionals can explain that the type of work is less important than the setting for work adjustment, and so on, it is discomforting for many relatives of formerly apparently productive people to see them working at simple bench assembly and packaging.

Another question that also is more likely to be raised by a parent or other relative than by the patient is why he or she must work alongside people with handicaps, particularly the physically handicapped or the severely mentally handicapped. The mentally ill share the same attitudes toward handicaps and peculiar behavior as does the general public. These questions can best be dealt with as part of counseling or treatment services. In my own experience they occur infrequently, but they can be troublesome. They are not restricted to the mentally ill and their relatives and advocates. I have had them raised by parents of the severely mentally retarded complaining about the "boring" nature of the work being done in a sheltered workshop, and also about the mentally retarded being placed next to psychiatrically ill people.

The Changing Federal Scene in the United States

Two changes in the recently enacted amendments to the Vocational Rehabilitation Act (see *NARF Rehabilitation Review,* October 13, 1986) hold much promise for work-related services to the mentally ill. First is the clear inclusion of mental illness among the physical and mental disabilities listed in the act and the broadening of the definition of "employability" to include whether "the individual is likely to enter or retain, as a primary objective, full-time employment, and when appropriate, part-time employment, consistent with the capacities or abilities of the individual in the competitive labor market or any other vocational outcome the Secretary may determine consistent with this Act." The second is the inclusion of a section, "Supported Employment," that defines such employment as "competitive work in integrated settings," and that states "such term includes transitional employment for individuals with chronic mental illness. For the purpose of this Act, supported employment as defined in this paragraph may be considered an acceptable outcome for employability."

These changes should eliminate many barriers in understanding between the vocational rehabilitation and mental health authorities as to the resources available for the mentally ill. It should make possible greater support for transitional work and supported work programs that serve the very chronically mentally ill, for whom placement in outside employment may not be feasible for the foreseeable future.

Finally

After a somewhat dormant period in the 1970s that followed great strides in the development of sheltered work services for the mentally ill and mentally handicapped during the 1960s, there is again increasing interest in the use of work as a senior partner in the care systems in the United States. A variety of forms of work programs have evolved, and I do not doubt that other forms will arise. The old argument as to which format is best is of little regard, for all models seem to have successful use for some patients in some settings. The federal government has given an impetus to the supported work format, but I do not think that there will be any lessening of the use of sheltered workshops, work activity centers, transitional employment programs, or even of the Fairweather Lodge groups. Work programs have earned their place as part of the mental health system.

The problems of balance between business and therapy will always be with us, however. As a component of the social welfare system of our society these programs are of the highest order. Moses Maimonides, the renowned religious scholar of the twelfth century, defined as most meritorious the charity that prevented poverty by teaching a trade or setting up in business "so that he may earn an honest livelihood; and not be forced to the dreadful alternative of holding out his hand for charity." If we define "honest livelihood" as embracing "productive participation in society," we have the essence of work programs in rehabilitation of the mentally ill.

References

Advisory Committee on Sheltered Workshops. 1983. *Statement of Principles.* WH Publication 1373, revised. Washington, D.C.: U.S. Department of Labor, November.

Akabas, Sheila H. 1984. *Study of the Role of the Private Sector in Relation to the Rehabilitation of Physically and Emotionally Disabled Persons: The Experience in Canada and the United Kingdom.* Final Report, World Rehabilitation Fund. New York.

Allen, Claudia Kay. 1982. "Independence through Activity: The Practice of Occupational Therapy (Psychiatry)." *American Journal of Occupational Therapy* 36, no. 11.

Altro Health and Rehabilitation Services. 1984. *Annual Report.* New York.

American Psychiatric Association. 1980. *Diagnostic and Statistical Manual of Mental Disorders.* DSM III. Washington, D.C. (Revised as DSM III-R, 1987.)

Anthony, William A. 1980. *The Principles of Psychiatric Rehabilitation.* Baltimore: University Park Press.

———. 1983. "New Perspectives on the Young Adult Chronic Patient." Paper presented at the Annual Meeting of the American Orthopsychiatric Association, August, session 513.

Anthony, William A.; Cohen, Mikal R.; and Cohen, Barry F. 1984. "Psychiatric Rehabilitation." In John Talbott, ed., *The Chronic Mental Patient: Five Years Later.* New York: Grune and Stratton.

Argyle, M. 1969. *Social Interaction.* London: Methuen Press.

Asuni, Tolani. 1967. "Aro Hospital in Perspective." *American Journal of Psychiatry* 124, no. 6.

Azrin, N.; Flores, T.; and Kaplan, S. 1975. "Job-Finding Club: A Group-Assisted Program for Obtaining Employment." *Behavior Research and Therapy* 13, no. 1.

Azrin, N., and Phillip, R. 1979. "The Job-Club Method vs. a Lecture-Discussion-Role Play Method of Obtaining Employment for Clients with Job-finding Handicaps." *Rehabilitation Counseling Bulletin* 23, no. 2.

Babayan, Edward, and Shashina, Yu G. 1985. *The Structure of Psychiatry in the Soviet Union.* New York: International Universities Press.

Bates, Mariette, and Whiteside, Duncan. 1985. "Health and Disabilities in Cuba: Impressions from a Visit." *Center Magazine* (New York, National Center for Health Education).

Bauman, Gerald, and Grunes, Ruth. 1974. *Psychiatric Rehabilitation in the Ghetto: An Exceptional Approach.* Lexington, Mass.: D. C. Heath and Co., Lexington Books.

Beard, J. H. 1976. "Psychiatric Rehabilitation at Fountain House." In J. Meislin, *Rehabilitation Medicine and Psychiatry.* Springfield, Ill.: Charles C. Thomas.

Beard, J. H.; Schmidt, J. R.; and Smith, M. M. 1963. "The Use of Transitional Employment in the Rehabilitation of the Psychiatric Patient." *Journal of Nervous and Mental Diseases* 136:507–14.

Bellak, Leopold; Black, Bertram J.; Lurie, Abraham; and Miller, Joseph A. S. 1956. "Rehabilitation of the Mentally Ill through Controlled Transitional Employment." *American Journal of Orthopsychiatry* 26 (April).

Bemak, Fred. 1982. *Mental Health Lessons from the Third World: The Experience of Community Psychiatry in India.* Final Report. New York: World Rehabilitation Fund, Inc.

Benchmark. 1985. *The Benchmark: A Quarterly Report on Occupational and Continuing Education in New York State* (New York State Education Department) 5, no. 2.

Bennett, Douglas. 1973. "The European Program." In *International Conference on Productive Participation Programs for the Mentally Ill.* Amsterdam: Excerpta Medica.

Berkowitz, Monroe. 1980. "The Economics of Work." In John E. Lapidakis, James B. Ansley, and Julian Lowitt, eds., *Work, Services, and Change.* Proceedings of the National Institute on Vocational Facilities, University of Notre Dame, Notre Dame, Ind., November 3–5, 1980. Washington, D.C.: National Association of Rehabilitation Facilities, November.

———. 1981. "Disincentives and the Rehabilitation of Disabled Persons." In Elizabeth L. Pan, Thomas E. Backer, and Carolyn L. Vash, eds., *Annual Review of Rehabilitation,* vol. 2. New York: Springer Publishing Co.

———. 1985. *Social Insurance and Rehabilitation: The Netherlands, Sweden, Finland, and Israel.* New York: World Rehabilitation Fund.

Black, Bertram J. 1956. "Post-Hospital Transitional Workshop Employment for Psychiatric Patients." In Edward L. Chounard and James F. Garrett, eds., *Workshops for the Disabled: A Vocational Rehabilitation Resource.* U.S. Department of Health, Education and Welfare, Office of Vocational Rehabilitation Services, series 371. Washington, D.C.: U.S. Government Printing Office.

———. 1959. "The Protected Workshop." In Milton Greenblatt and Benjamin Simon, eds., *Rehabilitation of the Mentally Ill: Social and Economic Aspects.* Washington, D.C.: American Association for the Advancement of Science.

———, ed. 1963. *Guides to Psychiatric Rehabilitation: A Cooperative Program with a State Mental Hospital.* New York: Altro Health and Rehabilitation Services.

———. 1965. "The Workshop in a Changing World: The Three Faces of the Sheltered Workshop." *Rehabilitation Literature* 26, no. 8.

———. 1966. *Industrial Therapy for the Mentally Ill: Observations on Developments in Western Europe and Significance for Programs in the U.S.* New York: Altro Work Shops.

———. 1970. *Principles of Industrial Therapy for the Mentally Ill.* New York: Grune and Stratton.

———. 1971. "Milieu Therapy." *Encyclopedia of Social Work.* 16th issue, vol. 1. New York: National Association of Social Workers.

———. 1977. "Substitute Permanent Employment of the Deinstitutionalized Mentally Ill." *Journal of Rehabilitation* 43, no. 2.

———. 1982. "Roads to the World of Work for the Chronically Mentally Ill: Feasibility of a Transitional Manpower Training Program." *Community Support Journal* 2, no. 2.

———. 1983. "Rehabilitation of the Mentally Ill in Australia." In Diane E. Woods, ed., *Rehabilitation in Australia and New Zealand: U.S. Observations.* Monograph no. 21. New York: World Rehabilitation Fund.

Black, Bertram J.; Carpenter, Mary D. ; and Robinson, Paul E. 1986. *Using Manpower Training Programs in the Vocational Rehabilitation of the Mentally Restored.* New York: Altro Health and Rehabilitation Services.

Black, Bertram J., and Kase, Harold M. 1973. *Vocational Rehabilitation Services in Community Mental Health Centers: Partnerships in Industrial Therapy.* New York: Altro Health and Rehabilitation Services.

Black, Bertram J.; Meyer, Henry J.; and Borgatta, Edgar F. 1960. "Altro Health and Rehabilitation Services: Case Study of a Protected Workshop." *Journal of Social Issues* 16, no. 2.

Bleuler, M. 1978. *The Schizophrenic Disorders: Long-Term Patient and Family Studies.* New Haven: Yale University Press.

Boffey, Philip M. 1984. "Treating Mentally Ill: Trieste's Lessons." *New York Times,* January 17, sec. B, p. 2.

Bond, Gary R.; Witheridge, Thomas F.; Setze, Paul J.; and Dincin, Jerry. 1985. "Preventing Rehospitalization of Clients in a Psychosocial Rehabilitation Program." *Hospital and Community Psychiatry* 36, no. 9.

Bordieri, James E. 1986. *Employment Alternatives for Workers with Disabilities: An International Perspective.* Research Report, Stout Vocational Rehabilitation Institute. Menomonie, Wis.: University of Wisconsin—Stout.

Bowe, Frank. 1986. "The Beat Goes On." *Interchange* (World Rehabilitation Fund), no. 12 (Summer).

Buckner, John C.; Trickett, Edison J.; and Corse, Sara J. 1985. *Primary Prevention in Mental Health: An Annotated Bibliography.* DHHS Publication no. (ADM) 85–1405. Washington, D.C.: National Institute of Mental Health.

Burti, Lorenzo; Garzotto, Nicola; Siciliani, Orazio; Zimmerman-Tansella, Christa; and Tansella, Michele. 1986. "South Verona's Psychiatric Service:

An Integrated System of Community Care." *Hospital and Community Psychiatry* 37, no. 8.

Burtless, Gary T. 1986. "Job Tax Credit Stigmatizes Workers." Letter to the Editor. *New York Times*, January 7.

Campbell, William, and Dillon, Arthur. 1983. "Psychiatric Rehabilitation: A Time for Change." *Industrial Therapy* (London, British Institute of Industrial Therapy) 8, no. 1.

Canadian Human Rights Advocate. November 1985. "Workshop Found Guilty of Unsafe Conditions." Vol. 1, no. 11.

CARF. 1985. *The Standards Manual for Facilities Serving People with Disabilities.* Tucson: Commission on Accreditation of Rehabilitation Facilities.

Carpenter, M. D. 1978. "Residential Placement for the Chronic Psychiatric Patient: A Review and Evaluation of the Literature." *Schizophrenia Bulletin* 4, no. 3.

Carpenter, M. D., and Black, B. J. 1983. "Community Placement of Chronic Schizophrenics." In "Partial Hospitalization and Acute Day Hospital: A Response to the CSS-Eligible Patient." Proceedings of a Conference at World Trade Center, New York City, February 18, 1983. Albany: New York State Office of Mental Health. Mimeo.

Carpenter, Mary D., and Black, Bertram J. 1986. "Review of Research and Evaluation." In *Work as Therapy and Rehabilitation for the Mentally Ill.* New York: Altro Health and Rehabilitation Services.

Carter, Kent. 1982. "Workfare: An Urban League Analysis." *Washington Social Legislation Bulletin* 27, no. 37.

Chanoit, P. F. 1983. *Analyse instrumentale des hopitaux de jour de la M.G.E.N.* Paris: Mutuelle Generale De L'Education Nationale.

Chapple, Eliot D. 1970. *Rehabilitation: Dynamic of Change: An Anthropological View.* Ithaca: Center for Research in Education, Cornell University.

Ciompi, L. 1980. "The Natural History of Schizophrenia in the Long Term." *British Journal of Psychiatry* 136: 413–20.

Clements, Harry R. 1977. "NISH Finds Its Niche." *Journal of Rehabilitation* 43, no. 2.

Cohen, Carl I. 1984. "Schizophrenia and Work." *Hospital and Community Psychiatry* 35, no. 10.

Coker, Charles C., and Blakemore, Thomas F. 1985. "Computer Software for Assessing and Shaping Motor Performance in Vocational Evaluation and Adjustment Programs." In *The Issues Papers.* National Forum on Issues in Vocational Assessment, September 20–22, 1984, Atlanta, Ga. Menomonie, Wis.: University of Wisconsin—Stout.

Cole, Margaret. 1984. "Vive la France." *Industrial Therapy* (London, British Institute of Industrial Therapy) 9, no. 1.

Comptroller General. 1977. *Returning the Mentally Disabled to the Community: Government Needs to Do More.* HRD 76–152. Washington, D.C.: U.S. Government Printing Office.

Comptroller General. 1981. *Stronger Federal Efforts Needed for Providing Employment Opportunities and Enforcing Labor Standards in Sheltered Workshops.* Report to the Hon. Barry M. Goldwater, Jr., House of Representatives.

HRD 81–99. Washington, D.C.: U.S. Government Printing Office, September 28.

Conte, L. 1982. "Manpower Policy and the Disabled Person: An International Perspective." *Rehabilitation Literature* 43, nos. 5–6.

Cornes, Paul. 1984. *The Future of Work and Disabled Persons.* Monograph no. 28. New York: World Rehabilitation Fund.

Cornes, Paul, and Hunter, John, eds. 1985. *Work, Disability, and Rehabilitation.* East Lansing, Mich.: University Center for International Rehabilitation, Michigan State University, May.

Coudroglou, Aliki. 1984. *Abilitating the Disabled: Policy Issues and Program Realities: The View from Greece.* Fellowship Report. New York: World Rehabilitation Fund.

Crawford, Jeffrey L. 1980. *Mental Health Reform in Trieste, Italy.* Final Report. New York: World Rehabilitation Fund.

Croxen, Mary. 1985. "Employment and Disability: A European Perspective." In Cornes and Hunter 1985.

Danish, S. J.; Galambas, L.; and Lagustra, I. 1983. "Life Development Intervention: Skill Training for Personal Competence." In R. D. Felner et al., eds., *Preventive Psychology: Theory, Research, and Practice.* New York: Pergamon Press.

DeJong, Gerben, 1984. *Independent Living and Disability Policy in the Netherlands: Three Models of Residential Care and Independent Living.* Monograph no. 27. New York: World Rehabilitation Fund.

Denber, H.C.B., and Rajotte, P. 1962. "Problems and Theoretical Considerations of Work Therapy for Psychiatric Patients." *Canadian Psychiatric Association Journal* 7, no. 1.

Dencker, S. J. 1980. *Hospital-based Community Support Services for Recovering Chronic Schizophrenics: The Experience at Lillhagen Hospital.* New York: World Rehabilitation Fund.

Dickerson, Altamont. 1979. *Independent Living and Industrial Sheltered Employment.* Final Report. New York: World Rehabilitation Fund.

Dickinson, Nancy S. 1986. "Which Welfare Work Strategies Work?" *Social Work* 31, no. 4.

Dincin, Jerry. 1975. "Psychiatric Rehabilitation." *Schizophrenia Bulletin,* no. 13 (Summer).

———. 1985. "Psychiatric Rehabilitation Today." In Joan P. Bowker, ed., *Evaluation for Practice with the Chronically Mentally Ill: What Works?* Washington, D.C.: Council on Social Work Education.

"A Discussion Concerning Sheltered Workshops: A State and National Perspective." 1982. A Report to the Secretary of Human Resources by Department of Rehabilitation Services, Department of Welfare, and Department of Mental Health and Mental Retardation. Richmond, Va., June 1. Mimeo.

Doniger, Joan M. 1970. "Is a Halfway House Therapeutic? The Woodley House Philosophy." In E. Robert Sinnett and Angela D. Sachson, eds., *Transitional Facilities in the Rehabilitation of the Emotionally Disturbed.* Lawrence, Kans.: University Press of Kansas.

Doughty, Carolyn, and Hayes, Elizabeth. 1979. *Proceedings of the Conference on Psychosocial Clubs, September 18–20, 1979.* Albany: The Training Unit, New York State Office of Mental Health.

Dunn, Dennis J. 1981. "Current Placement Trends." In Elizabeth L. Pan, Thomas E. Backer, and Carolyn L. Vash, eds., *Annual Review of Rehabilitation.* Vol. 2. New York: Springer Publishing Co.

DuRand, Lance, and DuRand, John. 1978. *The Affirmative Industry.* St. Paul: Minnesota Diversified Industries.

Durlack, J. A. 1983. "Social Problem Solving as a Primary Prevention Strategy." In R. D. Felner et al., eds. *Preventive Psychology: Theory, Research, and Practice.* New York: Pergamon Press.

Early, Donal F. 1985. "Medical Report." *Twenty-fifth Annual Report.* Industrial Therapy Organisation (Bristol) Ltd.

Eddy, Thomas. 1815. *Hints for Introducing an Improved Therapy for the Insane in the Asylum.* New York: Samuel Wood and Sons.

Eisler, R. M.; Herson, M.; and Miller, P. M. 1973. "Components of Assertive Behavior." *Journal of Clinical Psychology* 29 (July).

Eisler, R. M.; Herson, M.; Miller, P. M.; and Blanchard, E. R. 1975. "Situational Determinants of Assertive Behavior." *Journal of Consulting Clinical Psychology* 43, no. 3.

Eldred, D. M. 1945. "Vermont's Program for Psychoneurotics." *Journal of Rehabilitation* 11, no. 9.

———. 1957. *Background and Progress Report.* The Vermont State Hospital Project for the Rehabilitation of Chronic Schizophrenic Patients. September. Mimeo.

Elton, F. 1948. *Work Therapy.* New York: American Rehabilitation Committee.

Elwyn Industries. 1983. *Profile of a NISH Contract.* Elwyn, Pa.: Elwyn Industries.

Erikson, Erik S. 1950.*Childhood and Society.* New York: W. W. Norton and Co.

Etzioni, Amitai, and Lehman, Ethna. 1968. "Dual Leadership in a Therapeutic Organization." *International Review of Applied Psychology* 17, no. 1.

Evans, Olive. 1984. "Relationships: Motivating Mentally Ill to A 'Life.' " *New York Times,* May 28, Style section.

Fairweather, G. W., ed. 1964. *Social Psychology in Treating Mental Illness: An Experimental Approach.* New York: Wiley.

———, ed. 1980. *The Fairweather Lodge: A Twenty-Five-Year Retrospective.* New Directions for Mental Health Services, no. 7. San Francisco: Jossey-Bass.

Fairweather, G. W., et al. 1960. "Relative Effectiveness of Psychotherapeutic Programs: A Multicriteria Comparison of Four Programs for Three Different Groups." *Psychological Monograph* 74, no. 5.

Fairweather, G. W., and Simon, R. 1963. "A Further Follow-up Comparison of Psychotherapeutic Programs." *Journal of Consulting Psychology* 27, no. 2.

Fairweather, G. W.; Sanders, D. H.; Maynard, Hugo; Cressler, D. L.; and

Bleck, D. S. 1969. *Community Life for the Mentally Ill: An Alternative to Institutional Care.* Chicago: Aldine Publishing Co.

Falloon, Ian R. H. 1985. *Family Management of Schizophrenia: A Study of Clinical, Social, Family, and Economic Benefits.* Baltimore: Johns Hopkins University Press.

Federal Register. 1984. Title 20, CFR Parts 404 and 416. May 29, pp. 22268–75.

Federal Register. 1985. Title 34, CFR Part 373. February 28, pp. 8300–8302.

Field, M. G., and Aronson, J. 1965. "Soviet Community Mental Health Services and Work Therapy: A Report of Two Visits." *Community Mental Health Journal* 1, no. 1.

Fortushniak, James. 1983. Personal correspondence with the author. Sanco Industries, Deckerville, Mich., December 7.

Fountain House Foundation. 1984. "Transitional Employment: The Role of Projects with Industry in the Rehabilitation of the Vocationally Disabled Psychiatric Patient." *Survey Memorandum* 269, August 20.

Freeman, Hugh L.; Fryers, Thomas; and Henderson, John H. 1985. *Mental Health Services in Europe: Ten Years On.* Public Health in Europe, 25. Copenhagen: Regional Office for Europe, World Health Organization.

Freud, Sigmund. 1953. *Civilization and Its Discontents.* London: Hogarth Press.

Frost, E. S. 1965a. "Viewpoint on Mental Health." Transcript of television interview, Channel 31, WNYC-TV, New York City, March 31.

———, ed. 1965b. "A Workshop: Industry in the Mental Hospital." Proceedings of a Workshop on Industry in the Mental Hospital, New York, April 22, 1965. Brockton, Mass.: Brockton Veterans Administration Hospital.

Gallagher, Rosemary. 1977. "The Allied Services Experience." *Journal of Rehabilitation* 43, no. 2.

Gannik, Dorte; Holst, Erik; and Wagner, Mersden. 1976. *The National Health System in Denmark: A Descriptive Analysis.* DHEW Publication no. (NIH) 77–673. Washington, D.C.: U.S. Government Printing Office.

Gellman, William. 1956. "Job Adjustment of 'Apparent Unemployables' through a Vocational Adjustment Workshop." In Edward L. Chounard and James Garrett, eds., *Workshops for the Disabled.* Rehabilitation Services Series no. 371. Office of Vocational Rehabilitation, U.S. Department of Health, Education, and Welfare. Washington, D.C.: U.S. Government Printing Office.

———. 1967. "The Principles of Vocational Evaluation." In *Vocational Evaluation Curriculum Development Workshop.* Menomonie, Wis.: Stout State University, 1967.

———. 1983. *Changes in the British Job Placement Program for Disabled Persons during a Period of Economic Dislocation and High Unemployment.* New York: World Rehabilitation Fund.

Gellman, W.; Gendel, H.; Glaser, N. M.; Friedman, S. B.; and Neff, W. S. 1955. *Adjusting People to Work.* Monograph no. 1. Chicago: Jewish Vocational Service and Employment Center.

Gervey, Robert; Wartenberg, Daniel; and Gabler, Arthur. 1985. *Community*

Support Services Enhancement Project: Program Evaluation Final Report. New York City Department of Mental Health, Mental Retardation, and Alcoholism Services, Contract 83191. June.

Ginsburg, Sol W. 1963. *A Psychiatrist's View on Social Issues.* New York: Columbia University Press.

Gittelman, Martin. 1975. "Recent Developments in European Rehabilitation." In L. Bellak and H. Barren, eds., *Progress in Community Mental Health.* New York: Brunner/Mazel.

Glasscote, R. M.; Cumming, E.; Rutman, I. P.; Sussex, J. N.; and Glassman, S. M. 1971. *Rehabilitating the Mentally Ill in the Community.* Washington, D.C.: Joint Information Service of the American Psychiatric Association and National Association for Mental Health.

Goertzel, V.; Grumer, M.; Hiroto, D. S.; and Moes, J. H. 1967. "Coordinating Hospital and Community Work Adjustment Services." Final Report of a Joint Study by Camarillo State Hospital and the Jewish Vocational Service of Los Angeles. VRA Project No. RD-1156. January. Mimeo.

Goldstein, Arnold P.; Sprafkin, Robert P.; and Gershaw, N. Jane. 1976. *Skill Training for Community Living: Applying Structured Learning Therapy.* New York: Pergamon Press / Structured Learning Associates.

Goodwill Industries of Orange County, Santa Ana, California. 1985. Brochures and Program Materials.

Greenblatt, Milton. 1983. "Psychiatric Rehabilitation: Some Personal Reflections." *Psychiatric Annals* 13 (July).

Gudmundsson, Johann. 1985. *Cooperatives of Disabled Persons: A Guide for Promotion and Organization.* United Nations Decade of Disabled Persons, 1983–1992. Rome: Center for Social Development and Humanitarian Affairs, U.N. Department of International Economic and Social Affairs.

Hagner, D., and Como, P. 1982. "Work Stations in Industry: An Alternative for the Training and Employment of Handicapped Individuals." Menomonie, Wis.: Materials Development Center, University of Wisconsin—Stout, May. Offset.

Hammerman, Susan R., and Maikowski, Stephen. 1983. "The Economics of Disability from an International Perspective." In Elizabeth L. Pan, Thomas E. Backer, and Carolyn L. Vash, eds., *Annual Review of Rehabilitation.* Vol. 3. New York: Springer Publishing Co.

Harding, Courtenay M.; Brooks, George W.; Ashikaga, T.; and Strauss, John S. 1984. *Chronic Mental Patients in the Community for Twenty Years.* Progress Report, NIMH 29575, July 31.

Harding, T. W. 1976. *Rehabilitation in the W.H.O. Mental Health Programme.* Geneva: Office of Mental Health, World Health Organization, June.

Hoffman, Paul R. 1970. "Where Do We Go from Here?" In Ralph N. Pacinelli, ed., *Vocational Evaluation and Work Adjustment Service in Manpower, Social Welfare, and Rehabilitation Programs.* Washington, D.C.: International Association of Rehabilitation Facilities.

Howard, George. 1975. "The Ex-Mental Patient as an Employee: An on-the-Job Evaluation." *American Journal of Orthopsychiatry* 45, no. 3.

Huber, G.; Gross, G.; Schuttler, R.; and Linz, M. 1980. "Longitudinal Stud-

ies of Schizophrenic Patients." *Schizophrenia Bulletin* 6, no. 4.
ILO. 1978. *Cooperatives for the Disabled: Organisation and Development.* Geneva: International Labor Organization.
———. 1979. *Vocational Rehabilitation of the Mentally Restored.* Geneva: International Labor Organization.
Industrial Therapy. Autumn 1983a. "Rehabilitation: The Way Ahead or the End of the Road?" Vol. 8, no. 2.
Industrial Therapy. Autumn 1983b. "Steps to Work." Vol. 8, no. 2.
Institute for the Crippled and Disabled. 1967. *TOWER: Testing, Orientation, and Work Evaluation in Rehabilitation.* New York: ICD Research Center.
International Conference on Productive Participation Programs for the Mentally Ill. 1973. Helsinki, Finland, October 12–15, 1971. Amsterdam: Excerpta Medica.
International Rehabilitation Review. 1983a. "Disabled Computer Programmers Successful in Czechoslovakia." Third Quarter.
———. 1983b. "Special Employment Measures, German Democratic Republic." Third Quarter.
———. 1983c. "Successful Vocational and Placement Program in New Zealand." Third Quarter.
Jansen, Mary A. 1986. *European Mental Health Policies and Practices: Rehabilitation of the Chronically Mentally Ill.* New York: World Rehabilitation Fund, February.
Jarvikoski, Aila, and Lahelma, Eero. 1980. *Early Rehabilitation at the Workplace.* Monograph no. 6. New York: World Rehabilitation Fund.
Jewish Employment and Vocational Services. 1962. "*A Work Adjustment Center for Disabled Persons with Emotional Problems: Final Report.*" OVR Project no. 355. Philadelphia, July 2. Mimeo.
———. 1968. *Work Samples: Signposts on the Road to Occupational Choice.* Philadelphia: Jewish Employment and Vocational Services.
Job Training Legislative Transition Conference. 1985. *Conference Report.* New York State Employment and Training Council, New York City, December 14–15.
Jolly, Bill. 1985. "Industrial Therapy at Crown Hill: A Pathway to Normality." *Industrial Therapy* 10, no. 1.
Jones, Kathleen, and Poletti, Alison. 1986. "The Italian Experience in Mental Health Care." *Hospital and Community Psychiatry* 37, no. 8.
Jones, M. 1953. *The Therapeutic Community.* New York: Basic Books.
Jones, M., and Stoller, A. 1952. "Rehabilitation in Psychiatry." World Health Organization Monograph (in English only), WHO/Ment/30, July 7. Mimeo.
Journal of Applied Rehabilitation Counseling. Fall 1986. "A Special Issue: Disability Management and Rehabilitation in the Workplace." Vol. 17, no. 3.
Kanter, Joel. 1985. "The Process of Change in the Long-term Mentally Ill: A Naturalistic Perspective." *Psychosocial Rehabilitation Journal* 9, no. 1.
Kase, Harold M. 1970. "The Distinction between Sheltered and Rehabilitation Workshops." *Social Work* 15 (October).

Kase, Harold M., and Gerber, Norman M. 1977. "The Altro Experience." *Journal of Rehabilitation* 43, no. 2.

Kemp, Bryan J. 1981. "The Case Management Model of Human Service Delivery." In Elizabeth L. Pan, Thomas E. Backer, and Carolyn L. Vash, eds., *Annual Review of Rehabilitation*. Vol. 2. New York: Springer Publishing Co.

Kennedy, M. 1985. "Moving Out on the Eden Express." *Tables* (National Restaurant Association), no. 2 (August).

Knudson, A.B.C. 1959. "Rehabilitation of the Mentally Ill in the Veterans Administration." In M. Greenblatt and B. Simon, eds., *Rehabilitation of the Mentally Ill: Social and Economic Aspects*. Washington, D.C.: American Association for the Advancement of Sciences, Publ. no. 58.

Krahl, Wolfgang. 1980. "Reintegration of Chronic Patients into the Malaysian Community." *Proceedings, Second National Society for Neurology, Psychiatry*. Jakarta.

Kulkarni, Madhav R. 1982. *Quota Systems and Employment of the Handicapped: Experiences in Three Countries*. East Lansing, Mich.: University Center for International Rehabilitation, Michigan State University.

Kunce, J. T. 1970. "Is Work Really Therapeutic?" *Rehabilitation Literature* 31, no. 10.

———. 1983. *The Mexican-American: Cross-Cultural Rehabilitation Implications*. New York: World Rehabilitation Fund.

Kwitny, Jonathan, and Landauer, Jerry. 1979a. "Sheltered Shops: Pay of the Blind Often Trails Minimum Wage at Charity Workrooms." *Wall Street Journal*, January 24.

———. 1979b. "Sheltered Shops: How a Blind Worker Gets $1.85 an Hour after 20 Years on a Job." *Wall Street Journal*, January 25.

———. 1979. "Minimal Wage: Some Workshops Pay Handicapped as Little as 10 Cents an Hour." *Wall Street Journal*, October 17.

Lahore Mental Health Association. 1985. *Fountain House, 1971–1985: A Project*. Lahore, Pakistan: Lahore Mental Health Association.

Lamb, H. R., et al. 1971. *Rehabilitation in Community Mental Health*. San Francisco: Jossey-Bass.

———. 1976. *Community Survival for Long-Term Patients*. San Francisco: Jossey-Bass.

Lamb, H. Richard, and Peele, Roger. 1984. "The Need for Continuing Asylum and Sanctuary." *Hospital and Community Psychiatry* 35, no. 8.

Landy, David, and Raulet, Harry. 1959. "The Hospital Work Program." In *Rehabilitation of the Mentally Ill; Social and Economic Aspects*. Publication no. 58. Washington, D.C.: American Association for the Advancement of Science.

Lee, H. 1963. "Two Rehabilitation Programs for the Chronic Services." Second Progress Report. NIMH Grant OM-547-2, Medfield Foundation, Inc. Dittoed.

Lereim, K. 1980. "Norway." In John G. Cull et al., eds., *International Rehabilitation*. San Antonio: Clinical Prediction Press.

Leshner, Saul. 1970. "The Relationship of Work Evaluation to Work Adjustment." *Journal of Rehabilitation* 31, no. 1.

Levitan, S. A., and Magnum, G. T. 1969. *Federal Training and Work Programs in the 1960s.* Ann Arbor: University of Michigan Press.

Liberman, Robert P., and Fry, David W. 1983. "Psychiatric Rehabilitation for Chronic Mental Patients." *Psychiatric Annals* 13, no. 7.

Liberman, Robert P., and Phipps, Catherine C. 1984. "Innovative Treatment and Rehabilitation Techniques for the Chronically Mentally Ill." Presentation at the National Conference on the Chronic Mental Patient II, American Psychiatric Association. Kansas City, Mo., August 12–14.

Lin, Tsung-yi, and Eisenberg, Leon, eds. 1985. *Mental Health Planning for One Billion People: A Chinese Perspective.* Vancouver: University of British Columbia Press.

Liu, Shi-Ji. 1985. "An Outline of the Grass-Roots Health Care System in the People's Republic of China." In Lin and Eisenberg 1985.

McCann, R. V., ed. 1963. *Sheltered Workshops in Massachusetts: A Descriptive and Functional Study.* Boston: Massachusetts Rehabilitation Commission.

McCray, Paul M., and Blakemore, Thomas F. 1985. *A Guide to Learning Curve Technology to Enhance Performance Prediction in Vocational Evaluation.* Research Utilization Report, Research and Training Center, Stout Vocational Rehabilitation Institute. Menomonie, Wis.: University of Wisconsin—Stout.

McCreath, James. 1984. "The New Generation of Chronic Psychiatric Patients." *Social Work* 29 (September–October).

McFarlane, William R., ed. 1983. *Family Therapy in Schizophrenia.* New York: Guilford Press.

Mackota, Cecile. 1976. "Using Work Therapeutically." In Lamb et al. 1976.

Marx, Karl. 1961. "Preface to a Contribution to the Critique of Political Economy."In Erich Fromm, *Marx's Concept of Man.* New York: Frederick Ungar Publishing Co.

Maryland vs. Wirtz. 742 U.S. 112 (1968).

Massachusetts Rehabilitation Commission. 1974. *A Statewide Plan for Rehabilitation Facilities.* Supplement no. VI, January.

MCW News. March 1984. Marin County Workshops, Mill Valley, Calif.

Meyer, H. J., and Bergotta, E. F. 1959. *An Experiment in Mental Health Rehabilitation.* New York: Russell Sage Foundation.

Mitchell, Ken. 1983. "A Study and Analysis of Rehabilitation Laws, Rehabilitation Services, and Work-Return Strategies for Individuals Disabled by Industrial Accidents or Occupational Disabilities in New Zealand." In Diane E. Woods, ed., *Rehabilitation in Australia and New Zealand: U.S. Observations.* New York: World Rehabilitation Fund, Inc.

Moriarty, Francis M. 1970. "A Token Economy Program for Chronic Schizophrenic Patients." In E. Robert Sinnett and Angela D. Sachson, eds., *Transitional Facilities in the Rehabilitation of the Emotionally Disturbed.* Lawrence, Kans.: University Press of Kansas.

Mosher, L. R. 1986. "The Current Status of the Community Support Program: A Personal Assessment." *Psychosocial Rehabilitation Journal* 9, no. 3.

Muthard, John E., and Salomone, Paul R. 1969. *The Roles and Functions of the*

Rehabilitation Counselor. Special issue of the *Rehabilitation Counseling Bulletin* 13, no. 1-SP.

Myers, J. K.; Weissman, M. M.; et al. 1984. "Six-Month Prevalence of Psychiatric Disorders in Three Communities." *Archives of General Psychiatry* 41 (October): Appendices.

Nadelson, Carol C. 1986. "Psychiatry across Borders." *Hospital and Community Psychiatry* 37, no. 2.

Nadolsky, Julian M. 1985. "Vocational Evaluation: An Experimental Trend in Vocational Assessment." In *The Issues Papers.* National Forum on Issues in Vocational Assessment, September 20–22, 1984, Atlanta, Ga. Menomonie, Wis.: University of Wisconsin—Stout.

NARF. 1984a. *Federal Wage and Hour Law: A Guide for Vocational Rehabilitation Facilities.* Washington, D.C.: National Association of Rehabilitation Facilities.

———. 1984b. *National Directory of RSA-Funded PWIs, 1984.* Washington, D.C.: National Association of Rehabilitation Facilities.

———. 1985a. *From Theory to Implementation: A Guide to Supported Employment for Rehabilitation Facilities.* Washington, D.C.: National Association of Rehabilitation Facilities.

———. 1985b. *A Supported Work Approach: Employer-Based Rehabilitation Facilities Services.* Washington, D.C.: National Association of Rehabilitation Facilities.

NARF Tech Brief. 1984. No. 11. Washington, D.C.: National Association of Rehabilitation Facilities.

NARF Voc/Dev Management Review. April 1985. "Town Meeting on Supported Work Raises Unanswered Questions." Vol. 2, no. 4.

———. July 1985. "Non-Profit Competition Issue Still Alive." Vol. 2, no. 7.

———. September 1986. "Employment Outlook: What's Ahead." Vol. 3, no. 9.

NARF Voc/Dev Rehabilitation Review. May 21, 1984. "JWOD Committee Reviews NISH, NIB." Vol. 1, no. 20.

———. June 4, 1984. "Advisory Committee Publishes Statement of Principles." Vol. 1, no. 22.

———. June 11, 1984. "SBA Agrees with NARF on Nonprofit Competition Issues." Vol. 1, no. 23.

———. November 12, 1984. "NISH Awards First Loans." Vol. 1, no. 44.

———. June 25, 1985. "Elder Remarks Reported in News Magazine." Vol. 1, no. 25.

———. July 15, 1985. "Wehman Justifies Supported Work Programs." Vol. 2, no. 27.

———. August 12, 1985. "Real Work for Real Pay." Vol. 2, no. 31.

———. September 9, 1985. "Judge Continues Deliberation of NARF Suit." Vol. 2, no. 35.

———. September 16, 1985. "Judge Rules in NARF Suit." Vol. 2, no. 36.

———. September 23, 1985. "HHS Issues Mental Impairment Categories." Vol. 2, no. 37.

———. October 21, 1985. "Judge Issues Clarification in NARF-JWOD Suit." Vol. 2, no. 41.

———. October 28, 1985. "OSERS Proposes New Criteria for PWI." Vol. 2, no. 42.

———. December 16, 1985. "NISH Holds Board Meeting in Washington." Vol. 2, no. 49.

———. December 23, 1985. "Nickles to Introduce FLSA Bill." Vol. 2, no. 50.

———. January 20, 1986. "Congressman Introduces Set-Aside Bill." Vol. 3, no. 3.

———. January 27, 1986. "GAO Reports Problems in Labor's Enforcement of FLSA." Vol. 3, no. 4.

———. February 10, 1986. "JTPA Impact Assessed by GAO." Vol. 3, no. 6.

———. March 10, 1986. "PWI Evaluation Positive." Vol. 3, no. 10.

———. March 17, 1986. "OMB Seeks to Restrict Set-Asides." Vol. 3, no. 11.

———. March 24, 1986. "Weiker Introduces Set-Aside Bill: Opposition Expected." Vol. 3, no. 12.

———. March 31, 1986. "Bartlett, Dole Introduce Sec. 1619 Bill." Vol. 3, no. 13.

———. May 26, 1986. "TJTC Included in Tax Bills." Vol. 3, no. 21.

———. September 1, 1986a. "Final Report on TJTC Program Released." Vol. 3, no. 34.

———. September 1, 1986b. "1619 Study Completed by HHS." Vol. 3, no. 34.

———. October 6, 1986a. "Congress Enacts Sec. 14(c) Bill!" Vol. 3, no. 39.

———. October 6, 1986b. "Tax Bill Passes: Targetted Jobs Tax Credit." Vol. 3, no. 39.

———. October 13, 1986. "New Provisions of Rehabilitation Act of Special Interest for Rehabilitation Facilities." Vol. 3, no. 40.

Nash, Kenneth R. 1983. *A Study of the Netherlands National Policy towards the Handicapped.* Final Report. New York: World Rehabilitation Fund.

National Council on Employment Policy. 1985. *The Job Training Partnership Act: Some Encouraging Signs but Important Questions Still Remain.* A Policy Statement. Washington, D.C., July.

National League of Cities vs. Usery. 426 U.S. 833 (1976). Neff, Walter S. 1968. *Work and Human Behavior.* New York: Atherton Press.

Neilson, Lester John, Jr. 1978. *Development and Evolution of Vocational Rehabilitation and Its Service Delivery Systems in the United Kingdom: A Ten-Element Examination.* Final Report. New York: World Rehabilitation Fund.

Nelson, Nathan. 1971. *Workshops for the Handicapped in the United States: An Historical and Developmental Perspective.* Springfield, Ill.: Charles C. Thomas.

Nessel, Julius J. 1985. "IAPSRS and CARF: A New Relationship." *Psychosocial Rehabilitation Journal* 9, no. 2.

New York Association of Rehabilitation Facilities. 1980. "A Compendium of Service Provision Models for the Mentally Ill." Albany: NYSARF, May. Mimeo.

New York Times. 1986. "Jobless Program Seen as a Failure." April 5, sec. A.

Nunn, Harold D. 1977. "The Abilities, Inc., Experience." *Journal of Rehabilitation* 43, no. 2.

OWL Handbook. 1983. Lexington, Ky.: Opportunity Workshop of Lexington.

Ozawa, Martha N., and Lindsey, Duncan. 1977. "Is SSI Too Supportive of the Mentally Ill?" *Public Welfare* 35, no. 4.

Palmer, Frances, and Gatti, Donna. 1985. "Vocational Treatment Model." *Occupational Therapy in Mental Health* 5, no. 1.

Papiasvili, Avtandil, and Papiasvili, Eva D. 1986. "Therapeutic Communities for Neurotic Patients in Eastern Europe." *Hospital and Community Psychiatry* 37, no. 7.

Paquette, A., and Lafave, H. 1964. "Halfway House." *American Journal of Nursing* 64, no. 3.

Paul, Gordon L., and Lentz, Robert J. 1977. *Psychological Treatment of Chronic Mental Patients: Milieu vs. Social Learning Programs.* Cambridge: Harvard University Press.

Pepper, B.; Ryglewicz, H.; and Kirshner, M. C. 1982. "The Uninstitutionalized Generation: A New Breed of Psychiatric Patient." In B. Pepper and H. Ryglewicz, eds., *The Young Adult Chronic Patient.* New Directions for Mental Health Services, no. 14. San Francisco: Jossey-Bass.

Piercy Committee. 1973. *Sheltered Employment for Disabled People: A Consultative Document.* London: Department of Employment, Disabled Persons Branch, DPS.

Plume, B. 1965. *Edgar J. Helms, The Goodwill Man.* Minneapolis: T. S. Dennison.

PRA 1986. *Twenty-ninth Annual Report, 1984–1985.* Redfern, New South Wales, Australia: Psychiatric Rehabilitation Association.

Productive Participation for the Mentally Ill. 1973. International Conference, Helsinki, Finland. Amsterdam: Excerpta Medica.

Profile. May 1985, October 1985, and January 1986. Reading, Pennsylvania: Threshold Rehabilitation Services.

Propst, Rudyard N. 1984. *Enriching the Fountain House Model through a Two-Way Exchange: The U.S. to Northern Europe and Northern Europe to the U.S.* New York: World Rehabilitation Fund.

Pruitt, Walter A. 1977. *Vocational (Work) Evaluation.* Menomonie, Wis.: Walt Pruitt Associates.

———. 1983. *Work Adjustment.* Menomonie, Wis.: Walt Pruitt Associates.

Public Law 78–113. Vocational Rehabilitation Act Amendments. U.S. Congress, 1943. (Borden-LaFollette Act.)

Public Law 83–565. Vocational Rehabilitation Act Amendments. U.S. Congress, 1954.

Public Law 84–911. Health Amendments Act. U.S. Congress, 1956. (Title V.)

Public Law 88–164. Community Mental Health Centers Act. U.S. Congress, 1963.

Public Law 90–391. Vocational Rehabilitation Act Amendments. U.S. Congress, 1968. (Projects with Industry demonstrations.)

Public Law 92–28. Javits, Wagner, O'Day Act. U.S. Congress, 1971.

Public Law 93–203. The Comprehensive Employment and Training Act (CETA). U.S. Congress, 1973.

Public Law 95–524. CETA Amendments. U.S. Congress, 1978.

Public Law 95–602. Rehabilitation, Comprehensive Services, and Developmental Disabilities Amendments (Title II, Part B). U.S. Congress, 1978.

Public Law 97–300. Jobs Training Partnership Act. U.S. Congress, 1982.

Public Law 98–8. Emergency Jobs Appropriations Bill. U.S. Congress, 1983.

Public Law 99–150. Fair Labor Standards Act Amendments. U.S. Congress, 1985. (Wage and Hour Laws.)

Public Law 99–506. Rehabilitation Act Amendments. U.S. Congress, 1986.

Rackow, Leon. 1959. "The Art and Science of Rehabilitation." In Milton Greenblatt and Benjamin Simon, eds., *Rehabilitation of the Mentally Ill: Social and Economic Aspects*. Publication No. 58. Washington, D.C.: American Association for the Advancement of Science.

Reagles, Kenneth W. 1980. *Evaluation Measures of Community-Based Programs of Psychiatric Rehabilitation in England*. Monograph No. 23. New York: World Rehabilitation Fund.

Redke, Henry. 1975. "Sheltered Workshops Abroad: What We Might Learn about Sheltered Employment." *Rehabilitation World* 1, no. 2.

Reitsma, Walter H. 1984. "Organization and Administration of Rehabilitation in Holland." *Quarterly Bulletin* (Association of Medical Rehabilitation Directors and Coordinators) 23, no. 3.

Reubens, Beatrice G. 1970. *Special Job Creation for the Hard-to-Employ in Western Europe*. Manpower Research Monograph no. 14. Washington, D.C.: U.S. Department of Labor/Manpower Administration.

Rhoades, Lawrence J. 1981. *Treating and Assessing the Chronically Mentally Ill: The Pioneering Research of Gordon L. Paul*. Rockville, Md.: U.S. Department of Health and Human Services, ADAMHA, Division of Scientific and Public Information.

Richmond, D. T. 1983. *Inquiry into Health Services for the Psychiatrically Ill and Developmentally Disabled*. Part 1, General Proposals; and Part 3, Mental Health Services for the Mentally Ill. Sydney, Australia: New South Wales Department of Health, March.

———. 1985. *Policies for Mental Health Services*. Sydney, Australia: New South Wales Department of Health, January.

Rise Reporter. May 1983. Vol. 6, no. 2. Minneapolis: Rise, Inc.

———. December 1985. Vol. 8, no. 4. Spring Lake Park, Minn.: Rise, Inc.

Robinault, Isabel P., and Weisinger, M. 1978. "Selected Approaches to Vocational Rehabilitation." *Community Resources: Multifaceted Model for Mentally Ill*. New York: Research Utilization Laboratory, ICD Rehabilitation and Research Center.

Rood, L. 1983. *The Unsheltered Workshop: A Guide to Work Stations in Industry*. Omaha: The Media Resource Center, Meyer Children's Rehabilitation Institute, University of Nebraska Medical Center.

Rowlands, Vernon. 1985. "SITO: Initiation and Operation." *Industrial Therapy* 10, no. 1.

Royal College of Psychiatrists. 1980. *Psychiatric Rehabilitation in the 1980s: Report of the Working Party on Rehabilitation of the Social and Community Section.* London: Royal College of Psychiatrists.

Rush, Benjamin. 1812. *Medical Inquiries and Observations upon the Disease of the Mind.* Philadelphia. Reprinted in Sidney Lich, ed., *Occupational Therapy Sourcebook.* Baltimore: Williams and Wilkins Co., 1948.

Rutman, I. G., and Armstrong, K. 1985. "A Comprehensive Evaluation of Transitional Employment Programs in the Rehabilitation of Chronically Mentally Disabled Clients." Final Report, Mary E. Switzer Research Fellowship Project. Philadelphia: Matrix Research Institute, March. Mimeo.

Sands, Harry, and Radin, Jerome. 1979. *The Mentally Disabled Rehabilitant: Post Employment Services.* New York: Postgraduate Center for Mental Health.

San Francisco Examiner. 1979. "Blind Workers Trying to Increase Wages to Minimum Level." Nation. June 6.

Sartorius, Norman. 1983. "Mental Health in the Early 1980s: Some Perspectives." *International Rehabilitation Review.* Second Quarter.

Schulman, Eveline D. 1981. *Rehabilitation of the Mentally Ill: An International Perspective.* Report of the President's Committee on Employment of the Handicapped. Washington, D.C.

Science News. 1985. "An Optimistic Twist for Schizophrenics." Vol. 127, June 1.

Sheets, John; Prevost, James A.; and Reichman, J. 1982. "Young Adult Chronic Patients: Three Hypotheses for Subgroups." *Hospital and Community Psychiatry* 33, no. 3.

SK&F Psychiatric Reporter. 1962. "How to Bring Industrial Projects into the Hospital—and How to Get Them Done." September–October.

Smith, Harry P. 1982. *Examination of the Republic of Ireland's Special Education, Vocational, and Rehabilitation Delivery Systems.* New York: World Rehabilitation Fund.

Soloff, A. 1968. *A Work Therapy Research Center.* Summary. Chicago: Jewish Vocational Service. January 11. Mimeo.

Souder vs. Brennan. 367F (Supp. 808 and 813) U.S. Court for the District of Columbia (1973).

South Shore Rehabilitation Center. 1985. Brochures and Annual Report. Quincy, Mass.

Speijer, N. 1959. "Some Views on Sheltered Workshops for the Mentally Handicapped." *International Journal of Social Psychiatry* 5, no. 2.

Spence, Sue, and Shepherd, Geoff, eds. 1983. *Developments in Social Skills Trianing.* London: Academic Press.

Srole, L. 1962. *Mental Health in the Metropolis: The Midtown Manhattan Study.* New York: McGraw Hill Book Co.

SSRC News. Spring 1984. Quincy, Mass.: South Shore Rehabilitation Center.

Stefanis, C. N.; Madianos, M. G.; and Gittelman, Martin. 1986. "Recent Developments in the Care, Treatment, and Rehabilitation of the Chronic Mentally Ill in Greece." *Hospital and Community Psychiatry* 37, no. 10.

Steinmeyer, Heinz-Dietrich, and Tracy, Martin B. 1985. "Rehabilitation Program Issues in the Federal Republic of Germany." *Journal of Rehabilitation* 51, no. 3.

Strauss, John S.; Hafez, Hisham; Liberman, Paul; and Harding, Courtenay M. 1985. "The Course of Psychiatric Disorder, III: Longitudinal Principles." *American Journal of Psychiatry* 142, no. 3.

Stubbins, Joseph. *The Clinical Attitude in Rehabilitation: A Cross-Cultural View.* Monograph no. 16. New York: World Rehabilitation Fund.

Stude, E. W. 1986. "Special Education and Vocational Rehabilitation in the Federal Republic of Germany." *Journal of Rehabilitation* 52, no. 2.

SUNY. 1978. "Evaluation of a Workshop Subcontract Operation." Personal Communication. Regional Economic Advisory Service, State University of New York.

Szklarczyk, Eugeniusz. 1978. "Economic Self-Sufficiency of Invalids' Cooperatives." *Cooperatives for the Disabled: Organization and Development.* Geneva: International Labor Office.

Tate, Denise G., and Letsinger, Jane. 1983. "Rehabilitation in a Developing Country: An Overview of Brazil's Efforts and Needs." *Rehabilitation/WORLD.* Fall.

Toomba, Ken. 1984. "The New Dawn." *Industrial Therapy* 9, no. 1.

Toyamil, Manuel. 1983. Presentation at Montefiore Hospital and Medical Center, Bronx, New York, April 12.

Turley, John. 1985. "Chairman's Report." *Twenty-fifth Annual Report.* Industrial Therapy Organization (Bristol) Ltd.

Turner, J. E. 1976. Memorandum, "Working Conference on Community Support Systems for Adults with Seriously Disabling Mental or Emotional Disorders." Arlington, Va., January 13–15, Human Resources Management, Inc., under contract with National Institute of Mental Health.

Turner, J. E., and TenHoor, W. J., 1978. "The NIMH Community Support Program: Pilot Approach to a Needed Social Reform." *Schizophrenia Bulletin* 4, no. 3.

Turner, R. J. 1973. "The Implications of Psychiatric Disorder for Employment: An Assessment of the Degree and Nature of Their Relatedness." Presentation at the Annual Meeting of the Society for the Study of Social Problems, New York, August.

U.S. Department of Education. 1980. *Summary of Existing Legislation Relating to the Handicapped.* Publication no. E-80-22014, August. Washington, D.C.: U.S. Government Printing Office.

U.S. Department of Labor. 1963. *Manpower Report of the President and a Report on Manpower Requirements, Resources, Utilization, and Training.* Washington, D.C.: U.S. Government Printing Office.

U.S. News & World Report. 1979. "Blind Workers Cry: End Exploitation!" Labor. June 11.

Vash, Carolyn L. 1977. *Sheltered Industrial Employment: Emerging Issues in Rehabilitation.* Washington, D.C.: Institute for Research Utilization (a division of the Washington Transportation Alliance), December.

———. 1984. *Yugoslav Self-Management in Rehabilitation.* Final Report. New York: World Rehabilitation Fund.

Versluys, Hilda P. 1986. "Thuishulpcentrale: A Dutch Model for Practical Family Assistance." *Rehabilitation Literature* 47, nos. 3–4.

Volovik, V. M., and Zachepitskii, R. A. 1986. "Treatment, Care, and Rehabilitation of the Chronic Mentally Ill in the U.S.S.R." *Hospital and Community Psychiatry* 37, no. 3.

Wadsworth, W. V.; Wells, B.W.P.; and Scott, R. F. 1962. "The Organization of a Sheltered Workshop." *Journal of Mental Science* 108, no. 457.

Wallace, Charles J.; Nelson, Connie J.; Liberman, Robert P.; Aitchison, David L.; Elder, John P.; and Farris, Chris. 1980. "A Review and Critique of Social Skills Training with Schizophrenic Patients." *Schizophrenia Bulletin* 6, no. 1.

Wansbrough, Nancy, and Cooper, Philip. 1980. *Open Employment after Mental Illness.* London: Tavistock Publications.

Whitehead, Alan. 1984. "Industrial Therapy and Community Care." *Industrial Therapy* 9, no. 1.

———. 1984/85. "Care in the Community." *Industrial Therapy* 9, no. 3.

WHO. 1978. *The WHO Medium-Term Mental Health Programme, 1975–1982.* Interim Report, 1978. Geneva: Division of Mental Health, World Health Organization.

WHO. 1980. *International Classification of Impairments, Disabilities, and Handicaps: A Manual of Classification Relating to Disease.* New York: World Health Organization.

Williams, Henry. 1983. *Village System in Nigeria: An Approach to the Rehabilitation of the Mentally Ill.* Final Report. New York: World Rehabilitation Fund, Inc.

Williams, Richard H. 1953. *Vocational Rehabilitation in a State Mental Hospital: Analysis of a Program.* Staff Memorandum for Administrative Use. U.S. Department of Health, Education, and Welfare, Public Health Service, NIH-NIMH-10/14:300, November.

———, ed. 1962. *The Prevention of Disability in Mental Disorders.* Mental Health Monograph no. 1. U.S. Department of Health, Education, and Welfare, Public Health Service Publication no. 924. Washington, D.C.: U.S. Government Printing Office.

Williamson, Pauline. 1984/85. "Wise Words from Worcester." *Industrial Therapy* 9, no. 3.

Wing, John, ed. 1975. *Schizophrenia from Within.* Surrey, Eng.: National Schizophrenia Fellowship.

Witheridge, T. F., and Dincin, J. 1981. "The Bridge: An Assertive Home-Visiting Program for the Most Frequent Psychiatric Recidivists." Final Report to the Hospital Improvement Program. National Institute of Mental Health. Chicago: Thresholds, December 1.

Wolpe, J. 1958. *Psychotherapy by Reciprocal Inhibition.* Stanford: Stanford University Press.

World Federation for Mental Health. 1984. "News from the Regions." *Newsletter* (Alexandria, Va.). June.

———. 1985a. "News from the Regions." *Newsletter,* February.
———. 1985b. "News from the Regions." *Newsletter,* November.
———. 1986a. "World Information Bulletin." *Newsletter,* February.
———. 1986b. "News from the Regions." *Newsletter,* February.
———. 1986c. "World Information Bulletin." *Newsletter,* April.

Wortis, J., and Freundlich, D. 1964. "Psychiatric Work Therapy in the Soviet Union." *American Journal of Psychiatry* 121, no. 2.

Xia, Zhen-Yi. 1985. "Primary Mental Health Care in Shanghai." In Lin and Eisenberg 1985.

Yood, Barry, and Esposito, Tony. 1986. "Multidisciplinary Rehabilitation Treatment Format." Presentation at Queens Colloquium on Rehabilitation of the Mentally Handicapped, St. John's University, Queens, New York, June 18.

Index

Designed by Martha Farlow.

Composed by Brushwood Graphics Inc., in Palatino.

Printed by Thomson-Shore, Inc., on 50-lb. Warren's Olde Style
and bound by John H. Dekker & Sons, Inc., in Holliston Roxite A.